David Evans   2010

From the Cult of Waste to the Trash Heap of History

From the Cult of Waste to the Trash Heap of History

*The Politics of Waste in
Socialist and Postsocialist
Hungary*

Zsuzsa Gille

*Indiana
University
Press*

BLOOMINGTON AND INDIANAPOLIS

This book is a publication of

Indiana University Press
601 North Morton Street
Bloomington, IN 47404-3797 USA

http://iupress.indiana.edu
Telephone orders   800-842-6796
Fax orders   812-855-7931
Orders by e-mail   iuporder@indiana.edu

The paper used in this publication meets
the minimum requirements of American
National Standard for Information
Sciences—Permanence of Paper for
Printed Library Materials,
ANSI Z39.48-1984.

Manufactured in the United States of America

Library of Congress Cataloging-in-Publication Data

Gille, Zsuzsa.
From the cult of waste to the trash heap of history :
the politics of waste in socialist and postsocialist
Hungary / Zsuzsa Gille.
p. cm.
Includes bibliographical references and index.
ISBN 0-253-34838-2 (cloth : alk. paper)
1. Environmental policy—Hungary. 2. Refuse and
refuse disposal—Social aspects—Hungary. 3. Post-
communism—Hungary. I. Title.
GE190.H9G55 2007
306.4'6—dc22   2006026312

1 2 3 4 5 12 11 10 09 08 07

To the loving memory of my parents

Contents

Acknowledgments

This book has been in the making for a long time. I tried to do something that I had no model for, and therefore I am indebted to many people who not only found the development of a social theory of waste worthwhile but also encouraged me and lent their support in various forms over the years. I am first of all grateful to my mentors at UC Santa Cruz—Ronnie Lipschutz, John Brown Childs, Andy Szasz, James O'Connor, Anna Tsing, Mark Cioc, and Ravi Rajan—for teaching me critical views of society and environment and for their encouragement in sticking with the seemingly idiosyncratic topic of waste. For help in quantitative analysis I am indebted to Hiroshi Fukurai. I am grateful to James Clifford for showing me the difference cultural studies can make, and to Martha Lampland and William Cronon for thinking with me about how the interaction of culture and economy could be conceptualized in my research design. It was however mostly the one and only Michael Burawoy who nurtured my inner ethnographer and who taught me so much about the emancipatory potential of theoretically infused fieldwork. I am forever in his debt for his believing in me, for his generosity with his time, and for his consistent critical advice. I thank Michael Goldman, David Sonnenfeld, John Gulick, Alan Rudy, and the collective of the Global Ethnography book project for reading very early interpretations of my data and for giving me constructive feedback. Peter Evans and David Stark boldly compelled me to try out theoretical perspectives that I would not have risked on my own, especially in rethinking the role of the state in my history. I am grateful to my colleagues at the University of Illinois–Urbana Champaign—Matti Bunzl, Michael Goldman, and Andy Pickering—whose advice propelled this project to new, exciting directions. I thank Martha Lampland and anonymous reviewers of my manuscript for insisting on mobilizing my somewhat hidden ethnographic voice. I have tremendous appreciation for my graduate students who have given me feedback on my theory of waste: Annie McCloskey, Lisa Asplen, Keith Guzik, and Jong-Young Kim.

This research however would not have been possible without the confidence and generosity of my informants, primarily the residents of three villages, Garé, Bosta, and Szalánta. I am also humbled by the trust the leaders of the Budapest Vegyimũvek and Hungaropec had in me, and their generosity in opening their doors and archives to me. But fieldwork was only one source of the history I am retelling in this book. Without the incredibly professional and mostly unappreciated labor of the archivists in the archives of Hungary, of the Communist Party, and of Baranya County I would not have been able to reconstruct either the story of Garé's dump or the changing concept of waste in Hungary. I am also grateful to the Országos Széchenyi Könyvtár for allowing me to use illustrations from their poster collections. Finally, I would not have been able to finance this immense research project on my own. The International Exchanges Board, the Fulbright Commission, the Wenner-Gren Foundation, the American Council of Learned Society, and the University of Illinois have given me generous financial support in these last ten years.

Most importantly, I would not have accomplished much without the warm support of my husband, Rick Esbenshade, and my two children, Shara and Abel, who faithfully accompanied me on my many research trips leaving friends and home behind. Rick not only has shown patience and empathy toward my daily "paradigm shifts" and intellectual crises but also has been a keen and critical reader of my manuscript. Since I embarked on this journey I lost many of my loved ones, including my parents, and I myself went through a life-threatening illness. I don't know how I would have survived without the emotional sustenance I received from my Hungarian family, especially my two aunts and three cousins, among whom Zoltán Balogh also lent generous help with digitalizing my illustrations. This list is far from complete, and in closing, all I want to emphasize is that I hope to return the kindness of all the people who helped me turn this project into the book I always dreamed about writing.

From the Cult of Waste to the Trash Heap of History

one
Was State Socialism Wasteful?

Upon an island hard to reach,
the East Beast sits upon his beach.
Upon the west beach sits the West Beast.
Each beach beast thinks he's the best beast.

Which beast is best? . . . Well, I thought at first
that the East was best and the West was worst.
Then I looked again from the west to the east
and I liked the beast on the east beach least.

   Dr. Seuss, *West Beast East Beast*

A Puzzle

Soon after I came to the United States in 1988 as a Hungarian émigré,
state socialism collapsed, not only in my country but also in the entire
socialist camp of Europe. In reading American news about the region, I
was struck by the persistence of the metaphor of waste. State socialism was
described as having been a wasteful economic order and polluted to the
extreme by its wastes. Visual representations of state socialism invoked the
image of the state socialist landscape most familiar in the West—a gray still
life composed of shoddy goods; people wearing poor, idiosyncratic clothes

surrounded by houses that looked like they could fall apart at any time; and piled-up garbage and filth. Images are not timeless snapshots, however; they tell a story. Here, the juxtaposition of images—"backward" production technologies, represented by horse-drawn carts and smokestacks burning coal; power plants; poverty with debris, dirt, and toxic wastes; and degraded nature—tell a story about state socialism that has been told for many decades, portraying it as megalomaniac yet outdated industrialization that left society in poverty, generated tremendous amounts of waste, and caused environmental destruction.

Textual representations in journalistic accounts, policy papers, and scholarly works rarely go further than the confirmation of this imagery. The main culprits are usually poor management of the economy and outdated technology. "Open hearth steel manufacturing and other outdated, inefficient technologies are still widely used by East European and Soviet industries," states the World Watch Institute in a 1991 study explaining state socialist wastefulness and pollution (World Watch Institute 1991). In addition to backwardness, a "faulty, mismanaged economic system" has been invoked as a key cause of environmental degradation. "Lack of efficiency in East German factories is a major pollution factor. On the average, they use twice as much energy as necessary, burning huge amounts of coal to generate the needed electricity," says the director of research for the West German Federal Ministry of the Environment (Mutch 1990, 4).

Scholarly works and studies made by international financial and aid hubs applying statistical data often point out that state socialist countries' emissions/GDP, emissions/capita, and waste/GDP indexes, as well as material and energy intensity indexes,[1] have been significantly higher than— and often multiples of—Western equivalents.

> Data on gross emissions suggest that sulphur dioxide emissions per head of the population are higher for Czechoslovakia, the GDR and Poland than for any other countries in the world. These emissions are the consequence of a wasteful use of energy combined with a reliance upon coal, especially brown coal, for a large fraction of total primary energy consumption. (Hughes 1990, 4)

The World Watch Institute adds, "The Soviet Union and East European countries generally use 50 to 100 percent more energy than the United States to produce a dollar of gross domestic product (GDP) and 100–300 percent more than Japan" (French 1990). The result is, as a *New York Times* author puts it: "Mountains of garbage. Literally, garbage" (Lewis 1990, A21).

The textual, visual, and statistical representations all suggest, therefore, that state socialism was wasteful, both in the sense of squandering resources and in the sense of being full of wastes: producing too many rejects, too much waste and garbage, and too many outdated and/or super-fluous goods. But too many compared to what? In the great majority of representations, state socialism's wastefulness is not only confirmed but, implicitly or explicitly, it is also contrasted with the cleanliness, efficiency, and thriftiness of Western capitalism. In the above-quoted *New York Times* piece, for example, the author admits that these "mountains of garbage" (400,000 tons of detritus and 40,000 tons of toxic waste per year) were imported from West Germany, yet this fact does not stop her from conclud-ing that the performance of Western capitalism is superior: "After all, mar-kets, cost-consciousness, the need to please the customers, turn out to be more effective than central command even on such basic social questions as pollution" (Lewis 1990, A21).

Scholarly representations attributed this inferiority to the overreach of the state in the East. Most authors stipulated that state ownership and especially the lack of market-controlled prices led to a squandering of resources, since enterprises were always bailed out if they operated with a deficit. Scholars ultimately explained the environmental problems of state socialism as the failure of Marxist ideology, not only because the dictator-ship of the proletariat served as justification for a hyperactive and omnipre-sent state but also because the labor theory of value saw work as the only source of value and thus tended to treat natural resources as free and inexhaustible.

Convincing as these representations may be, it is not easy to reconcile such findings with memories of my youth spent in Hungary: the numerous waste collection campaigns in school, in which we competed among our-selves to collect the most paper waste and metal scrap; the hours I spent standing in line to return empty jars and bottles to the grocery store (I got to keep the deposits); the fact that you took your own bags when you went shopping because the stores offered none. I also remember the shortages and the electricity-saving campaigns. What was wasteful about these prac-tices? I went to Hungary to investigate.

The Case Study

When I first saw a picture of the Garé dump site in 1993, I was reminded of familiar images in the media: dirty, barren lands with oozing waste drums, surrounded by some of the poorest villages of the country. (To locate Garé on the map, please see figs. 8.1 and 8.2, chap. 8.) Was the story of this case similar to the narratives told by those media images? How was it interpreted and made use of by various actors? Since Garé's toxic dump made the national news on a weekly basis in the 1990s, it seemed to be an excellent example for answering questions such as these. Garé is a small village in Baranya County in the south of Hungary, a relatively under-developed and multiethnic region of the country. In 1968 the Budapest Chemical Works (BCW) established a disposal site next to the village for its pesticide by-product, tetrachlorobenzene (TCB). The metal drums even-tually corroded and started to leak, causing the contamination of ground-water and a nearby spring. In addition to the stench, according to villagers, the dump was to be blamed for mysterious illnesses among domestic ani-mals and an increase in the incidence of cancers among residents. Though the environmental authorities ordered BCW to clean up the dump in 1990, the firm instead decided to use the Garé dump as a rationale for establishing a toxic waste incinerator next to the dump. A French cor-poration formed a joint venture with BCW for this purpose, generating a decade-long battle around the permits for this facility.

Garé's dump was a case that, on the surface, seemed to confirm the view that state socialism was dirty, and that the West was going to clean up by providing high-tech solutions and capital. Tetrachlorobenzene was pro-duced by a state-owned enterprise through a rather inefficient production process, in which the ratio of the waste to the final product was about 50 percent. Furthermore, it was a French company that was supposed to solve Garé's twenty-year-old problem. It was in such a Cold War frame of refer-ence that the case was evoked in supranational organizations' or foreign governments' policy recommendations. Yet, if one looked at the history of the case, it proved wrong many of the same assumptions and clear-cut binaries. First, the pollution was not of the paradigmatic type associated with state socialism, that is, the acid rain–causing emissions of outdated, coal-based heavy industry. Rather, BCW was among the most modern chemical firms of the country, and TCB was the by-product of a herbicide intermediary, a rather modern product at the time. Second, state owner-ship and Marxist ideology had little to do with this waste. The state may have been the producer of the by-product in a legal sense, to the extent that BCW, like all large enterprises in Hungary before 1989, was in state owner-ship; but TCB production actually arose out of BCW's need to make up for subsidies it requested but never received from the state. The firm turned to the West to address this deficit, and the TCB that was eventually dumped in Garé resulted from the manufacturing process of a good that had actu-ally been produced for Austrian, that is, capitalist, export. This already indicates that the West's role in this case is a little more complex than was assumed in the mainstream representations I introduced above. The herbicide Austria produced out of this intermediary was not an ordinary peacetime tool of agricultural modernization; rather it was said to be Agent Orange, which Hungary's Western neighbor sold to the U.S. Army. Due to the toxicity and the sheer volume of the by-product, there were no Western companies willing to manufacture TCB; BCW, however, desperate for hard currency, accepted the offer.

Not only is it impossible to make sense of the origins of the dump with an exclusive reference to domestic circumstances and the shortcomings of socialism, it is also difficult, at the other end of the story, to see the West solely in the role of savior. After all, the French incinerator firm's goal was not to clean up the village's dump site but rather to build a profit-oriented waste-burning facility, using an end-of-pipe technology[2] that had been known to cause serious environmental and public health risks, thus adding to rather than attenuating the toxic load on the region. But the West's ambiguous role does not end here. After a decade-long struggle, the villagers and Greens won in this local case, and the incinerator plan failed.[3] However, no sooner did the ink dry on the ultimate rejection of this facility than the government drew up an ambitious plan to establish more toxic waste disposal sites and incinerators in order to make Hungary conform to the European Union's environmental standards. While on paper the European Union prefers preventative approaches to waste problems such as waste minimization, reuse, and recycling, its actual practice has favored end-of-pipe technologies that deal with already existing pollutants, but only incompletely. While the European Union has provided no aid and loans for waste prevention, it has provided Hungary (as well as other East European candidate countries) with millions of Euros to establish an extensive network of dumps and incinerators, all of which are to be built by Western European capital and technology. The local victory in the Garé case was in vain to the extent that it had no effect on national-level policy. To properly appreciate the tragedy of this turn of events, we must consider that socialist Hungary could actually boast an extensive infrastructure of waste collection and reuse—as I referred to it from my childhood memories—in practice embodying a preventative rather than an end-of-pipe approach to by-products.

My point is not that all environmental problems of state socialism ultimately originate in the West or in the East's economic dependence on the West, but rather that we cannot make sense of Eastern Europe's past record on waste without considering the geopolitical as well as local contexts and the many unintended consequences of building both socialism and capitalism. The Garé case thus problematizes our previous notions of state socialism and capitalism and suggests that a more nuanced terminology is needed if one is to account for the contradictions and the puzzle I started with—a terminology that takes into consideration the cultural, ideological approaches to waste as well as the material agency of by-products. Let me illustrate.

Contrary to my expectations, within the first month of doing archival work in Hungary, I realized that waste not only existed as a concern to the planners but also had become something of an obsession. The number of studies that appeared on the problem of waste production, the number of institutions and authorities dealing with waste, the depth and comprehensiveness of waste legislation and data collection, and the amount of propaganda materials just within the first few years of state socialism made it clear that my hypothesis, according to which waste problems were denied until reform economics started worrying about lowering production costs, could not even stand the first test of the historical record.

As I continued with my historical investigation, it slowly dawned on me that the industrial waste the early socialist planners talked about, measured, collected, and regulated to the extreme was somehow different from the waste the later reformers talked about, and it was definitely different from the industrial waste we talk about in the United States. This waste seemed to consist of a different material and occupied a different place in the planners' cognitive maps of the economy. The planners talked mostly about metal wastes, while in the United States, when we hear the term industrial waste, we immediately think of hazardous wastes. The planners' waste was always thought of as being within production, while, in the United States, we usually talk about industrial waste outside the context of production. In sum, the way in which the question of waste was posed in public discourse sounded entirely exotic.[4]

The contemporary Hungarian newspapers were full of reports on workers finding wastes in the factory yards and ingeniously making something out of them. The celebratory tone of these articles reminded me of the tone of essays about major scientific or geographic discoveries. The socialist dailies made waste collection and reuse sound like an exciting adventure, and they reported these "events" in the genre of detective stories. In contrast, everything that appears in the U.S. media about industrial waste portrays it as a material that pollutes and poisons, and not only is it not supposed to be collected, it should be displaced and eliminated. Between January 1982 and October 1998 in five U.S. newspapers,[5] forty-one articles addressed industrial waste. Out of these, only ten were not about hazards, disposal, or cleanup, and only four addressed recycling or waste minimization explicitly.

While in early state socialism the reduction but especially the reuse of waste were subject to numerous regulations, in the United States such regulations have remained suspect. When, for example, in the seventies the need to federally regulate waste streams finally became acknowledged, the idea that it was waste disposal and not waste production that needed legislative attention won out, despite a theoretical agreement that regulating waste generation is a more advanced, more preventative approach (Szasz 1994). DuPont's argument before a U.S. Senate committee is quite telling of this attitude:

> We believe that the disposal of wastes ought to be regulated instead of regulating the nature and use of the product or the type of manufacturing process used . . . greatest emphasis should be placed on establishing standards which assure that the ultimate disposal method is satisfactory . . . it is unreasonable in most instances to require the use of certain types of processes solely based on the waste generated . . . product standards could have severe economic effects . . . [which would] not be in the overall interest of the consumer . . . [there would be] a detrimental effect on the development of new materials and innovative uses of existing materials. (Szasz 1994, 19)

While in the United States, and in most Western countries, waste production was off-limits to public scrutiny, and the generated wastes were only arrested once outside of production, in Hungary, and in other state socialist countries, waste *disposal* was the taboo item.

Chalking these differences up to some vague notion of cultural diversity would only short-circuit the analysis. The really interesting question is how and why these varying concepts of waste appear, metamorphose, and disappear. For this reason, studying the question of wastefulness in a country such as Hungary that has experienced both state socialism and capitalism can provide a much-needed thick description of such historical changes and their relationship to waste issues. However, socialism was not seamless, but rather it went through its own metamorphoses, about many of which it is reasonable to expect that they had an impact on how waste was conceptualized and managed. Most scholars tend to identify two main phases of state socialism: Stalinism and the reform periods. Stalinism, a totalitarian political regime that accompanied a rigid and even militarized central planning model, is probably the more familiar face of state socialism to Western readers. However, the larger part of Eastern Europe's postwar history can be more accurately identified as the softened, reformed version of socialism characterized by the loosening of economic control, the opening toward the West, industrial modernization, and a cautious political and cultural liberalization. This transformation of state socialism followed a different time line and occurred with varying degrees of intensity and irreversibility in different countries. Hungary, Poland, and the German Democratic Republic have been identified as countries where these two forms and periods of state socialism were the most ideal-typically present. Therefore, a Hungarian case study not only offers us a more nuanced understanding of the regime but also is likely to demonstrate change processes and their effects on waste discourses in a more crystallized manner than a case study of countries with no significant change in their economic and political orders.

The Hungarian communists implemented totalitarian rule by the end of 1948 following a series of electoral and political manipulations. They expropriated capitalists and landlords, turning state ownership into the dominant form of property in industry. In agriculture, cooperative and state farms were established, often with violent measures. A forced rapid modernization was carried out in the country, people of peasant background were brought into urban factories in massive numbers, and professionals, now treated as class enemies, were expelled from managerial positions and the political leadership. Largely due to the threat of a Third World War and to a Western embargo on certain metal exports, central planning funneled all human and material resources into the heavy industries, causing severe shortages in consumer goods. The party treated the failures in plan fulfillment as political sabotage and "culprits" as spies, creating a pervasive atmosphere of fear. In October 1956, Hungarians took to the streets seeking socialism with a human face and even independence from the Soviet Union, but they were defeated by the Soviet Army. By early November, János Kádár was put in power by the Soviet Union, and he ruthlessly avenged the revolution in the next three years. In order to gain legitimacy and to prevent another revolution, Kádár nevertheless started to give more concern to consumption. This, in return, required the loosening of the party-state's control over production and distribution leading to a series of reform steps that culminated in the New Economic Mechanism of 1968. Enterprises gained more say in what they produced and who they traded with, price setting became more flexible, and private ownership was tolerated and in agriculture even encouraged. Hungary also opened up trade with the capitalist countries, which not only earned it hard currency but also made available coveted consumer goods from Western Europe. By the mid-1960s Kádár's regime was turned into a type of consumer socialism, earning Hungary the name "the happiest barrack in the camp." The reforms continued in a stop-and-go fashion, but overall, the tendency was toward greater liberalization. The year 1989, the collapse of the regime in Hungary, is often interpreted as the breaking point at which many small changes added up to a radical transformation, whose effects could no longer be contained. The history thus told tends to be a narrative in which freedom and the accession to EU membership were the inevitable telos of events.

This rather sketchy and standard history of Hungarian state socialism will look somewhat different when viewed from the perspective of waste. One cannot deduce all aspects of a social regime, including its environmental record, simply from its macroeconomics and political institutions (or, according to Marxist terminology, its mode of production). Therefore I will replace the capitalism/socialism and the totalitarian/reform socialism dichotomies with a typology in which the central organizing concept is that of waste regimes. These are delineated according to how—that is, through what economic, political, and material dynamics— waste is produced, how it is conceptualized, and how it is politicized. I will elaborate on this concept in chapter 2. When history is viewed through this conceptual lens, rather than through, for example, the notion of mode of production, we gain a different periodization of the forty years of Hungarian state socialism.

I will identify three waste regimes in Hungary during the years between the advent of socialism in 1948 and 2004, the year when the country definitively became capitalist by joining its former political nemesis, the European Union. The metallic waste regime prevailed from 1948 to 1974, and its key characteristic was an identification of waste with metal scrap, leading to a cult of waste that hailed all garbage and by-products as "free" materials to be mobilized for the fulfillment of the plan. It is in this period that the state implemented a vast infrastructure that registered, collected, redistributed, and reused both production and consumer wastes. From the second half of the seventies, waste was primarily seen as inefficiency; policy attention shifted from reuse to reduction; and waste dumping started to be legalized. Finally, by 1985, the regime fully in operation was the chemical waste regime, which treated by-products as inherently useless and toxic and thus as something to be disposed of or incinerated. From 1989, through a curious synergy between the chemical waste regime and marketization, the waste recycling infrastructure was demolished, effecting the first appearance in Hungary of a throwaway culture. The narrative here is rather that of a loss or regression rather than that of a teleological progression toward freedom and affluence.

After the next chapter that develops a social theory of waste and places the present study in the context of the scholarship on state socialism, the book follows the history of the three waste regimes from the beginning of Hungarian state socialism in 1948 to 2004. This narrative will be told in three parts, each of which will consist of a chapter on the respective waste regime, and one on its contradictions and unintended consequences, especially as they were exhibited through the Garé case. The Conclusion summarizes the shortcomings of both socialism and capitalism on the terrain of waste politics, and ends with a call for the democratization of decisions made about production.

two
Toward a Social Theory of Waste

State Socialism and the Environment in Academic Scholarship

That socialism's "demonstrated" wastefulness could turn into yet another ideological weapon demonstrating Western economic and moral superiority in the Cold War and in the postsocialist transition has much to do with the poverty of the scholarship on environmental issues in Eastern Europe. In fact, the question whether state socialism was wasteful was never really explicitly raised but rather was assumed or deduced from the uncritical application of general and outdated economic and political science approaches to state socialism.

This, in turn, is the result of the mutual ignorance of East Europeanists and environmental studies scholars. Though there were studies documenting horrendous ecological disasters, mostly in the Soviet Union, environmental concerns were lacking from the agendas of sociologists, anthropologists, historians, and, to a lesser degree, political scientists. Fatally, the reverse has also been true. The few studies that have focused on ecological problems have remained uninformed by the achievements of the empirical studies done on Eastern Europe and untouched by the theoretical sophistication and methodological rigor that accrued to research on the economy, social inequalities, and culture.

A key problem with the fledgling field of study of ecological problems in the former state socialist world was its assumption that the state and the enterprises had shared interests:

> Instead of serving as a referee between polluters and conservationists, government officials usually support the polluters. It is necessary to remember that the state is the manufacturer, and so there is almost always an identity of interests between the factory manager and the local government official. (Goldman 1972, 69–70)

Though economists and political scientists had long since proved this view wrong and even the official ideologues in socialist countries had stopped automatically assuming an identity of interests, studies in this vein (DeBardeleben 1985; Goldman 1972; Jancar 1987; Völgyes 1974) continued to ignore the interests and constraints of enterprises.[1] As a result, they assumed that it was sufficient to concentrate on the failures of the state, that is, on policy. Had these authors paid more attention to sociological, economic, and anthropological studies of state socialism, they would not have established simplistic causal relations between the poor environmental record of state socialism and either Marxism-Leninism or the absence of market mechanisms.[2] Readers could deduce two things from such studies: either that the regime was the practical implementation of Marxist-Leninist philosophical principles, including, for example, the labor theory of value; or, alternatively, that the regime was a deficient copy of capitalism that failed in so many respects exactly because it lacked the law of value (for Marxian analysts) or the wisdom of the "invisible hand" (for more liberally minded observers) (DeBardeleben 1985; Szlávik 1991; Taga 1976; Ziegler 1992).

Narrow policy analysis continued to dominate environmentally oriented social science studies even after 1989, and these studies demonstrated the same disregard for empirical research on other aspects of the regime change. These studies primarily focused on laws and other regulative measures and paid little attention to new economic interests (especially multinational corporations), the radical shift in environmental discourse, and the reappearance of the local in politics (DeBardeleben 1991; Feshbach and Friendly 1992; Klarer and Moldan 1997).[3] While the early 1990s saw a simple description of environmental movements and their issues, including their prominent role in bringing down state socialism, today the field boasts several theoretically informed and critical empirical studies (Harper 1999; Lipschutz and Mayer 1996; Schwartz 2006).

Even so, much remains to be done in updating the field with the advances made in sociology, anthropology, geography, and political science in the study of postsocialist economic formations and relations (Böröcz 1992; Burawoy and Hendley 1992; Burawoy and Krotov 1992; Dunn 1999; Gábor 1990; Humphrey 2002; Lampland 1995; Ledeneva 1998; Ries 1997; Stark and Bruszt 1998; Verdery 1996; Woodruff 1999), social inequalities (Barany 1994; Humphrey 1999; Lemon 2000), regional inequalities and the spatiality of power (Bodnár 2000; Humphrey 1999), new and old identities and cultural and discourse analysis (Böröcz 2001; Hann 2002), and East-West power relations (Böröcz 2001; Sampson 1999; Wedel 1998). To my mind, there are two tasks that are especially urgent. First, we ought to subject environmental discursive formations to historical scrutiny. Here key questions are how and why certain issues come to be seen as "environmental" and become a part of public discourse. A corollary is the question of how and why other issues remain taboo or are seen as not environmental in nature and therefore undeserving of policy attention. We ought to be able to account for the disappearance of certain issues from public discourse.

Second, we ought to see these issues as having a material existence. A problem does not receive regulatory attention out of the blue, but rather because somebody somewhere produced something and used, changed, or destroyed a part of the natural and physical world. Such interventions are material and tend to occur in production. That is, the problem of the exclusive focus on policies and movements is not only that these authors assume to know a priori what constitutes an environmental problem but also that they see solutions in terms of post facto management. For example, the authors study emissions standards but not the production process and the local, national, and global economic contexts in which this production is deemed necessary and beneficial. Or else, they might study the unequal distribution of toxic waste (as, for example, in studies on ecological racism) but ignore the question of why and for whose benefit goods with toxic by-products are generated. That is, both policy and movement approaches suffer from an end-of-pipe approach and lack a focus on the realm of production (Gottlieb 2001).

While the question of state socialism's wastefulness clearly has political implications, my intention is not merely to use waste as a lens to reveal features of socialism and capitalism. Waste plays different roles in constituting what we refer to in a rather objectified manner as "socialism" and "capitalism." To put it more precisely, waste is not only a representational perspective I will use in this book but also a constitutive element of the social orders whose material culture and economy I am interested in investigating. Waste and society will be shown to mutually constitute each other and will be analyzed as such.

The Problem of Waste

In U.S. environmental sociology, struggles around waste dumps and incinerators have been among the most researched issues, and it is to the resulting studies that we can credit the discipline's systematic approach to environmental justice (Aronson 1997; Bryant and Mohai 1992; Bullard 1990; Costner and Thornton 1993; Di Chiro 1996; Kuletz 1998; Luton 1996; Pellow 2002a; Pellow 2002b; Szasz 1994; Walsh, Warland, and Smith 1997; Weinberg, Pellow, and Schnaiberg 2000). In Europe, the most influential school of environmental sociology, ecological modernization theory, turned its attention to a shift from end-of-pipe remedial approaches to preventative, that is, economically and technologically built-in, environmental solutions, in which wastes and by-products were a key concern. In 1992 Ulrich Beck argued that in the "overdeveloped" countries, social struggles increasingly center not on the distribution of goods but on the distribution of bads, such as toxic waste and other health risks (Beck 1992). Individual strategies of avoiding such risks and a newly developing consumer consciousness of the waste-generating effects of certain commodities and services have also enjoyed new attention in a promising new scholarship on consumption (Dürrschmidt 1999; O'Brien 1999; Schor 2000). In sum, waste—both as a moral category and as a polluting material —has received much scholarly attention in the last twenty years.

Yet, the way we think about waste has not changed much, and today Michael Redclift would still argue, as he did in 1996, that "we lack a theoretical understanding of sink functions, matching that of resources" (Redclift 1996, 14).[4] Scholars studying waste in one form or another have been speaking at cross-purposes because they operate with different implicit definitions of waste. Especially unfortunate has been economists' assumption that waste is merely an attribute of efficiency, but public discourse has also been hampered by an environmentalist impulse to reduce the problem of waste to a problem of pollution. Most detrimental is the way a distinction has been drawn between production and consumption wastes (or industrial and municipal wastes). That distinction assumes that consumers actually have control over how much and what kinds of waste they generate.

The Problem of Data

Academic writing often establishes the merit of studying a social problem by quoting statistics on the matter. Such data then are used to demonstrate the "pervasiveness" of the social problem at hand; or, as in relying on longitudinal data, to show some kind of a crisis tendency. While there is extensive circumstantial evidence that we keep producing more wastes, that their toxicity is increasing, and that they constitute an ever-greater menace to the environment and thus to public health, the tried-and-true statistical manner of introducing a social problem is not feasible when the subject at hand is waste.

First, there are no statistics on overall waste volumes. Instead, data are published on seemingly distinct categories, such as municipal waste, manufacturing waste, mining waste, energy production waste, nuclear waste, hazardous waste, landfilled waste, and incinerated waste, just to mention the most common categories of data. Statistical practice also breaks down these categories according to their source, toxicity, preferred method of disposal, physical state, recycling rate, and so forth.

Comparing countries and time periods within is equally problematic. There is no agreed classification of even the smaller categories of waste, and even these incommensurate classifications are constantly subject to change, which makes both cross-national and longitudinal comparisons impossible. The data published by the OECD (Organization for Economic Cooperation and Development) and the European Environment Agency have so many qualifying footnotes that their explanation takes up more space than the tables themselves. Two different teams in the European Environment Agency drew the conclusion that the respective waste data were not sufficient to allow valid comparisons either cross-nationally or longitudinally (Brodersen, Crowe, and Jacobsen 2001; Weissenbach 2001).

Most statistics, such as those used in policy papers, concentrate on the waste/GDP ratio, that is, the amount of waste generated by unit of Gross Domestic Product (GDP). The difference between socialist countries and capitalist countries does seem considerable enough to warrant a suspicion that state socialism was more wasteful.[5] But was this difference a systemic one, due to the mode of production, or was it due to "backwardness"? Running a regression analysis, one would find that the level of development, measured by GDP/capita, does not have any effect on the level of waste/GDP ratio. However, the mode of production—that is, whether a country was state socialist or capitalist—does have an effect. That relationship seems statistically significant ($F=0.007$), with the mode of production explaining about 60 percent of the change in the amount of waste per GDP.

There are, however, other quantitative findings that do not fit nearly so well with the conclusion that state socialism was more wasteful than capi-

Table 2.1. Annual Nonmunicipal Waste Production and Its Ratio per GDP and per Capita (1,000 Tons). The three highest values are highlighted.

Country	Year	Waste	Waste/GDP	Waste/capita
Canada	1990	1,079,390	1.90	40.55
USA	1990	9,880,710	1.81	39.33
Japan	1985	312,251	0.23	2.59
Austria	1990	33,852	0.21	4.39
Belgium	1988	30,989	0.20	3.11
Denmark	1985	3,836	0.34	0.75
Finland	1990	55,910	0.41	11.21
France	1990	559,800	0.47	9.92
West Germany	1990	96,736	0.06*	23.74
Greece	1990	15,974	0.24	1.58
Iceland	1990	135	0.02	0.53
Ireland	1984	26,500	1.49	7.51
Italy	1991	34,710	0.03	0.60
Luxembourg	1990	1,300	0.14	3.40
Netherlands	1990	28,819	0.10	1.93
Norway	1990	29,000	0.27	6.84
Portugal	1990	1,044	0.02	0.11
Spain	1990	195,902	0.40	5.03
Sweden	1990	66,475	0.29	7.77
Switzerland	1990	1,000	0.00	0.15
UK	1990	271,400	0.28	4.73
Czechoslovakia	1987	630,150	12.08	40.47
Hungary	1989	107,493	3.69	10.13
Poland	1990	143,861	2.31	3.77
East Germany	1990	34,064	0.24*	2.10

Source: My calculations from OECD Environmental Data (1993).

*The GDP values for East and West Germany are based on UN estimates which were the same for current and constant prices (World Development Report, 1990).

talism. First of all, the enormous variation within both the capitalist and socialist blocs suggests that factors other than the mode of production might be quite relevant.[6] Second, the mode of production does not seem to affect another measurement of wastefulness, the waste/capita ratios. On that dimension of wastefulness, Canada and the United States actually surpass all but one of the socialist countries. Which data are we to believe? Can we believe statistical findings at all? Or does the answer to the question "was socialism wasteful?" depend a great deal on what notion of wastefulness we presume? Should we insist on using quantitative data? These in particular can be used to prove the mainstream claim about socialism's wastefulness, but just as easily can be used to show the opposite.

This insufficiency and chaos in waste data collection is not accidental. To some extent, it is the result of what Susan Strasser, a key historian of trash, calls the invisibility of waste (Strasser 1999). However, this invisibility is not simply cultural. The idea that production data, including data on waste, should be shared with the state, the public, and potential competitors contradicts the sanctity of private property and corporations' rights to protect their industrial secrets. In some countries certain waste-related data are classified (Brodersen, Crowe, and Jacobsen 2001; Weissenbach 2001), and the United States has never even collected comprehensive manufacturing waste data as the European Union countries have done. Finally, wastes are impervious to being consistently classified, registered, and measured, which also has something to do with the fact that the complexity of materials we produce intentionally or unintentionally increases faster than the capability of our classificatory systems.

In sum, it is time for the tail to stop wagging the dog, that is, it is time for us to develop theory that could inform data construction, rather than allowing the existing and rather faulty data collection practices to keep impoverishing theory and limiting space for social critique. In that spirit, I will advance a sociological theory of waste, first by identifying waste fetishism as the main fault in our thinking about waste, and then by distinguishing among three key aspects of waste: its spatiality, its materiality, and its temporality.

Waste Fetishism

Before defining waste as a social category, let me indicate the general theoretical direction in which I wish to proceed. First of all, it is important to insist that it is possible to define what waste is even in a theoretical framework that on the whole is sympathetic to social constructivism. That is, while at a certain level of argumentation, it is sensible to maintain that waste is in the eye of the beholder, at another, metatheoretical level we do need to be able to define what it is that is seemingly in the eye of the beholder. Social constructivism should not become an excuse either for theoretical sloppiness or for a view from everywhere but accountable to no one (Haraway 1991). Defining waste at a metatheoretical level is not free of politics. In fact, identifying and challenging the metaconcept of waste that silently underlies and sanctions existing statistical practices and knowledge-production about waste is in itself a political step.

Not only does statistics attend to waste only in its seemingly distinct embodiments (such as municipal waste, nuclear waste, and so forth), but, as I argued above, most specialized lexicons also fail to include the term "waste," or if they do they immediately refer the reader to other entries, such as radioactive waste, air pollution, and other terms. The problem is not only the one identified by K. A. Gourlay, namely, that by breaking up the concept of waste and spreading it over dictionary entries on distinct tasks of "waste management," the waste problem is presented as not only manageable but already being managed, thus solved (Gourlay 1992). More importantly, this extreme operationalism (Marcuse 1964) suggests that what is at fault is the material: it is toxic, it is useless, it is stinky, and there is just plain too much of it.[7] However, if we ask why it is toxic, useless, stinky, and too voluminous, we ought to admit that the answer is, "because we, humans and society, have made it so." That is, materials are not "born" to be waste: they are transformed into waste by identifiable material and social processes. Therefore, the focus must shift from waste as a certain kind of material to the activities from which waste emerges. As I will later qualify, this does not undermine the material agency of waste.

To the extent that we have taken the "wasteness" of some discarded materials for granted, and to the extent that this view has justified an environmentally and socially damaging politics of waste, we can register a prevalent waste fetishism in most contemporary societies. Therefore, any step, no matter how small, that leads us away from the reification of waste and toward an inquiry into the activities that make waste is a bold political move.

I credit Gourlay with the first step. In his book *World of Waste* (Gourlay 1992), he reunites all the disaggregated and concrete manifestations of waste and defines it as something that we have failed to use. However, we cannot stop here, because there are many ways in which we fail to use something and many reasons why we do so. For this reason, I will now start not only to shift the focus from waste to the act of wasting but also to delineate what we may call the elementary forms of wasting.

First, we turn something into waste when a material has been used up, worn out, broken, and so on. This material has therefore fulfilled the human need for which it was produced. This is probably the most common way to think about waste. If we eat a banana, the immediate waste we create is the peel. If a shirt gets torn from having been worn, the whole shirt tends to become waste. The question here is how "well, how 'fully'" this product been used. A half-eaten banana or a shirt that is still in "working condition" but is no longer fashionable are turned into waste "before their time."[8] Second, we turn some things into waste even when they have never fulfilled the human need for which they was created. Defective products belong to this category. A shirt that was produced with a defective textile that causes it to rip the first time we wear it becomes waste. Bananas that spoil en route to the supermarket become waste as well. Third, we can also turn into waste well-made products that are perfectly capable of fulfilling the human need for which they were created when we don't find uses for the items. This is the case with goods for which there is no demand—either because they are overproduced or because of some of their qualitative aspects, such as aesthetic or sensory appeal.

In reality these elementary forms of wasting combine in complex ways. For example, we may use something in a way that was not intended by the producers of the product, and this can happen after the product in question was already used to fulfill the human need for which it was created, or we can "misuse" the object from the beginning. We can use a shirt as a rag for dusting in all three elementary cases, that is, without ever having used the shirt as a shirt even though it was capable of fulfilling the human need for clothing; or using a defective but new shirt; or having used the shirt as a shirt first and then as a rag.

To bring in yet another complicating factor, the "original" human need that a shirt is supposed to fulfill can change from culture to culture, and from individual to individual. Furthermore, as Appadurai points out, commodities can go back and forth between being waste and being useful—so that temporarily usefulness and waste can share the same register of signification (Appadurai 1986). As a sociologist, I am, however, primarily interested in complicating this rudimentary classification by connecting seemingly individual acts of wasting to others, and by theorizing the relationship between micro-level or individual acts of wasting and macro-level wastings. To do so, I will now identify three main aspects of wastes: spatiality, materiality, and temporality. Still remaining at the level of metatheory, I will make an argument in relation to each: first, that waste is liminal; second, that waste is hybrid; and third, that waste's circulation and metamorphosis are not only socially specific but also impart unique features to, and thus are constitutive of, society.

Waste Has an Immanent Spatiality

Various scholarly conceptualizations have all suggested that waste is the opposite of some concept or quality (Moser 2000). That is, it has been understood to occupy the negative side of a number of different dichotomies, such as efficiency/inefficiency; usefulness/uselessness; order/disorder; gain/loss; clean/dirty; alive/dead; fertile/sterile. By and large, there is a curious though not counterintuitive affinity among disciplines and the choice of a binary. Economists tend to identify waste as cost inefficiency and low productivity; natural scientists, ecologists, and environmental sociologists think of waste as pollution and thus as the opposite of cleanliness and hygiene; and anthropologists and humanists see waste as the opposite of order and value.

As individuals we also accomplish some classification when we are engaged in an act of wasting. Historian Susan Strasser (1999) argues that trash is created by the act of separating the usable from what is to be thrown out, and she demonstrates how, why, and with what effect the social agents involved in this sorting have changed over time in the United States. This, I must add, involves a selection along multiple criteria of utility. There is, obviously, utility in the sense of using something for its originally intended purposes, but there is also a secondary utility, such as using a discarded tire as an outdoor flowerpot, or the many artistic uses of trash—by now a well-accepted art form (Neville and Villeneuve 2000; Yaeger 2003). Another element of utility is emotional: we often prevent a thing from passing into the sphere of objects to be discarded because it has "sentimental value." It is when we decide that the object in question is not useful to us in either of these senses that we cognitively turn it into waste.

Besides these different classes of utility, however, the cognitive task of wasting includes a certain planning, a certain calculation. What will it imply to throw an object out? How much will it cost to get rid of it, to replace it, or how much will I have to pay for fixing it, maintaining it, or storing it if I decide to hold onto the object? Will the value of this object increase again in the future? Will it become fashionable again? What emotional work will it cost me to convince a packrat spouse to get rid of the object? Will the dog get sick if I feed it to him or her? The cost-benefit calculations again are made from multiple perspectives, not simply from that of monetary value. While it may seem that these are fairly individual and even psychological decisions, they are obviously influenced by society.

How often fashion changes, how important it is to follow it, how affordable it is to replace a discarded good, or how strongly animal rights are protected not only change over time, or from one social order to the next, but also depend on class, religion, age, and potentially many other factors, all of which are fundamentally social.

Another calculation and classification we engage in involves comparing the consequences of different acts of wasting and then choosing based on some criterion. A schizophrenic case is when we waste for hygienic and environmental purposes. When mad cow disease broke out in England or when bird flu broke out in Asia, just to mention cases still fresh in collective memory, hundreds of thousands of animals were slaughtered to prevent the spread of the disease—resulting in TV images that are not for the squeamish. We do the same with forests facing an epidemic and with food suspected but not confirmed to be contaminated. In these cases, we might say that we waste in order to avoid a larger and more devastating form of waste: untimely death, whether of people, animals, or trees.

Geoffrey C. Bowker and Susan Leigh Star (1999) demonstrate through numerous fascinating examples that classification is a fundamentally social activity. We fail to see it as such, because most of the time it is invisible and moralized. In order to make it visible, they suggest, we must inquire into (a) what allows classificatory systems and standards to fit together and cooperate (see also Molotch 2003), (b) who does the classificatory work, and (c) what happens when cases don't seem to fit existing classification (Bowker and Star 1999). Projected against this conceptual background, Strasser's argument that wasting involves sorting is simplistic. Is it always the free choice of the waster to create that classification? When one has to throw out a toaster three months after purchasing it because it doesn't work, who really did the sorting—the manufacturer or the consumer? It is therefore imperative that a sociological study of waste answers these questions rather than taking the answers for granted, as is done when we take as our point of departure seemingly self-explanatory waste statistics, such as data on "consumer waste" or "municipal waste."

The act of wasting always involves some classification and displacement, and this is where the figurative spatiality of waste (that is, classification) transitions into its physical spatiality. The reclassification of the object implies placing it not only into a different category of things but also into a physically different place, one that is sufficiently removed from where it was kept while still used. In our modern society, the trash can, or recycling bin, is the most common destination for wastes, but of course it is only an intermediary one en route to the "final" location of disposal: the municipal dump, the recycling center, or the incinerator. A more final (though, from a longue-durée perspective, only transitional) destination is of course our air, soil, and water.

Sometimes, rather than throw them out, we give away our "wastes" by leaving them on the curbside, handing them down to kin and friends, or donating them to charity. Nevertheless, as the adverb "away" implies, the primary goal is still to get the unwanted stuff displaced and preferably out of sight. Wasting therefore always has a spatial aspect. It is to this extent that cultural approaches to waste (Argyrou 1997; Moser 2000; Murray 1999; Strasser 1999; Thompson 1979) have been correct in adopting anthropologist Mary Douglas's definition of dirt as matter-out-of-place (Douglas 1966). Carrying the argument further, the way people external to the act of wasting know that something has been classified as waste is by looking at where it is. Most people will not take a baby's car seat left in the garage or in a car outside someone's home, but anyone living in the United States will know that a car seat left on the curb next to trashcans or recycling bins is unwanted and thus free for the taking. A newcomer to this country may not know this, and an American visiting abroad might not immediately be able to realize what the proper place of waste is in that locality. We can however be sure that waste has a relatively distinct space assigned to it in most cultures, and that serious moral indignation and resistance will result should a culture impose its own spatial arrangements on another (Argyrou 1997). Just as there are culturally specific norms about utility, there are culturally specific signals about what is the correct place for waste.

For this reason, places for waste are usually marginal spaces—marginal to whatever mainstream activity is taking place in a particular location. In the United States, for example, trash bins are left on the curb for pickup; dumpsters are placed at the back of a restaurant; and dumps, recycling centers, and incinerators are located on the outskirts of town. But just how separated or shunned waste is spatially has much to do with the dominant cultural evaluation of waste. So far, I have only mentioned cases in which waste is identified as the negative side of certain paired opposites. That certainly tends to be the case in market economies in the West. Socialist economies, on the contrary, saw waste as a benevolent deus ex machina, "a gift of nature" to be used in fulfilling quotas in their efforts to establish communism. For them, scrap and by-products were fertile and useful materials, and the state saw one its key economic tasks as registering, collecting, redistributing, and organizing the reuse and recycling of wastes (Gille 1997). From news accounts and a few scholarly studies we know that this positive valuation also dominates among poor countries. In such cases, waste is much less segregated from the main areas of life, and objects pass back and forth between the realms of useful objects and wastes with a greater ease.[9]

But let's not underestimate the difficulty involved in this sorting. In the United States it is estimated that 0.5 percent of the population suffers from what is now identified as a new obsessive-compulsive behavior: compulsive hoarding. Though we may laugh at people like these and we may be less "compulsive," we have all experienced the anxiety over making the decision to throw things out. "Hesitation," however, also occurs at the social level. Disagreements on whether something can be thrown out (for example, demolishing a building), or whether a waste product can be reused (as with the insertion of a fluoride by-product into the drinking water to "protect the dental health" of Californians) have led to the involvement and fierce struggle of social movements and other political actors. That such debates quickly take on a moral rhetoric is not accidental but rather has to do with the unruliness of the concept of waste.

Waste, to wit, is not merely a matter out of place, as those following Douglas argue, but, more profoundly, a concept out of order. Similarly to other hard-to-classify events scrutinized by anthropology, such as hermaphroditism (Geertz 1983), or ritually marked points in an individual's or a group's life, in which they are suspended between two states (Turner 1990 [1969]; Van Gennep 1960), waste is a liminal or boundary object. I am not the first one to propose this: Thompson understands waste as being in a transitional position from the perspective of value, and Moser sees waste as a boundary object between inside and outside and between past and present (Moser 2000; Thompson 1979). Since for them this is simply an interesting fact with no further social consequences and with no roots in the larger social context, liminality becomes the end of the argument rather than its beginning. I would argue that waste's liminality goes deeper and is more complex. First, waste's liminality is multiple: that is, waste can be and is conceptualized as a "no-man's-land" between several dichotomies, such as the ones I listed above, which in practice means that there is a lot at stake in classificatory practices and struggles, certainly a lot more than technical and economic debates would have us believe. Second, the liminality of waste means that waste issues always involve the guarding or the breaking down of certain boundaries, that is, moral discourses will always play an important role in social struggles and policy decisions involving waste. Thus, dismissing morality as immaterial and secondary to some underlying economic conflict will skew our analysis of waste politics. Finally, because of this classificatory anxiety, waste may also prove to be a good lens through which social scientists can get a glimpse of other underlying social and cultural anxieties and moral dilemmas.

The Hybridity of Waste

That said, there is a danger in overemphasizing waste's liminality. Waste issues are not merely expressions of other, "deeper" social matters and moral anxieties. In fact, what I find sorely problematic in the anthropological and cultural studies scholarship is the dematerialization of waste. This in turn has a lot to do with the Durkheimian impulse to relate social facts only to other social facts, which denies the existence of nonhuman agency. This shortcoming was first acknowledged in sociology by environmental sociologists William Catton and Riley Dunlap (Catton and Dunlap 1978) and, more recently, by sociologists of science associated with posthumanism (Callon, Law, and Rip 1986; Goldman and Schurman 2000; Latour 2004; Latour and Woolgar 1979; Pickering 1995). Environmental history has also called for and done much to develop an understanding not just of the effect of society on nature but of the reverse, nature's effect on society (Cronon 1983; Cronon 1991; Merchant 1989; White 1980; Worster 1984; Worster 1985). In sum, we should not only treat waste as always material but also theorize what its material agency means.

This is all the more imperative because the economic model dominant in Western market societies has tended to deny waste's materiality. It is only through the concept of joint production that economists have addressed wastes or, more precisely, by-products. Usually, there is a main product in the manufacturing of which another product is generated that has a secondary importance. The fact that economic theories have been treating joint production as an exception rather than as the rule is in itself a telling sign of the extent to which economists make reality conform to their theoretical models.

The main problem that joint production has posed for economists is one of accounting, that is, the motivation in modeling joint production has been to answer the question of how to separate the function, and thus the costs, of jointly used resources (labor, raw material, energy, and so forth) for each jointly generated product. A common way to model such production and to grapple with this problem is to make the hypothetical assumption that the secondary product can be treated as a main product of another industry, and thus its costs and profits can be assigned to the appropriate industry as its single (nonjoint) product. When the existence of such an industry cannot be assumed, as indeed is the case with most wastes, modelers introduce a dummy industry in the input-output matrix that "uses *no* input and shows the secondary product as output" (Schefold 1987, 1030; my emphasis). Other models treat the secondary products as negative inputs.[10] To paraphrase, economics "solves" the problem of wastes by pretending that waste is produced from nothing or less than nothing.

This negative attitude toward waste gives rise to a practical impulse to "eliminate" it. Specialized dictionaries avoid defining waste itself, and tend to move quickly to the imperative and the techniques of disposal (for example, *Hawley's Condensed Chemical Dictionary* (Hawley 1993) and *Kingzett's Chemical Encyclopaedia* (Kingzett 1966).[11] Waste, as any form of matter, however, cannot be made to disappear, leaving as the next best thing getting it out of sight—that is, lifting it out from the actual milieu in which it was generated.

In the process of displacement, however, waste proliferates. Waste in landfills turns the soil into wastes, which is a well-known fact from cleanup cases, in which not only the originally deposited wastes but also the soil under and around the landfill have to be "cleaned up," usually incinerated. Incineration itself produces wastes, in the form of unburned wastes and in the form of emissions, which have to be screened and properly disposed of. In some cases, incineration reduces the overall waste volume by only 60 percent, and it can easily transform hazardous materials into even more hazardous ones. That is, the waste disposed of comes back to haunt us in newer forms and ever-greater quantities. In these dictionary entries, waste first is defined as negative (as useless), then it is suggested that it should be disposed of in one way or another; since it creates problems when it is disposed, its negativity (troublesomeness) is reinscribed. Waste is something bad, therefore it is something bad. Following Gourlay (1992), we can say that common sense identifying waste as negative and integrating disposal into its definition not only does not offer a solution but itself becomes part of the problem.

Marxist economists of the sixties and seventies differ from classical economists in that they see waste not as an anomaly but rather as a systemic problem (Baran and Sweezy 1966; Packard 1960; Toffler 1970). Nevertheless, by restricting waste to a cost of production, or a wasted resource (a wasted positive use value), both groups ignore that waste is also a negative use value that can harm nature and human health when disposed of or emitted through factory chimneys. Unfortunately even sociological accounts share this propensity to identify waste as inefficiency. Environmental sociologist Raymond Murphy's (1994) programmatic call for a sociology of waste locates the problem of waste in producing with more wastes than ideal engines do.[12] Murphy and Marxist economists therefore imply that waste as a polluting by-product would not exist if it weren't for the built-in wastefulness of capitalism.[13]

Not so much against them but to complement them, I would stress two things. First, simply increasing efficiency—that is, decreasing the amount of waste generated in the production of a unit of product—does not automatically decrease overall waste volumes. If the rate of growth exceeds the rate with which efficiency increases, we still have increasing volumes of waste output. Second, waste is generated even in cases of maximum efficiency, and in fact what type of material or energy efficiency we are talking about invites us to consider more seriously material agency. This, however, must go beyond reducing the materiality of waste to pollution, as is the case in most of environmental sociology. Here, the problem is the exclusive focus on the distribution of waste and ignoring its production. To this extent Monica Casper (2003) is right to argue the ecological justice literature I referred to above treats toxic materials as simply "a backdrop or spur to social action" and leaves their materiality and production unprobed (xvii–xviii).

Many of our wastes, to be sure, have as much to do with materials' tendency to rot, rust, and spoil as with our human intentions to use those materials before their time is over. Just as the author of the nineteenth-century volume *The American Frugal Housewife* did, we too still spend "an inordinate amount of energy battling mold, fermentation, and spoilage" (quoted in Strasser 1999, 33). We in the "overdeveloped" countries may be spending less time and energy combating spoilage, dust, and waste in our households now; however, society at large still has at least as much trouble with unwanted goods, by-products, emissions, and other wastes as those in charge of the premechanized, presynthetic kitchen. In a certain sense our troubles due to material agency have even intensified, inasmuch as the complexity and the danger of dealing with synthetic, nonbiodegradable, and toxic wastes are much greater than dealing with dust, mold, and rot. Recycling, dumping, or incinerating wastes requires collective efforts on a scale even beyond the sanitation of cities that took place in Western countries from the nineteenth through the twentieth centuries (Melosi 1981; Murray 1999; Tarr 1996). Dealing with nonorganic wastes not only demands scientific expertise and complex chemical and mechanical technologies that are hard for the layperson to grasp (Beck 1992), and whose costs are immense, but also requires cooperation among more geographical scales than did sanitation. This is for a couple of different reasons. First, the kinds of wastes we produce today are less perishable, many in fact will never decay on their own, and thus they have time to cross more natural and manmade boundaries. Second, the old rules of thumb according to which larger volumes and longer exposures to chemical hazards pose a greater threat to health do not seem to apply in the case of some material compounds. As Theo Colborn, Dianne Dumanoski, and John Peterson Myers (1997) demonstrate, estrogen-mimicking chemicals, for example, are more harmful in a certain developmental stage of an individual (human or animal); instead of slowly being eliminated and broken down, they are not only stored in the body for a lifetime but even accumulate over time and generations. Third, due to the increasing connectivity of our globe, wastes also cross borders more easily (Fagan 2004). Finally, new types of wastes, such as dioxin emissions or greenhouse gases, accumulate and circulate with much greater ease and pose greater health risks than human excreta. In this sense, it is not far-fetched to say that dealing with wastes has become a more collective and global task.

I am not proposing a simple historical trend of increasing volumes. Rather, it is the complexity of linkages, both among different scales and among different materials in circulation, that renders today's waste problems so much more daunting than they were for the nineteenth-century Sanitary Movement (Melosi 1981; Tarr 1996). This complexity therefore is of a hybrid nature: it is the confluence of ever-more numerous and complex materials, today's means of communication and exchange, and the new social structures that facilitate today's unprecedented global connections.

Waste itself is a hybrid entity, that is, it is simultaneously social and material. But let me be quite specific about what I mean by the term "hybridity." First, different societies tend to rely on a particular set of materials (Amato 1997) and thus tend to produce a certain range of wastes (Markham 1994; Tarr 1996). Second, the materiality of waste places a limit on how it may be classified or, as referred to above, spatialized. To put it simply, the materiality of waste has important implications for how we can go about safely dealing with it. Third, different societies ignore or misunderstand the nature of their material foundations and thus "misspatialize" wastes in unique ways. Waste's materiality is usually clouded by culture: by insufficient knowledge of the materials in use and/or by the ideologies, metaphors, norms, and values that blind us to one or another aspect of material agency. To appreciate the autonomy of the representational and cultural aspects of waste practices, I will refer to them collectively as "waste models." Fourth, such misrecognition and "malpractice" cause things to "bite back" (Tenner 1996), and the unintended consequences then limit and modify "purely social" relations and institutions. Fifth, all these manifestations of waste's materiality influence human and social intention, resulting in a constant "back-and-forth" between society and waste that Pickering calls the "dance of agency" (Pickering 1995). Sixth and finally, the processes by which waste metamorphoses from one form to another are also hybrid, and I will analyze them in the next part when discussing waste's temporality.

Let me demonstrate these arguments using the example of Hungarian state socialism. In the 1950s, the party-state assumed that waste materials were either metal or behaved like iron and steel scrap, that is, that they could be melted down and rerolled over and over again. This assumption of easy recyclability however did not hold for the chemical industries, whose by-products were the result of irreversible processes and whose reuse or recycling posed serious technical problems. Policymakers did not acknowledge this specificity of chemical wastes, and they imposed what I will term the "metallic waste model" on the chemical industry. In practice this meant that other ways of dealing with chemical by-products were not pursued, enterprises were prevented from dumping, and there was no incentive for ceasing technologies leading to nonrecyclable wastes. Chemical plants had no choice but to "store" their wastes in the hope of finding a reuse for them some day. The accumulation of these by-products in factory yards had serious ecological consequences. Waste, to summarize, is hybrid in the sense of having dual determination: social and material. Hungary might not have produced as much chemical waste as it did, and certainly it would not have accumulated this waste in such environmentally disastrous ways, if decision makers had let go of their metallic waste models.

Note that insisting on waste's hybridity is not reneging on the social nature of waste. Nor does the term "hybridity," which is borrowed from social studies of science, imply that the social and the material are mixing "in the same quantities" or are always on equal footing. Hybridity is the acknowledgment that the material and the social do not exist apart from one another; rather, they constantly create and reconstitute each other. The consequence of waste's hybridity for its theorization is that in order to understand how wastes become agents in history we need to pay attention to culture, materiality, and economy all at once. Analyzing the temporality of waste allows us to see just how materiality and economy work together over time. This is what I turn to next.

The Temporality of Waste

Most social scientists view the economy as a place where useful inputs turn into useful outputs and, as such, as a sphere in which value begets value. While we increasingly accept that useless outputs are also produced out of useful inputs, we have not understood properly how certain useless things turn into other useless ones. In this part I will propose that besides the circulation of value, we also find in any economy a circulation of waste. This is no simple circulation of the same waste. Rather, it is a circulation in which one form of waste metamorphoses into another form.

Joel Tarr (1996) is on the right track when he demonstrates how historically "solutions for one pollution problem often generated new pollution problems in different localities in different media" (8). However, the circulation of waste doesn't simply mean the transformation of *one waste material into another* (for example, when waste incineration generates toxic ashes). It also, and even more fundamentally, implies that *different forms of waste* are continually transformed into each other. Waste as excess turns into waste as material, as in the environmental consequences of overconsumption. Waste as inefficiency can change into waste as material and vice versa. I will attend to just such processes in this discussion.

The ways in which waste begets waste are rendered unique by the characteristic social relations of a society. I will demonstrate the systemic forms of waste in two ideal-typical societies—capitalism and state socialism—only to then reconstruct these societies as constituted by waste. I will rely on Hungarian economist János Kornai's (1980) modeling of the modus operandi of centrally planned economies, though he himself has not studied the problem of waste. In his seminal work, *Economics of Shortage*, Kornai (1980) defines central planning, as it existed, as a resource-constrained economy, in which producers competed for resources allocated through taut plans by the center. The tautness of the plans and the sanctions associated with their nonfulfillment forced enterprises to develop several survival strategies, primarily hoarding, substituting inputs, and hiding capacities. In order to make sure resources were at their disposal to fulfill plans, enterprises hoarded materials, even those that they did not have immediate need for, because these could be bartered for those needed. When inputs were missing, enterprises had to find substitutes for them in order to fulfill their quotas. Management not only had to worry about existing plan quotas but also had an interest in preventing their increase. In order to do so, they hid their capacities. Kornai then demonstrates how each of these strategies created and recreated chronic shortages in an endless cycle.

The modus operandi of the system was such that the same logic and motivations that create and recreate shortages simultaneously generated waste. Kornai does not discuss the waste-generating dynamics of centrally planned economies, but they can easily be deduced from his work, especially if supported by other studies on the subject, such as Donald Filtzer's

(1992) and Hillel Ticktin's (1992). When an enterprise accumulated inputs that it did not necessarily need in the present plan period (whether it was a month, half-year, or a year), in order to ensure itself against future shortages, it simultaneously deprived another producer from the inputs required to fulfill its quotas. Substituting inputs, besides possibly producing a product that did not meet technical standards, had the same effect. However, it was not only shortage that was reproduced in this way but also waste. As plans could not be fulfilled due to shortage in one or more inputs, available inputs were transformed into what Kornai (1980) calls slack. The slack that could not be mobilized in a later plan period or in another production process within the same plant became waste. This waste is a broader category than what Kornai calls "bad slack," unmobilizable slack due to shortages in other inputs, because it also includes "good slack," which in the process of storage lost its qualities: it rusted, rotted, broke, or evaporated.

For Kornai, shortage is not simply a discretely produced phenomenon, but it ripples through the entire economy. Just like any material, shortage is not lost, it only transforms within the plant or outside it. Ticktin (1992) and Filtzer (1992) make a parallel argument about waste. Both emphasize the far-reaching effect of retaining rather than discarding deficient products. In capitalism, if a defective product is sold but not used, it turns into waste, while still letting the manufacturer profit from the sale of this product. In socialism, however, a defective product had to be kept in use because of shortages, but the use of this product incurred further costs; that is, it absorbed resources that were not in surplus to begin with. The defective product thus reinforced shortage. Ticktin thus explains both shortage and waste as the flip-side consequences of the same social relations of production.

Filtzer (1992) distinguishes among the following concrete forms of waste: lost work time, the duplication of labor, overconsumption of raw materials, incomplete production, physical loss of materials, and defective production. He presents these forms of waste as interconnected stages of production. The prevalence of defective materials and equipment forces workers to spend their work time rectifying these problems—changing the size of input materials, searching out tools and parts to fix machines—and these efforts necessitate the use of more raw materials than technological specifications require. In addition, some products may not be completed due to missing or defective materials and loss of work time, and they have a strong likelihood of turning into wastes.

These diverse forms of waste snowball through not only a production process but also the entire economy. "The cycle through which this form of waste [resulting from the use of defective materials] is reproduced is virtually never-ending, and the losses which it inflicts on the economy are probably far more serious than those caused by outright defective production" (Filtzer 1992, 135); that is, the losses are more serious than they would have been if defective materials were left unused to begin with. In sum, these microforms of waste are transformed into each other, spiraling upward to reproduce waste as a key macro-level characteristic of centrally planned economies.[14]

For an analysis of systemic causes of waste in capitalism, I turn to Paul Baran and Paul Sweezy's 1966 book, *Monopoly Capital*. Their argument is that in monopoly capitalism there is a tendency for the surplus to rise, but the systemic guarantees for the absorption of this surplus are missing. Unlike in Bataille's (1988) treatment, where surplus originates in nature, surplus here is specific to capitalism, especially its monopolistic version. Furthermore, the reason why it needs to be "absorbed"—that is, wasted—is not due to some essential expediency in nature, but rather because capitalists strive to make returns on their investments. Thus, to keep the economic system from collapsing, the capitalist class and the state develop certain sinks to drain this surplus, such as ever-newer strategies to sell consumer goods (or what Baran and Sweezy term the "sales effort"), the civilian government, and militarism and imperialism.

Baran and Sweezy (1966) thus implicitly argue that in monopoly capitalism, waste results from unabsorbed surplus that materializes in unemployment and unutilized productive capacity. An important implication is that capitalism is an inherently wasteful society, and that it produces waste in the indirect form of generating both consumer goods and productive capacities that remain unutilized. But how does this abstract waste transform into waste as a tangible material in capitalism? In the wasteful absorption of surplus, products are manufactured to turn obsolete faster, which directly increases the amount of waste generated. Furthermore, the manufacturer adds extras onto the product, extras that are not necessary for the product's ability to fulfill a particular function or need, for example, an attractive metal strip on the side of a car. When the product is used up and discarded, it turns into an increased amount of material waste.[15] However, there are other, more subtle processes at work.

Alvin Toffler's (1970) and Vance Packard's (1960) micro-level illustrations nicely fill out the abstract macroeconomic theory of Baran and Sweezy. Documenting the rise of a throwaway culture all across the most developed countries, Toffler (1970) argues that accelerated technological development and planned obsolescence created powerful pressures toward moving away from an economy based on permanence to an economy based on impermanence, in which the "man-thing relationship" becomes ever more "ephemeralized." Packard (1960) documents corporations' strategy to make us overconsume through numerous case studies, resulting in veritable best-sellers. Concerned as these scholars are about inappropriate uses of our resources, this inappropriateness is meant only in terms of consumer, or at most investment, choices, and not in terms of ecological consequences. Locating the source of this prodigality in the macrostructural features of market economies and in the overall culture of capitalism —a materialist, if not hedonist ethos—they present waste less as a concrete material than as an abstract economic, and even moral, category. As with most Marxists of their generation, they do not oppose growth in principle, as long as its benefits fulfill human needs, mostly basic ones, and especially as long as these goods are enjoyed more or less equally.

They do not carry their argument further to conclude, as James O'Connor (O'Connor 1988; O'Connor 1989a) and other Marxist ecologists later do, that capitalism will necessarily run up against the shortage of natural resources wasted away in such a manner. Instead, they suggest that capitalism will ultimately fail to absorb the entire surplus it produces and that this will inevitably bring about its collapse. For both camps, the conclusion is the inevitable and fatal crisis of capitalism due to waste: capitalism will suffocate in its waste—literally for leftist ecologists and figuratively for Baran and Sweezy (1966). When we make the two camps speak to each other, what is clearly demonstrated is that one form of waste, that of surplus materializing as unnecessary and unproductive goods, will turn into actual waste, thus immensely increasing the burden on nature. The chief waste circulation pattern of capitalism is thus the metamorphosis of waste as unutilized excess into waste as pollution.

To summarize, in centrally planned economies, shortage caused waste in two main forms. First there was the waste of resources that could not be used due to the lack of other resources necessary for their useful use in production. While waiting to be utilized, many of them spoiled, rotted, or evaporated; that is, they turned into garbage. Second, waste resulted from producing rejects with substituted or insufficient resources. In capitalism, waste is primarily produced by market economies' tendency to overproduce and by the objective necessity of absorbing surplus through planned obsolescence and accelerated need creation.

Both economic orders play an interesting game with time, with systemic consequences for waste generation. In state socialism, time's passing was thought to be harnessed and controlled through plans—five-, three-, or one-year plans, which were then broken down into monthly, weekly, and daily production quotas. The goal here was to squeeze as much output out of each period as possible. There was a constant pressure on society to overfulfill the plan: to cheat time, if you will. Factory managers were instructed to cut the time iron and other inputs spend in each process of steel manufacturing, with the result that the final product was more brittle. This caused rejects and wasted resources used in the process. Managers were also encouraged not to amortize machinery quickly; that is, they were to keep it in production even after the point at which it could produce only in a faulty, hazardous, and inefficient manner. Materials' temporality was thus not only sped up but slowed down as well.

Capitalists also want to "cheat time," but since their problem is insufficient consumption, they want to accelerate not so much the production of materials as their consumption. They intentionally produce "rejects"— broadly understood—so that we will keep buying more. As I have already demonstrated, this too results in waste. Materials "bite back" in both cases. Forcing materials to convert into each other faster, and making them "age" and "spoil" faster, equally create wastes. Waste thus results from manipulating materials' and nature's temporality.

But temporality can be tampered with in other ways, as well. It could be argued, for one, that recycling and reusing wastes reverses or slows down time. First, reusing and recycling moves materials back to the sphere of useful goods, which they had once left. To the extent that things tend to "progress" in the opposite direction, recycling and reuse turn the clock back or, more abstractly, as Brian Neville and Johanne Villeneuve (2000) put it, mix temporalities. Second, such material conservation practices will have the effect of slowing down the depletion of nonrenewable resources or will harmonize the pace of depletion and the pace of regeneration of renewable ones. This, to be sure, is not always the case: adopting an energy transformation perspective, we'll find that recycling can sometimes take more energy than the production of new materials, as with glass recycling, for example.

Such modifications of temporality through various waste management techniques are never absolute. Whether and to what extent the clock is "turned back" depends on our point of view. It is not just that measuring, classifying, and managing time express larger cultural concerns and values, but that there is no single, objective viewpoint from which we can say with absolute certainty what constitutes speeding up, slowing down, reversing, or skipping time in a particular material practice. With the case of glass recycling, for example, if our viewpoint is not focused on energy, but rather on raw materials for making glass, by recycling glass we have indeed slowed down time. In fact, practices of "saving materials" or "saving time" that are well-meaning but are based on different assumptions can and will work at cross-purposes and thus lead to even more waste.

Waste Regimes

In conclusion, let me summarize the key propositions that have emerged and that form the foundation of a social theory of waste. First, I have argued that waste is a social category. This is not a simple social constructionist argument, however. Rather, I claim that there are social patterns of the social nature of waste. What appears to be unique in different time periods and different societies are the types of wastes produced (their material composition); the key sources of waste production (for example, unutilized surplus or insufficient inputs) and the dominant mode of waste circulation and metamorphosis; the socially and culturally determined ways of misperceiving waste's materiality; the ways in which, as a result, waste tends to "bite back"; the cultural, political, and moral inclination to resolve waste's liminality (inscribed negativity or positivity); and, finally, key struggles around waste (in the sphere of production or in the sphere of distribution).

To systematically study these patterns I propose the term "waste regime." The concept serves to stand Oran Young's (1982) concept of "resource regime" on its head.[16] Social institutions determine what wastes and not just what resources are considered valuable by society, and these institutions regulate the production and distribution of waste in tangible ways.

Waste regimes differ from each other according to the production, representation, and politics of waste. In studying the production of waste, we are asking questions such as what social relations determine waste production and what is the material composition of wastes. When we inquire into the representation of waste, we are asking which side of key dichotomies waste has been identified with, how and why waste's materiality has been misunderstood, and with what consequences. Also to be investigated here are the key bodies of knowledge and expertise that are mobilized in dealing with wastes. In researching the politics of waste, we are first of all asking whether or to what extent waste issues are a subject of public discourse, what is a taboo, what are the tools of policy, who is mobilized to deal with waste issues, and what nonwaste goals do such political instruments serve. Finally, no waste regime is static, thus we must study them dynamically, as they unfold, as they develop unintended consequences and crises.

The concept of waste regimes will move us away from a too-rigid, mode-of-production-type concept to allow the investigation of the changing materiality and discourses of waste within either socialism or capitalism. By emphasizing that multiple regimes of waste may develop within one mode of production, we'll be better able to understand the local variations (such as reliance on certain types of material) and resistances to seemingly ubiquitous relations of production. Ultimately, we'll be better equipped to understand how institutions and people in different social situations understand the sources of our waste-related problems, and thus we may develop solutions that are socially more just.

Comments on Methodology

The empirical data on which my arguments are based come from multiple sources. Yet, this book is primarily ethnographic. For us sociologists, ethnography is perhaps less sacred than it is for anthropologists; after all, we tend to aim for the understanding of larger social structures than those manifest in a particular locality. As a result, we are more liberal and less self-reflexive in "mixing and matching" methods, and we tend to be relentless realists when it comes to fieldwork. We have, as have anthropologists, had our own debates about the relationship between theory and method, macro- and micro-levels; and all this has put a stamp on the sociological practice of ethnography. The tradition that has influenced me the most is the extended case method, and its adaptation to the study of transnational linkages in what has come to be known as global ethnography (Burawoy et al. 1991; Burawoy et al. 2000). Both place the researcher primarily in one particular site, though fieldwork is also done in other places that are involved in the case. Both place special emphasis on ties between various localities and analyze those relations in order to make arguments at a level of analysis higher than either of these localities. Their purpose is not to generalize from one case, so to speak, but rather to critically evaluate the observed macro–micro, global–local connections that, in turn, allow the researcher to construct a theory of the reality in which these connections are forged.

Given the topic of my research—the changing concept of waste in Hungary, and not in a particular locality, from 1948 to 2004—ethnography has been extended in space and in time. That my research is ethnographic means two things. First, employing the sense of ethnography as a concrete methodological tool, I have used participant observation to complement data and insights gained from other methods, such as archival research and interviews. I have used archival materials to reconstruct the discourses on waste at various points in time, as reflected in laws, policies, institutions, and practices. Archival research lets me make inferences about the contradictions and limits of these waste discourses and institutions, but it had limited use in demonstrating the processes by which these unfold and produce specific outcomes. For my project, the value of fieldwork was primarily to understand how these waste discourses played themselves out in real places and in concrete situations. How did people interpret these discourses and what local conditions, if any, were reflected in actual waste practices?

Yet ethnography has not been reduced to simply one of the methods applied. My intention was to make use of ethnography as an epistemological position. Doing ethnography is a commitment to study an issue at hand by understanding it from the perspective(s) of people whose lives are tied up with the issue or affected by it. This concept of understanding requires an inquiry that is a lot more open-ended than an inquiry based on the Weberian notion of *Verstehen*, which imputes meaning to action based on the structural position of an individual or on the historical characteristics of a social order. Ethnography is the researcher's commitment to let herself be surprised, to be caught off-guard, and to be swept up by events that occur in the field as a result of which even the original directions of the inquiry may significantly change. This commitment is rooted in an insistence on the significance of from-below and partial perspectives for the understanding of an issue as well as for the construction of theory. In this sense, ethnography can be a master method or an epistemological imperative that guides the research even as that research relies on other methods.

My practice of ethnography as epistemology means three things in particular. First of all, following other anthropologists (Comaroff and Comaroff 1992; Des Chene 1997), I have extended the temporal boundaries of ethnography as traditionally understood by using an ethnographic sensibility in studying written records from the past. My fieldwork and, in particular, the way in which villagers and company representatives talked about the past thoroughly informed my choice of archival records to research. For example, many in Garé could not separate the opening of the toxic waste dump in their village from the fact that they had previously become administratively subordinated to the neighboring larger village, Szalánta. This compelled me to look at local and county archives, especially those that pertained to regional development and settlement rationalization projects.

Second, I have also transgressed the spatial boundaries of classical ethnographic practice, inasmuch as I did fieldwork in multiple sites. The choice of what sites to study was again motivated by my initial interactions with various informants. However, my research is not what Marcus (1998) calls "multi-sited ethnography." First of all, my choice of sites was not based on the constructivist approach he recommends, but on actual social relations that existed among sites. Second, I found that since these social relations transformed the sites over time, I had to focus as much on these relations in a historical context as on the localities themselves. Ultimately, by transgressing the temporal and spatial boundaries of ethnography, I have come to adopt a nonessentialist concept of site, much informed by geographer Doreen Massey's (1994) "global sense of place." She proposes four key arguments: places are not static; places do not have the kind of boundaries that warrant a simple counterposition to the outside; the identity of a place is not homogeneous; yet places are unique, and their specificity resides in the distinct mixture of local and wider social relations. In practice, my field became the changing bundle of social relations among various sites, such as the villages, the company, the county leadership, and the party, rather than the individual sites as isolated localities.[17]

Third, ethnography as epistemology to me also means a critical analytical perspective. Following Donna Haraway (1991), James Scott (1998), Jim Thomas (1993), and Henry Wolcott (1999), I give priority to a from-below view because it is only from a seemingly "parochial" perspective that one may question a hegemonic from-above definition of a social problem in a grounded and accountable manner. For example, as I have shown in my theoretical introduction, the problem of socialism's wastefulness is fraught with ideological blind spots that we can only start eliminating by asking what waste meant to concrete social actors in a concrete time and place—to the Communist Party, to company managers, and to villagers living next to a waste dump. Waste will then be seen as a terrain of power, and its definition as a political act in itself. Ultimately, my aim has not been to question or undermine the ethnographic method, but to empower it by modifying its self-imposed limitations.

Part 1

Discipline and Recycle (1948–1974)

Head of the metal scrap processing plant to the visiting Party official: "Steel production starts here: this is the scrap heap. All that you see here will be smelted down into high-grade steel. We'll make tractors from this steel to plough our fields and more washers so you can wash your overalls. These are our volunteer workers, mostly of bourgeois origin. We'll also smelt them down into a new kind of people."

Larks on a String, dir. Jiri Menzel

three
Metallic Socialism

If by some miraculous time machine you could go back to the Hungary of the 1950s and walk around Budapest, you would keep bumping into dingy little shops with large orange signs proclaiming "MÉH," which in Hungarian means "bee." Yet if you decided to peek into one of these shops, you would not find bees or honey, but rather piles of dog-eared books, newspapers, metal scraps, and textiles, pails of grease, and bags of feathers, bones, and human hair. That's when you would look at the sign more closely and realize that MÉH was an acronym that stood for the By-Product and Waste Utilization Company (Melléktermék -és Hulladékhasznosító Vállalat).

Still dizzy from the sight of such a chaotic stockpile, you might hop on a truck with the same orange sign heading for a factory. You would know this was no ordinary industrial site when, instead of finding workers absorbed in a manufacturing process, you would encounter them buzzing around like bees in the factory yard, scavenging among metal and wood scraps and then sorting and carting the scraps to another end of the plant. Going inside the plant, you would spot women sewing together pieces of leather fished out from a huge container, and every once in a while, when the foreman wasn't watching, you would see some of these same workers escaping to the changing rooms, concealing small or large scraps.

On the walls, you would see posters (such as figures 3.1–3.7) and intricate tables indicating which brigade collected how much waste and who had the best idea to reuse it. If you stumbled into the office of a manager, you'd most likely find his desk covered with various pieces of legislation prescribing waste quotas, which wastes were to be delivered to which company, how to calculate the price of wastes, what to do with still unregulated waste materials, and how much material reward could be given to those who collected wastes beyond the planned amount. You might also find treatises on the economics of waste reuse and on waste statistics and accounting that were published in scholarly journals. Just then a young lad would reach over you to deposit a slip in a box labeled "Gazda idea box."

Since "Gazda" means "caretaker," you might wonder, "the caretaker of what?" Then suddenly you notice the cover page of the daily *Szabad Nép* (Free People), featuring a photo of a middle-aged man and the caption "Comrade Gazda." Reading on, you would find out about the waste reuse movement he started and the popularity of his campaign. Skimming through past issues of the daily, you would find at least one article on the Gazda movement every day. This is what it would be like to experience the cult of waste in Budapest in the summer of 1951.

Yet, this is not the image of state socialism those in the West have. It's not that works on the political economy of state socialism have ignored waste; in fact several authors identified waste as a rather essential concomitant of central planning (see chapter 2). They also haven't ignored Stalinism's production movements, that is, contests or competitions to mobilize workers for improving their performance (Filtzer 1986). In fact, Iván Pető and Sándor Szakács (1985) provide an exhausting if not exhaustive list of such campaigns.[1] Rather, what stands to be revised in these accounts is, first, the lack of recognition that, while state socialism did produce wastefully in certain senses, the party-state had a rather explicit interest in solving the "waste problem"; and second, that up until now socialism has been treated as a vacuous political and economic structure independent of and even subordinating to itself the very materiality it created, mobilized, and came to be dependent on. In order to make sense of the manifestations of the cult of waste described above, and especially to make them jibe with the poor environmental record of state socialism, we must first understand how the official discourse constructed this waste problem. Then, we must comprehend how, in return, the materiality of production and of wastes shaped social institutions we have come to associate with the regime. In this chapter, I will analyze ethnographic and historical records to disclose what

FIGURE 3.1. "With the Gazda movement, with material conservation for more goods and for higher salaries! You too join the Gazda movement!" Courtesy of Országos Széchenyi Könyvtár, Hungary.

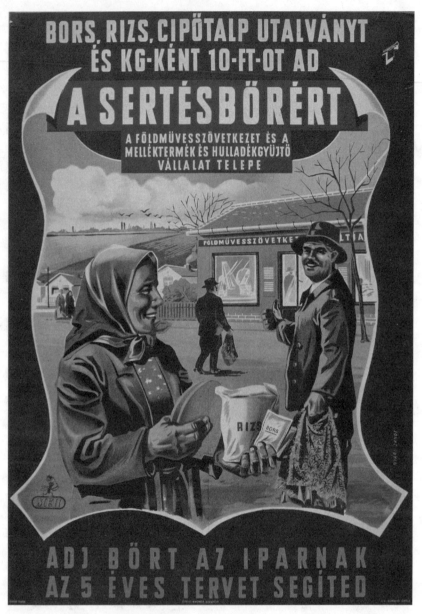

FIGURE 3.2. "The agricultural cooperative and the By-Product and Waste Collection Company will give you pepper, rice, and shoe coupons and 10 Forints for a kilo of hog leather. Give leather to industry and help the five-year plan." Courtesy of Országos Széchenyi Könyvtár, Hungary.

FIGURE 3.3. MÉH's flyer announcing the metal collecting campaign for November and December 1951. Headline: "Hand over the wastes collected now! The agricultural cooperatives will pay cash for them." Courtesy of Országos Széchenyi Könyvtár, Hungary.

FIGURE 3.4. Flyer of the Iron and Metal Waste Collection Company, 1951. "New bridges, factories, apartment buildings, and tractors are made from metal scrap. Let's fulfill the waste quotas." Courtesy of the Országos Széchenyi Könyvtár, Hungary.

FIGURE 3.5. Flyer of the Iron and Metal Waste Collection Company, 1951. "Don't leave iron and metal scrap in the workshop! You are serving the five-year plan by collecting them!" Courtesy of the Országos Széchenyi Könyvtár, Hungary.

FIGURE 3.6. Flyer showing goods made from iron and metal scrap, paper waste, rags, leather scraps, and bones, 1951. "Waste is raw material! It will become a new product. Collect waste! Provide the five-year plan with raw materials! You will also get cash for it!" Courtesy of the Országos Széchenyi Könyvtár, Hungary.

FIGURE 3.7. Flyer of the Iron and Metal Waste Collection Company, 1952. "Don't mix up the different iron and metal scraps!" Courtesy of the Országos Széchenyi Könyvtár, Hungary.

meaning and political potential waste held for various social actors in the Hungary of the 1950s and how these came to constitute the metallic waste regime.

The Material Production of Waste

It was in the 1948 rigged elections that communists became the ruling party in Hungary. Soon other parties were forced into illegality and their leaders were arrested or forced to emigrate. When the communists embarked on the journey to lead Hungary to communism they did not do so in a vacuum; the believed imminence of a Third World War on both sides of the geopolitical divide had an important effect on the nature of the newly emerging social and economic order in Eastern Europe. Postwar Hungary suffered from a scarcity of raw materials due to several factors: (a) the incapacitated production facilities; (b) the loss of territories,[2] that is, of raw material sources, productive capacities, and commercial relations; (c) the embargo by Western countries that made nonferrous metals especially difficult to obtain; and (d) war compensation to be paid to the Soviet Union. The need to build up the country's heavy industrial base amid the ruins left behind by the war and the embargoes put a tremendous strain on the country's economy.

The socialist mode of waste production did not originate in natural scarcity alone, however. Shortage always characterized other, much richer socialist countries as well, especially the Soviet Union, indicating that there were systemic causes of the chronic shortages that planned economies were famous for. In fact, a review of the contemporary rhetoric of shortages reveals that planners did not see anything but socially or, better said, politically produced shortages. Of course, such explanations dovetailed well with the Party's incessant need to construct enemy images within: workers, holdover fascists, and Social Democrats who were sabotaging production. The following section explains how social relations of and in production[3] governed the production of waste and the official discourse on waste.

The existing historical record on the manifestations of waste in early state socialist Hungary provides a rich source of data on the everyday life of industrial plants. Because production was a public issue, newspapers and frequently held employee conferences felt it to be their duty to disclose the irregularities of the fledgling economy, especially if they suspected sabotage. This, in turn, required that the authors or contributors describe in detail the problems they witnessed. Contemporary newspaper articles and documents, both public and classified, thus allow us to treat such records as "raw material" for what Jean and John Comaroff (1992) call "historical ethnography." On the one hand such records can be treated as curious kinds of public "journal entries"; on the other hand, because they clearly had to undergo substantial censorship and editorial process, the very fact of their selection for publication, their rhetoric, and their systemic silences allow us to subject them to discourse analysis. Accordingly, first I will scrutinize these records for the material manifestation of waste, and then I will attempt to "read between the lines" to reveal the social relations of waste production.

From such evidence two forms of waste emerge: allocative waste and material waste. A prevalent problem was wastes resulting from hoarding. In the May 8, 1951 issue of *Szabad Nép*, a letter by the Party secretary of the Ganz factory complained that "there [were] 30–40,000 kilos of high-alloy steel lying around on the yard, outside the warehouse in the open air, and when it rain[ed], there [were] 10-15-cm.-deep puddles under it. . . . [T]he rust [ate] away the etching [so no one could tell for sure what material it was]." If the weight of the material seemed to fit, they "baptized the material," otherwise they threw it on the pile of unknown goods. To make up for the missing amount, those taking the inventory cut off that much from other material and painted the number of the missing material on it. Since the other material was unlikely to be of the same quality as the missing one, the cut-off piece became "unfit" for the technology it was needed for and, if it was still used, it ruined the machines. This resulted in good-quality materials becoming useless and then sold at a discount to other plants.

Naturally, situations like this didn't help plan fulfillment: "Such [over-stocked] stockpiles divert materials from the more urgent uses, therefore, they impede the correct distribution of materials. Beyond this, however, overstocking involves such long storage times that during those the materials lose their quality and value" (Department of Wage, Production, and Economics of the Central Council of Hungarian Trade Unions 1953, 19).

Let us call this waste "allocative waste." Allocative wastes are the result of the relationship between the party-state and enterprise management. Taut plans and strict sanctions associated with nonfulfillment encouraged enterprises to hoard materials and replace the required input with others available. Hoarded materials and resources, which were originally available in appropriate quantities but could not be used due to shortage in another material, accumulated. Under such conditions, warehouse capacities also proved insufficient, and the stockpiles rusted, rotted, broke, or evaporated.

A second form was material waste, that is, the overconsumption of raw materials—the production of goods with a much higher material intensity than necessitated by technical prescriptions. Socialist economic actors had an explicit interest in producing with high material intensity. To the extent that enterprises had to fulfill the quotas given in use value, workers and management shared this interest. For example, they tended to manufacture heavier products than necessary because quotas in some industries were given in weight. A common practice among metallurgical companies was to produce large sheets rather than the sizes their buyers needed. Thus in plants where these sheets were cut into smaller pieces to make pipes, tools, and machines, the remainder of the sheets constituted a much larger amount of scrap than necessary.

In the May 6, 1951 issue of *Szabad Nép*, L. Gy. asked the question: "Why do some of our factories produce for the warehouses and not for the consumers?" The phenomenon he was trying to explain was why the customers could not buy much-needed two-to-three-liter pots. In the basement of the store

> pots and pans of 10–20 liters are towering still from 1944! But the factories—despite all the requests, begging and notices—keep delivering the pots with large cubic capacity. . . . Why can't the customer get the pot s/he needs? Because the factories [Lampart, the enamelware plants of Kőbánya, Budafok, and Bonyhád] fulfill their plan quotas measured in tons, ignoring the needs of the consumers, they only care about how they could fulfill their plans more easily. . . . And the warehouses of Vasért [the company running hardware stores] in Vadász street and Üllői avenue provide the same experience, where a whole range of important although smaller screws are not available, while they have an abundance of large screws. The Screw Mill, the Hungarian

Wagon and Machine Works fulfill their plans by weight: they deliver the
screws on order but they lag behind in the production of the important small
screws. (L. Gy. 1951, 5)

Economists have long ago called attention to this phenomenon both at
the macro-level (Drábek 1988; Gomulka and Rostowski 1988; Moroney
1990; Sláma 1986) and at the micro-level (Juhász 1981). Nevertheless they
always explained high material intensities with the irrationality of central
planning and/or with the region's backwardness, though they disagreed
whether it was a backwardness of technology or economic structure. In
contrast, from a from-below sociological perspective, producing with high
material intensity is a form of hidden resistance. Producing heavy goods
was a way in which workers and managers could fulfill plans formally,
while not fulfilling them substantially. In order to understand the power
struggles that manifested in this form of waste, we must first comprehend
the social relations of waste production. Taking my evidence from the
historical record, let me first establish the disciplinary potential of the
official waste-related campaigns.

The Discursive Production of Waste

Archival and journalistic evidence not only disproved my expectation
and common knowledge that the party-state was indifferent to waste in the
early period of state socialism but also forcefully testified to a rather keen
concern with collecting and reusing waste. The party-state established
numerous institutions, introduced pieces of legislation, and mobilized applied knowledge systems for organizing the large-scale registration, collection, distribution, and reuse of waste. The description of these institutions
and campaigns will allow me to sketch the historically specific waste model
that prevailed in Hungary between 1948 and the mid-1970s.

Waste Legislation and Administration

Between 1950 and 1959 thirty-four central regulations on the collection,
storage, delivery, and price of waste materials were issued. The No. 102.700/
1951 decree of the Director of the Central Planning Office on the obligatory collection of certain wastes was the first waste legislation. It obliged
companies generating certain types of wastes to collect them and offer them
for transfer in accordance with the national quotas established by the
Central Planning Office. These quotas were to be broken down into plan
targets for individual ministries and then for the firms. The enterprises had

to inform their workers about the firm's obligations in production conferences. The "waste-collecting organs" (ministries, councils) had to submit a monthly report to the Bureau of Material Savings, and could "use and trade waste materials under regulation only in accordance with the order of the Central Planning Office and the assigned material management office."

Subsequent laws extended both the circle of wastes subject to quotas and the circle of those firms subject to such laws. These laws threatened management with penalties for noncompliance or abuse, with fines starting at 3,000 Forints and soon rising to 5,000 Forints (average monthly income was a few hundred Forints). As for rewards, a law from 1954 (No. 2.500-21/1954) set the maximum reward an individual could get for fulfilling the delivery contract within the deadline. Persons who could be rewarded included the head of the trade department, the waste stewards, and the workers who collected, selected, or stored wastes. The reward was a certain percentage of the sale price, but there was an overall limit of 500 Forints per year per person.

Other decrees laid down the legal grounds for trading metal wastes and scrap metal. For example, the No. 107/1952 decree of the Central Arbitration Committee prescribed in a rather detailed manner the possible partners of a delivery contract, the time frame of the fulfillment of the contract, quality requirements, legal recourses for nonfulfillment, the legal entity entitled to negotiate nonfulfillment in terms of quality, the mode and place of transfer, the prices, and the transportation expenses. In sum, it created a whole cast of actors and mobilized a whole set of institutions whose task was to make sure that the waste laws were enforced.

A later regulation expanded the circle of wastes subject to planned distribution and reuse by specifying what "waste generators" had to do with wastes that had previously been left unused. The No. 2.500-21/1954 decree of the Director of the Central Planning Office on the collection and utilization of wastes was the first decree that provided a generally applicable definition of wastes, rather than merely listing the concrete wastes subject to regulation:

> a) the remnants of a material being processed or generated during any part of the production process, that are necessarily created due to the incomplete or insufficient use of the material,
>
> b) the materials, debris, and other products originating in repairs, demolition work, scrapping and cleaning, if the No. 105.600/1951 OT and the No. 5600-44/1952 OT decrees by the Central Planning Office do not apply to these,
>
> c) by-products whose utilization is unresolved.

It also argued that just because there was no explicit waste delivery quota assigned to producers of a certain by-product, that did not exempt them from the obligation to collect and transfer wastes. Those wastes that were not regulated or not used by the generators or could not be stored by them had to be transferred to the proper collecting company, such as MÉH (see below).

The other novelty of the decree was its effort to establish general instructions about who should reuse a certain waste material. Before, such decisions were made on a case-by-case basis without much regard for utility or economic returns on reuse.

The waste must not be reused in the place of its generation (within the enterprise) if

a) the present or other order prohibits it;

b) the production of goods made from that waste does not belong to the scope of activities of the waste generator and its use is uneconomical;

c) the waste has a greater value for consumption and is fit for the manufacturing of articles of a greater value by the local industry[4] than the value of those products that would be made out of it by the waste generator.

To execute laws, planners designed and established several institutions dealing with waste. In 1950 the Central Planning Office founded the Bureau of Material Conservation (Anyagtakarékossági Iroda). Its tasks included exploring artificial materials and substitutions for raw materials, elaborating proposals for developing and modernizing the capacities of substitutive material manufacturing, organizing and directing the necessary propaganda work, and solving the problems of reusing wastes fit for industrial utilization. The fact that the same office dealt with artificial materials, materials to substitute for metals—which at this time almost exclusively referred to synthetic material, such as plastics—and by-products once again demonstrates that wastes were seen as raw materials that could alleviate the shortage of metals so necessary for the heavy industrial ambitions of the party-state.

While this bureau was soon closed, another "waste institution," the By-Product and Waste Trading Company (MÉH), starting its operation simultaneously with the First Five-Year Plan in 1951, turned out to be a permanent feature of Hungarian state socialism. MÉH was obliged to buy the wastes of enterprises and sell them to others according to plan. The circle of wastes collected was very wide, including metal, paper, textiles, batteries, leather, wild berries, seeds, and nuts, as well as animal bones and human hair. It also paid individuals for domestic wastes.

The planners left no stones unturned to search out and lay control over wastes; therefore, the collection and reuse of waste from the very beginning was not merely a legislative or administrative task, but rather a task to involve laypeople.

Mobilizing the Population

In May 1951 the Democratic Youth Alliance (DISZ) organized a scrap metal collecting week, which had to be held "in every plant, every town and every village." On May 12, three days before the event's start, *Szabad Nép* published on the first page an article about the importance of the metal collecting week; the next day it reported that a metal collecting brigade consisting of DISZ members had been formed in the MÁVAG Company, and challenged the youth of the Ganz Train Factory to follow suit. From May 17 to May 27, as the "week" was extended, there was a report on the state of the competition every day, mostly on the first two pages.

Events like this were reported on not simply in a factual manner, listing pledges and further challenges, and their fulfillment, but were often put in a narrative format that was also supposed to encourage readers to get involved. The following quote describes a waste collection campaign as it occurred in a residential neighborhood, copying the genre of a revolutionary eyewitness account, or of a thriller.

> It's a sunny Sunday morning. On Béla Bartók Street, in the office of the DISZ's eleventh district committee, the youngsters are still sitting together. They have just finished the meeting; everybody is still bent over his or her notes. "Does everybody know his or her task?" asks Zoltán Kerekes, the field secretary of the DISZ committee. "Demand the utmost discipline and order from the youth." He looks at his watch. "It is 7:30, comrades; go!"
>
> Down on the street, a gay song resounds. The industrial apprentices are approaching in dense rows. In front of the DISZ building, about a hundred young boys and girls are already flocking together. . . . Within a quarter of an hour the youth from the Standard Factory and from the No. 33 Girl Apprentices' Hostel swarm onto Gellért Hill and Hamzsabég Street.
>
> . . . They are bringing out the "treasures," the rusted iron barrels, one after the other. They laugh at each other, "How nicely these will glow in the Martin furnace in Csepel!" (*Szabad Nép*, May 12, 1951c, 1)

The reported amount of scrap collected during the "week" was impressive indeed. The Mátyás Rákosi Steel Works placed first with a collection of 1,882.6 tons of iron, 177.6 tons of other metal, and 184.7 tons of copper scrap. However, the fact that, simultaneously with the evaluation of the collection campaign, articles began to appear reproaching primarily the middle- and high-level management and even ministers for not supporting the campaign sufficiently indicates that the movement was not going well enough.

There were sporadic pledges for material savings reported by the press, but July was practically idle, despite the establishment of a new award for realizing the material savings decree (cited earlier) by August 20, Constitution Day. As a confidential report of the Department of State Economy put it:

> In the majority of our plants we have encountered numerous initiatives that result in the better use of materials, and especially the reuse of wastes and by-products. The initiatives, however, became isolated; they were not sufficiently supported by either the Party organizations, or the trade unions, or the enterprise directors, and thus they have not become a mass movement of workers and technical employees. (MDP-MSZMP 1951, Fonds 276, group 116, preservation unit 8, document 2227, 1)

However, under the idle surface, the Party, the ministries, and some plants were busy giving another push to the material conservation movement by infusing it with charismatic power. As a directive put it, "The best material savers must be nominated for government and other awards and must be popularized as work heroes" (MDP-MSZMP 1951, Fonds 276, group 116, preservation unit 8, document 2215, 8). A directive by a steering committee of the Ministry of Heavy Industries went even further, suggesting that "following the example of the Soviet Union, a movement tied to the name of a person or a plant that foments material savings and is suited for being popularized must take off" (MDP-MSZMP 1951, Fonds 276, group 116, preservation unit 41, document 1667, 12.1). To be sure, this hero or plant could not be just anyone. The soon-to-be nationwide "movement" had to be initiated by "engineers, innovators or Stakhanovites of a heavy-industrial plant in which major construction or machine investment was still due in the second half of 1951 [that is, the same year]" (MDP-MSZMP 1951, Fonds 276, group 116, preservation unit 8, no document number, 14). The latter requirement was to create the appearance that championship in material savings could translate into additional investments, and/or to ensure that the hero would come from a "strategic," that is, a privileged, plant, which would prove again the correctness of the Party's preferences.

The plant from which the hero "emerged," unsurprisingly, was the Mátyás Rákosi Steel Works, and the hero himself was Géza Gazda, a foreman in the steel mill, soon named vice president of the mill.[5]

Géza Gazda began work as a teenager in the precursor to the Mátyás Rákosi Steel Works (hereafter referred to as "MR Works") in Csepel, the industrial island on the Danube, in the southern part of the capital. He suggested alleviating the plant's shortage of materials by taking scrap iron that would previously have been melted down into round-iron, and rolling it out without heating. According to a novel written about him as part of the propaganda campaign, he himself built the line of rollers out of waste metals, because the regular rollers were too fast to take in the scrap iron. The advantage of this recycling was that it saved energy, time, and labor, and it relieved the overburdened Siemens-Martin furnaces. To render wastes reusable in the very form in which they existed with a simple mechanical transformation, rather than putting them through further chemical processes, was indeed a step forward in waste reuse.

The MR Works turned Gazda's proposal in to the necessary departments of the Ministry, which evaluated it and recommended it to the Budapest Party Committee. The decision was made in early August. It was only at the time Gazda's proposal was considered that it was actually decided that "the main objective of the material savings movement should be the most practical use of materials, especially wastes and by-products" (MDP-MSZMP 1951, Fonds 276, group 116, preservation unit 8, document 2227, 2).

The schedule of the decree for spreading Gazda's movement was rather tight. Given that the decree itself was dated August 10, the only way in which the goal, "that the movement shows serious results already by mid-August" in the MR Works, could be achieved was if previous accomplishments were counted as the new success of the Gazda movement. In fact, the first round of firms for the movement to "spread" to had to be those "where such initiatives had [achieved] significant economic results already" (MDP-MSZMP 1951, Fonds 276, group 116, preservation unit 8, document 2227, 2).

A further guarantee against failure was the massive propaganda effort. "The Party Committee of Budapest should call on the Budapest Party organs to support the Gazda movement in a public decree. The decree should become public on August 15" (MDP-MSZMP 1951, Fonds 276, group 116, preservation unit 8, document 2227, 2). The Presidium of the Central Council of Trade Unions was directed to follow suit on August 17, while "the press, primarily the *Szabad Nép* [was] to place a great emphasis on the Gazda movement between August 15 and 20" (2).

> It should publish the history of the initiative, Gazda's work methods, the achievements of the Mátyás Rákosi Works and other plants, and should also evaluate the significance of the movement for the economy in an editorial. The articles must achieve that the Gazda movement is thrust to the center of the workers' attention and is spread as if from an explosion. The main organizer of the movement should be the press itself. (MDP-MSZMP 1951, Fonds 276, group 116, preservation unit 8, document 2227, 2–3)

If the press popularized it and organized the movement, the propaganda task forces within the individual plants that were selected to be the first to join the Gazda movement were there to make the movement simply un-avoidable. The Ganz factory included the following events and publica-tions in its schedule for organizing: leaflets, announcements and evalua-tions on the factory loudspeaker, articles in the company's paper, a movie about wastes and those shops that did not care about thrifty material use, an exhibition of the waste materials indicating their uses and the savings im-plied, weekly public education conferences, Party members' meetings, DISZ brigades and contests, and technical brigades.

In addition, just on a single day, the following bodies were scheduled to hold meetings about the material savings movement: the plant's Party committee, the Party secretaries, the propaganda secretaries, the factory trade union committee, the DISZ committee, and the top leadership of the Democratic Association of Hungarian Women (Magyar Nők Demo-kratikus Szövetsége).

It was claimed that the Gazda movement offered something special for each of these groups. A plan for the Ganz company, for example, suggested as a task for the Democratic Association of Hungarian Women to "agitate about women's achievements [in the material savings movement] and to point it out how they are protecting the peace of their children and families through the achievements of material economizing" (MDP-MSZMP 1951, Fonds 276, group 95, preservation unit 46, no document number, 75).

As if this wasn't enough, the Production Department of Ganz was to hold a daily evaluative meeting, the Party committee was to hold such meetings every third day, the trade union was to convoke a meeting of the entire membership, and the management of the company was to assemble the technical managers from numerous departments. Three employees were to be freed from their regular duties to supervise the movement, and the trade union and DISZ were to muster ten instructors, each of whom was also to have an orientation. In sum, this was total mobilization.

The Metallic Waste Model

Let us now stand back from these concrete discursive practices and dis-cover in them a unique representation of waste. Let us notice the waste model with which these practices operate. Textual representations quoted so far might have already struck the reader in their prevalent concern with metal wastes. Entries for the term "waste" in Hungarian dictionaries sup-port this suspicion. Definitions offered for waste are not abstract at all; rather, they amount to no more than a collection of examples from metal-lurgical and engineering waste practices. The 1962 edition of the *New Hungarian Lexicon*, for example, explains the concept of waste this way:

> The remainder of the processed material left after tailoring or working to a given size (e.g., metal shavings, waste sheets, etc.). The reduction of waste is an important economic interest, which can be achieved by, for example, precision casting and the appropriate composition of pattern designs. Depending on their quality and size, wastes can in many cases be utilized (e.g. re-smelting) and this has great economic importance. (Ákos 1962)

As if the metallic examples aren't enough, the lexicon refers the reader to the heading "Metal wastes," while making no mention of other types of waste.

If we revisit the pieces of waste legislation described in the previous section, we'll notice a similarly restricted field of view. Regulations tended to focus on metal wastes. Laws usually subjected the following waste materials to planning and regulation: scrap iron, scrap copper, scrap brass, scrap bronze, scrap nickel, lead waste, waste anchor, waste tin, aluminum scrap, used oil, all pollution-free paper waste, natron bags and natron bag waste, and bone waste. While a law from 1954 extended the circle of wastes to include formerly ignored chemical wastes, it alluded to only two waste materials, polyvinylchloride (PVC) and rubber wastes, and even these tended to be generated less in the place where they were produced (the chemical industry) than in the plants where they were used (in a great variety of industries).

Beyond the explicit identification of waste with metal scrap, waste tended to be visualized as metallic, or with the characteristics of metal waste—its solid state, its finality, its tangibility, its discrete nature—that were readily assumed to be universal for all production wastes. Liquid or gaseous wastes or wastes produced in a continuous flow, rather than in discrete batches, were ignored.

The primary methods of waste reduction and reuse could also be applied only to discrete and solid materials. This new approach, unlike recycling, gave priority to reusing waste materials in their original quality and function, without chemical or substantial mechanical transformation.

As Gazda put it:

> The correct interpretation of material conservation is to transform all those lay-away materials, that are found in iron scrap, for example, used axle materials, tracks and other steel materials, into useful materials *by by-passing the Martin furnaces, and occasionally even the rolling mills,* in the production process. (SZOT 1951, box 5, document 33, 3; emphasis mine)

This was applicable in other industries turning out discrete products, such as the leather, paper, textile, and wood product industries.

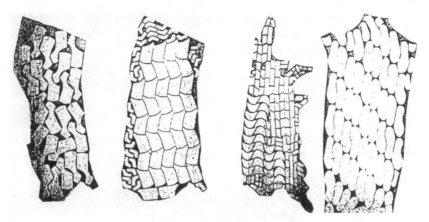

FIGURE 3.8. Cutting patterns for leather shapes. Source: Leather Workers' Union, 1951.

> We can also expect serious results from the innovation of Béla Märcz, a worker of the Artificial Leather Manufacturing Company. The essence of the innovation is that while so far the rejects . . . could be made recyclable only through grinding, now even the smaller pieces are sewn back into sheets, and this way there appears to be a saving of 19,000 Forints per year. (Bőripari Dolgozók Szakszervezete 1951, 4)

The few efforts to reduce the amount of waste produced were also more applicable in these industries. Source reduction was entirely restricted to redesigning the cutting pattern on sheets of metal, leather, and textile or changing their size so as to minimize the amount of material dropped during tailoring. (See fig. 3.8.)

> Most of the wastes are produced during tailoring. In the Ganz Shipyard they cut covers for switchboards out of steel sheets. Before, when they needed such a cover, the sheet was cut in half in the warehouse into two 1,000×1,000 mm pieces. Why? There was a misconception that the remainder was "easier to store." Since then they realized that exactly three covers could be cut out from a whole sheet, because the size of one was just a third that of a sheet. This way then there is no waste from cutting. (Vasmunkások Szakszervezete 1951, 23)

Why were the boundaries around waste drawn this way? A brief prehistory of the Gazda Movement will go a long way to answer the question. After the Party announced its search for a champion to carry its material conservation program to success, there were several contenders. The proposal that, based on its details and its references to earlier successes, I consider most serious was submitted by a team from the prestigious Chinoin pharmaceutical company. While Gazda's proposal listed one innovation, Chinoin's team listed several, all already successfully implemented. I will quote at length from the Chinoin proposal.

> Based on the decree of the Steering Committee, proposals must be made for initiating a movement that, following the example of the Soviet Union, promotes and is fit for popularizing the material conservation movement.
>
> Based on the above, I suggest initiating a movement on the entire terrain of the chemical industry, that strives to recycle in their entirety the wastes and by-products generated by chemical plants into products that are needed by either the generating plant itself or by other ones, or alternatively to have enterprises or chemical research institutions offer their [recycling] technologies to the Directorate of the Local Industries for helping to establish industrial cooperatives if such [recycling] tasks would prove unfeasible in the state sector, as suggested by the decree of our Party's Second Congress.
>
> It would be appropriate to name the movement Chinoin, because the Chinoin company has been implementing this movement successfully for a long time, and could fulfill its March plan by 114 percent, thanks to this movement.
>
> For example, Chinoin invented a method to produce ergosterin, previously made out of yeast, that used penicillin mold (mycelium), which had previously been regarded as waste and was left unutilized. The company also produced papaverin out of a by-product of tar.
>
> I recommend the above proposal with the concurrence and collaboration of the Plan Department of the Main Department of Inorganic Chemical Industry and the Chemical Workers' Union. (MDP-MSZMP 1951, Fonds 276, group 116, preservation unit 41, document 1667, 1)

The original endorsement by the Department of State Economy of the Party did not list more than two arguments in favor of Gazda, one of which was a tautological one, namely that Gazda enjoyed the support of the Party's Political Committee, and thus should be supported by the Party. The other argument claimed that Gazda had numerous innovations for material savings, but then so did the Chinoin team. The decision to turn down the Chinoin proposal is all the more surprising when we consider that the chemical industry was already doing well in waste reuse. The chemical industry had long been characterized by a significant amount of recycling of by-products and auxiliary materials. As a spokesperson said in a 1951 Party meeting in Chinoin, "we started our experiments concerning the reuse of by-products already before the Gazda movement took off, and with them we have made a huge step forward on the terrain of material conservation" (MDP-MSZMP 1951, Fonds 176/2, group 184, preservation unit 2, no document number, 15). Why was this fact ignored by the Party, and why was Gazda chosen over Chinoin?

One reason is that metallurgy was strategically the most important industry for the party-state. After 1948, heavy industry grew at a much faster rate than other industries; its proportion of all industries in 1949 far exceeded that in 1938, the last peace year. In 1938, metallurgy and engineering produced 23 percent of the Hungarian gross national product, while in 1949 their share was 32 percent (Berend 1979, 74). While this was to some extent a leftover trend from war preparations, and while Western European economies demonstrated similar trends, by 1950 the Hungarian plans indicated an exaggerated emphasis on the development of heavy industry, aptly captured in the contemporary slogan that Hungary would become "the country of iron and steel." In the First Five-Year Plan (1951–1955), 48 percent of all investments were in industry, and within that, 90 percent was in heavy industry. Even within heavy industry there was an imbalance: electronics and the chemical industry were neglected (Berend 1979, 97–99). Metal wastes were crucial because of the intended autarchy and for armaments, and their importance was further increased by the mentioned embargo on metals exports by Western countries. It seemed that if only all steel and other metal wastes could be collected, the rate of growth for the heavy industries could be maintained despite all difficulties.

We must also realize that the role of scrap in steel manufacturing was indeed very important, in that the Siemens-Martin process relied heavily on iron scrap as a raw material. The versions of Siemens-Martin types of manufacturing prevalent in the early period of state socialism needed two main raw materials: raw iron and scrap. Not only was the proportion of steel scrap waste high compared to the overall iron input (between 25 and 60 percent), but as more scrap was used, combustion was more efficient. In metallurgy, raw materials appear to be recycled over and over again, as acknowledged even in a U.S. advertisement: "The steel industry traditionally uses many million tons of waste, and thus our steel contains at least 25 percent recycled material. This is why we can say that steel is nothing else but material in a constant cycle" (Sebestyén 1973). Despite the uniqueness of steel manufacturing in this respect, it became the model for waste treatment in early state socialism. As my analysis in the following sections will show, this had some profound and very material intended and unintended consequences, some of them quite long-term.

Metallurgy was not only strategically important but also symbolically the most relevant industry of state socialism. The Soviet economic and political model that by then had been operating for three decades also suggested that a true socialist economy must be metallurgy-based, not just in the economic but also in the political sense. Communists considered metallurgical and metal workers the most trustworthy stratum of the working class, because of their skills and activist history. Metallurgy became an ideological metaphor for communism. Metal and mechanical symbolism grew strong initially in the early Soviet era in the futurist works of artists and poets such as Mayakovsky, but there were other numerous, lesser-known worker-poets, such as Aleksei Gastev, who used iron and steel as a metaphor for the worker's hard and hard-working body, and the metallurgical production process as a metaphor for the individual worker's identification with his tools and work task and his dissolution into the collective (Hellebust 1997, 505). Soviet leaders were also fond of assuming metallic names: "Molotov took his name from *molot* (hammer); and Stalin himself went from the Georgian Dzugashvili to a surname based on the Russian word for steel" (Hellebust 1997, 501).

The economic and geopolitical pressures, coupled with the cultural-aesthetic regime of Soviet state socialism, led to a modernization project that prioritized heavy industry and particularly metallurgy and engineering. As a result, the training of cadres emphasized the same industries, and the prevailing mental image of production became that of metal manufacturing: a production process relying on discrete production tasks rather than continuous production; mechanical rather than chemical transformation; and an emphasis on individualizable ("Taylorizable") performance. Following Stephen Gudeman (1986), we can identify the metallic waste model as metonymical. Gudeman calls those models of livelihood metonymical that are based on applying schemas from a concrete or partial reality to the entire sphere of livelihood. In them, the part stands in for the whole, hence the label.[6] Similarly, the scheme that planners in early state socialism applied to the economy was that of steel manufacturing.

As this knowledge and symbolism congealed into the institutional regime of state socialism (institutions, planning design, work discipline), a new society was produced. This discourse of production (knowledge, institutions, and persons) had a remarkable staying power, and it strongly affected later economic policies—in fact, the whole social and economic future of state socialism. As I will demonstrate in the subsequent chapters, this model had particular limitations and unintended consequences, some of which lingered on well into the reform period of state socialism. For now, however, let me turn to the kind of politics served by this metallic waste model and the mobilization of the population.

The Cult of Waste as a New Ethos

The mobilization of the population and the ubiquitousness of metal scrap symbolism led to what practically amounted to a cult of waste. The cult of waste was embodied in the rituals of waste-collection weeks and offerings of collected wastes to the Party or to Rákosi for his birthday; in the sacred objects of the waste reuse movement, such as the Gazda movement idea boxes; and in the whole cast of waste-reducing, waste-reusing characters—from the role of the class-conscious waste stewards mobilizing their less conscious colleagues for waste-related tasks, to the waste brigades regularly challenging their counterparts to more and more waste reduction or waste reuse ideas. In sum, the early socialist discourse of waste established a whole new material culture.[7]

In the atmosphere of this cult, it became entirely sensible for individuals to write to ministries with concrete waste reuse proposals, however small in nature; in fact, they were encouraged to do so. One worker suggested collecting burnt-out lightbulbs to reuse their inner parts, and matchboxes to be refilled. Another proposed to collect old tools from individuals, such as formerly independent craftsmen, and hand them over to industrial plants (MDP-MSZMP 1952, Fonds 95, group 4, preservation unit 103, no document number, 1).

It seemed as if the New Man envisioned by propaganda materials, "whose splendid feature is thriftiness" (Ember 1952), had already been born. An article in the weekly of the MR Works characterized a woman who turned in a proposal to reuse metal-cutting wastes this way: "Mrs. Rabcsák is one of the many who have understood the importance of material conservation, who have left behind the old, 'backward' way of thinking and dare to take the initiative" (*Szabad Nép* 1951c, 3).

Party activists often projected a society in which capitalist squandering ended, in which sparing materials was finally a worthwhile effort, since what is squandered is everyone's loss.

> "Such a movement never could have emerged before," says Géza Gazda, "because its conditions were absent." Today, in contrast, things are different: the country is ours, we are its stewards. We know that we are working for ourselves, for the benefit of our country. (Vasmunkások Szakszervezete 1951, 4)

A ministerial study compared capitalist and socialist scrap iron use, similarly concluding that the latter is superior.

[In capitalism] when for some reason huge scrap iron supplies are piling up, the heavy industrial plants shift to using increasingly more scrap iron, which now exists in large quantities and is cheaply available. Then the soaring demand and the rise in the profit rate [for the suppliers] generate a movement in the opposite direction in this industry, so that the use of scrap iron is "not profitable" for the furnaces anymore, and they decrease the use of scrap iron and stop purchasing it, thus leaving the supplies unsalable, for which reason the collection [of scrap] is terminated. (UML 1951, Fonds XIX-A-16a OT, group 25, box 446, no document number, 1–2)

Furthermore, waste collection in state socialism also was claimed to support the cause of peace, presumably by making socialism a worldwide regime faster and thus eliminating the threat of a Third World War. A ditty with this noble goal was written and reprinted over and over again, and remains well known even to the younger generations in Hungary. "Collect iron and [sic] metal, you defend peace with this, too." ("Gyűjtsd a vasat és a fémet, ezzel is a békét véded!"; note the rhyme.)

Based on such theorizations, socialism was identified as a morally superior society. Not only was it more just than other social orders, but it was the "thriftiest of all societies" (Ember 1952), and it "end[ed] the outdated view that worships new materials" (Jócsik 1977; Dömötör 1980). The absence of social antagonisms allegedly fomented a healthy, conscientious, and virtuous relationship with the material world.

Waste, in sum, became a symbol of a new ethos. Making new out of old by mobilizing the genius of workers became the encapsulation of what socialism was about: destroying the technological and human barriers, built by capitalism, to a democratically controlled and voluntaristically managed economy. This voluntarism manifested itself in an extreme social constructivist view of nature and of time. According to this position, socialism was the society that could overcome natural or technical obstacles in production, because those prevailed only in capitalism, where use value and exchange value were forcefully separated and came into conflict.[8]

The idea that simply by trying harder, which in turn was made possible by class consciousness, more could be produced from the same amount of resources and by the same number of workers presupposed and ultimately forced an extreme flexibility on both human and nonhuman nature. Party ideologues hailed the conquest of nonhuman nature, and the aesthetics of socialist realism openly celebrated the transformation of idle nature into useful, productive nature, with the industrial landscape advertised as the right natural environment for the Socialist Man. Morning or night, winter or summer, the industrial plants of Stalinism permeated the natural environment, creating what we might call socialism's second nature. As expressed in one of the production novels about Géza Gazda commissioned by the Party:

> The sky is clear. It was dawn not long ago, and now the summer sunshine is peeking into the wide yard of the morning. The factory however knows neither night, nor dawn, nor morning. It only knows shifts following on one another. The factory rules the entire landscape. (Vészi 1952, 11)[9]

> It was a beautiful summer night. The noise of the millworks almost belonged to the sound of nature around here. (Vészi 1952, 45)

Time was also something that, under the right social conditions, could be beaten. Wastes were to be mobilized for the fulfillment of plans and, if possible, for their overfulfillment, and thus the Party could achieve its objectives before plan deadlines. The concluding words of the above-quoted novel about Gazda put this political temporality thus:

> The capitalists said time is money. Therefore, they converted everything into money. Gazda now turns this around. He converts money into time. Because those who fulfill the plan, those who struggle for the overfulfillment of the plan, struggle for time. And those who get ahead of time and prove to be faster than the calendar year, those won't age. Just as Géza Gazda will not become old. Two weeks is not a lot in a man's life, but if a huge plant shortens the year needed for the fulfillment of the plan by two weeks, then it is clearly seen that we have got two weeks closer to socialism. (Vészi 1952, 54)

So it went with human nature as well. In socialism, workers supposedly had an objective interest in the development of the means of production, including technology and their own productive capacity, and thus gave their best to plan fulfillment and the building of communism. Workers' bodies were construed as flexible enough to work not eight but twelve to fourteen hours a day if necessary, and to break the records of the already backbreaking norms. What supposedly made this voluntary and painless for the workers was their identification with the productionist goals of the regime and the rigorous disciplining of their bodies. Representing workers' bodies as such was elevated to a new kind of aesthetics and ethics, materializing in paintings, sculptures, and literature that quickly filled public spaces and the shelves of libraries,[10] a fleet of loud monuments to the rule of mind over body and the rule of society over nature.[11]

The hidden value of the waste reuse movement for the Party was thus not merely to transform old material into new but also to mold old, unruly, and politically suspect human material into new, disciplined, and politically reliable human material. This recycled human material, however, in reality had very little to do with the self-governing, self-initiating New Man portrayed in official declarations.

The Politicization of Waste:
Disciplining Cooperatives and Private Shops

In the 1950s Mrs. Szabó worked as a young assistant in a privately owned jewelry shop. At the end of each day, one of her tasks was to carefully collect the fine powder left after processing gold. As she explained, she and the shop owner had to weigh this rather valuable by-product, record it in their books, and lock it away until "they came for it from the center," usually once a week (personal interview, Mrs. Szabó, Budapest, 2004).

Such small private or cooperative workshops and stores were among the key targets of the disciplinary waste politics of the early 1950s. In the plan for building socialism, cooperative and especially private forms of ownership were considered transitional; they were supposed to "wither away," a process that central planning hoped to speed up—first by the nationalization of larger units, and then by radically limiting the scope of activity for those remaining. At the same time, however, the cooperative form of ownership was looked upon as an economic unit that could hasten the entry of formerly private producers and others of non-working-class background into the state-owned industrial sector; therefore, the formation of cooperatives was encouraged. The economic function of these transitional forms was restricted to providing the local population with various services and high-quality consumer goods, which was expressed in the name of their superordinate ministry, the Ministry of Local Industry.

By mid-1951 there were 628 cooperatives with 20,042 members. Their production for that year consisted of the manufacturing of consumer goods (38 percent) and of construction materials (37 percent), the repair of consumer goods (17 percent), the manufacturing of nonconsumer goods (6 percent), and home improvement (2 percent) (Proposal by the Ministry of the Interior, Directorate of Local Industries, MDP-MSZMP 1951, Fonds 276, group 112, preservation unit 83, no document number, 68).

These producers and merchants were obviously treated as the stepchildren of central distribution who, if they wanted to survive, had to be content with materials and tools handed down from the state enterprises. As for what they produced, they were supposed to complement large-scale manufacturing by state enterprises, while their raw materials were supposed to be drawn from the wastes of the state sector (KSH 1952, 1953; Elefánti 1953). As a contemporary text put it, "one of the most fundamental tasks of the cooperative movement is to use local materials, remnants, wastes, rejects, and materials no longer in use" (*A szövetkezeti anyaggaz-dálkodás és értékesítés főbb kérdései* 1953, 56). The Central Statistical Bureau was ordered to collect data on whether the cooperative and private sector was fulfilling its obligation in this respect, and to write up its findings in confidential reports (KSH 1952, 1953).

From 1952 on, the control over some wastes (primarily nonmetal wastes) became the task of the Ministry of Local Industries; and, the same year, the Central Planning Office drafted a proposal to delineate the responsibilities for waste reuse between state-owned large-scale manufacturing (literally, "big industry") and local industry.

1) Big industry utilizes all wastes generated by itself if it can reuse them to manufacture products in accordance with its production profile, and if the reuse at the production units is advantageous both in terms of quality and in terms of profitability.
2) The raw material input basis of the Ministry of Local Industry is constituted by those waste materials that big industry does not utilize because:

a) the production of the product to be made out of waste does not belong to its scope of duties;
b) the reuse by big industry is not economical;
c) the technical conditions or free capacities are lacking; or
d) the waste can be used by the local industry to manufacture products that have a greater value for consumption or a greater importance than a product made out of it by big industry. (UML 1952, Fonds XIX-A-16-a, no document number, 1)[12]

Despite the declared aims for and the restrictions on the private and cooperative industrial sector, by the beginning of the fifties this sector was not only thriving but also started supplying state enterprises, paying preferential wages, and resembling large-scale manufacturing more than small-scale complementary services. According to officials, this was because the sector "neglected the use of waste materials" (KSH 1952, 1953). Another account criticized the view that "the cooperatives are not of a socialist nature, that they represent a superfluous and harmful competition for the state enterprises," but retained the idea that their role in building state socialism was to find uses for wastes. This author also did not miss the opportunity to reproach those cooperatives that blamed their failure to fulfill their plans on the shortage of raw materials: "At the same time, they fail to utilize the local materials and wastes which they have at their disposal in abundance" (Vályi 1951, 2).

From the planners' point of view, all this was a disadvantageous development, which they tried to combat by paroxysmally revising both the prices
of waste materials and the sale prices of recycled goods manufactured by
the private and cooperative sectors. In periods when officially calculated
prices for such materials were lacking, various offices could forbid private
businesses to sell them; those who did anyway lost their operating licenses,
as happened to textile tradesmen between January and October 1956. But
this iron-fisted policy backfired. As a chief accountant of the Ministry of
Domestic Trade complained, "since the enactment of the decree, at a
number of our enterprises wastes have been accumulating month after
month due to a lack of buyers, and are subject to dirtying and loss of quality
due to insufficient storage capacities" (UML 1956, Fonds XIX-A-48, document 1431-17-3/1956).

While a 1957 government decree maintained that state enterprises could
sell their waste materials at production cost to small-scale industry, it preserved the right to build sales tax into their prices "if the interests of the
economy should demand so" (UML 1957, Fonds XIX-A-48, document
2302/57). In a 1958 letter to the National Bureau of Materials and Prices,
the Industrial Ministry criticized the regulation that allowed private businesses to buy waste materials at the same price as the state enterprises, and
suggested they sell to private businesses at a price that contained a sales tax.
In reply, the Bureau revised the prices for most waste materials in question
(UML 1958, Fonds XIX-A-48, 9/7/1958, document 3470). The reply of the
Bureau and a letter from an industrial cooperative specializing in reusing
leather waste, however, indicate that too high a price for wastes and a
depressed price for consumer goods made out of them created paralysis.
The cooperative asked for a higher price on doormats to be made out of
leather wastes, arguing that at the present price it could manufacture these
only at a loss. If the Bureau approved of a higher price, it could produce
mats that were presently in great shortage and could simultaneously relieve
the shoe factories of their stored leather wastes, which, according to the
letter, amounted to 100 tons already and were causing storage problems
(UML Fonds XIX-A-48, document 5535/III-Ár).

These attacks on the nonstate sector, therefore, only opened up a can of
worms. The two contrasting interests of the state—keeping a lid on the development of the cooperative and private sectors on the one hand, and
making sure the wastes of the state-owned factories were utilized on the
other—made regulation of waste-use a contradictory business, ultimately
leading to overregulation and occasional paralysis.[13] In general, the private
and cooperative sectors' economic activity was tolerated as long as it tapped

the overflowing supplies of particular waste materials, but was looked at with suspicion when it competed with the state enterprises for wastes in high demand.

The Politicization of Waste: Disciplining Workers and Management

Take a trip to Maglód, outside Budapest, or any other Hungarian village that is or used to be near a machine factory or any plant using metals as raw material. You'll notice the curious geometrical designs of the fences, which, while featuring different patterns, all seem to be somehow similar. They all consist of vertical metal strips in which holes of the same shape follow one another as if punched out by a cookie cutter. "A friend who worked in the local metallurgical plant got it for me. These are the sheets that remained after they cut out the covers for a gauge used in buses," said a retired villager who had built his house and fence in the 1950s (personal interview, Anonymous, Maglód, 2004). Judging by the sheer abundance of such "cookie-cutter" fences, villagers either must have had a lot of friends and relatives working in the same plant, or else most of them worked in the plant themselves. Of course, another explanation would be that employees (who weren't actually that numerous, given the small size of the factory) hauled away such industrial wastes and bartered or sold them to fellow villagers. In either case, the pervasive, if creative, uses of such industrial by-products are manifestations of a curious material culture that valued used materials as well as the ingenuity required to make them function. This phenomenon also indicates the free rein of from-below initiatives in a society seemingly ruled and micromanaged from a dictatorial center.

Another example of employees manipulating wastes comes from a man who used to be a baker in a bread factory. As he explained, there was a certain slack in material norms, and if he swept up the flour from the floor and mixed it in the next batch of dough, he managed to produce more than the amount required by such norms. He then sold the bread produced in excess to shops and restaurants for less than the official price but at a price that still ensured an income worthy of assuming such risks. "You know, this way everybody came off well," he added with a wink and mischievous smile (personal interview, Maglód, 2004). The pride he took in providing me with the details of the production process and the business transaction suggested he felt he had a right to this extra money. After all, it resulted from his ingenuity and labor and, as he made it clear, the "bosses" always got away with so much more.

Such oral histories of waste reuse, and the landscape that still stands to testify to the prevalence of such practices suggest that a key terrain of the

FIGURE 3.9. Gate made of metal scrap, Maglód, Hungary, 2004. Photo by author.

politicization of waste was the shop floor itself. I have already hinted at the significance of workers' control over the production process in the preceding discussion of how social relations govern the material production of waste. In return, because waste was seen as, at least initially, escaping the rigorous registration other resources were subjected to, it became a crucial terrain on which to wrest some control away from the state and/or from one's supervisors. This resulted in a struggle around the distribution of already produced wastes. The Gazda movement and other waste collection campaigns were the state's reaction to "misuses" such as the ones introduced above, and in order to take charge, it politicized both waste production and waste distribution.

If the center was to regulate production down to its most minute details, it had to (a) introduce strong discipline, and (b) establish a rather stringent system of material norms. The material conservation and Gazda movements served both purposes.

> We must establish a political atmosphere in our plants in which the material squanderers and the reject producers cannot exist. The material squanderers must be subject to disciplinary action; the saboteurs must be brought to court and most severely punished. (MDP-MSZMP 1951, Fonds 276, group 116, preservation unit 8, no document number, 11)

As for the norms, they had to be as taut as possible since even small instances of slack, such as in the bread factory example, could add up to a great loss. As one contemporary expert put it:

> The primary task of material norms is to ensure that the material supply plans are technically grounded and to stop using average quotas based on statistical surveys in the planning methods, since those are only suited to offering free rein to incorrect directions in material use. (Elefánti 1952, 12–13)

Furthermore, economizing on material use was viewed as a key, albeit hidden, reserve for growth.

> The reduction in the per unit use of raw materials also makes it possible to ensure an increased production with the same supply of materials. . . . The battle fought for the thrifty and rational use of raw materials in this manner is a task of great importance for the national economy. The establishment of material norms plays a determining role in solving this task. (Elefánti 1952, 12)

It is important to emphasize, however, that the planners as early as 1951 already knew of the hoarding practices I mentioned before, providing yet another incentive to establish a system of material norms and, based on it, a system of material balances. Thus such rationalization of the use of materials was an early response of the Party to the survival strategies of the enterprises.

> We must admit that during practical planning we still often encounter phenomena that indicate that certain planning bodies "want to insure themselves"—and even, in the best case, out of shortsightedness—strive to acquire important materials beyond the needed amount. (Elefánti 1952, 21)

A Party report baptized this phenomenon "plant chauvinism."

> The other form of unconscientious material management occurs when the plants, out of negligence, carelessness or, in more than once case out of shortsighted plant chauvinism, accumulate superfluous supplies and irrationally insist on keeping them. Thus BAMERT [a firm], for example, keeps in storage stock worth four million Forints that it will not use in the foreseeable future, yet it clings tenaciously to it; what's more, it applies to its superordinate authority for even more materials. The Ganz Electric Engineering Plant has a stockpile that exceeds by 35 million Forints the stockpile it should have according to its current assets. (MDP-MSZMP Fonds 276, group 116, preservation unit 8, document 2215, 18)

To combat such problems, the Department of State Economy of the Party recommended the following steps: the ministries should keep establishing and implementing norms for the most important materials and tools; the plants should prepare quarterly plans for material savings; and planners should incorporate the registration and reuse of wastes and by-products into the planning system. These administrative measures were, however, not forthcoming at the expected speed. The Department pointed out that the already established norms applied to only a fraction of all materials used, that the methodology of calculating norms and controlling compliance with them was missing from the regulations, and even the few norms existing were 3 to 15 percent looser than the present actual use. In addition, complained a Party report, the norms were not trickling down to the workers. Party officials therefore suggested replacing normative administrative incentives with political ones by integrating material economizing in the already existing work competitions.

> The struggle for material savings must become the central issue of our work competition movement, along with the increase of productivity. Our Party organs and trade unions must mobilize the wide masses of workers in the battle for material savings. We must make the workers realize that saving materials does not only mean a reduction in expenses, as we have formulated this question so far, but within this, also the saving of a certain amount of copper, chrome, nickel, bronze, coal, rolled articles, leather and yarn. We must make the working masses realize that today material saving equals the fulfillment of our increased Five-Year Plan, the increase of the defense of our

homeland, and the acceleration of the building of socialism. (MDP-MSZMP 1951, Fonds 276, group 116, preservation unit 8, no document number, 11)

The proponents of "movementizing" material thriftiness, however, must have felt that simply expressing savings in terms of use values rather than cost reduction was not going to have enough incentive power. It was necessary thus to supplant the hitherto missing or "loose" norms with other individualized, quantifiable, and controllable prescriptions. This function was to be fulfilled by the "individual savings accounts."

> The results achieved in material savings must appear in demonstrable form for the workers. This depends on the introduction of individual savings accounts. No doubt, the lack of productive and overhead material norms makes it difficult to measure individual savings, and it is also indubitable that the bad circumstances of material storage and the looseness in the cutting workshops and around material allocation make possible numerous abuses. Despite all this, however, we must *bravely and determinedly start introducing the individual accounts because this is the grounds for the development of a wide competition movement.* (MDP-MSZMP 1951, Fonds 276, group 116, preservation unit 8, document 2215, 4; emphasis in original)

The individual savings accounts were much like bank accounts, except that instead of money, workers accumulated saved values. The worker received the materials and tools she or he individually needed for a certain period or job, then the supervisors individually measured her or his output and material use, and compared that to norms if they existed, or to a stepped-up version of actual use from a past period (year, quarter, month). Then, a percentage of the presumably positive balance between actual material use and norms—the suggested proportion was 10 to 20 percent, but for savings in strategic materials, such as nonferrous metals, it could amount to 50 percent—increased the credit of the account, while negative performance, supposedly, increased the debit side. While a positive balance translated into a monetary award, the latter possibility was never discussed, probably because there was little to do to workers who amassed large "debts." The individual balances or the brigade balances then would compete with each other within one plant, industrywide, or nationally.

But the same disciplinary actions were applied not only to the generation of wastes but also to the disposition of already existing wastes as well. That there was a struggle around owning waste, not just between the state and the private/cooperative sector, but also between the state on the one hand and workers and managers on the other, is indicated by numerous documents. The most common complaint—as evident, for example, from the minutes of meetings of the Party cells within MÉH—was that some workers were privately selling the wastes bought by the company (Dömötör 1980).

Until 1952, enterprises had been allowed to sell rejects and waste materials from demolition to their employees at a factor cost; after that, however, they had to hand over their wastes to the designated collection company. As ministry archives document, management felt pressured by workers to keep selling these materials to them, and, in order to cover themselves, they turned to the Bureau of Materials and Prices for clearance and for price suggestions. The Vehicular Bridge Maintenance Company, for example, requested permission to sell metal scraps (mostly scraps of tracks) to its employees at a factor cost, rather than having to hand them over to VAFÉM, the company in charge of collecting iron scraps, which would have made an 800-percent "profit" on its sale (UML 1957, Fonds XIX-A-48, document Gy72/709). The Council of the People's Economy (*Népgazdasági Tanács*, or NT), however, turned the request around and used it to increase its waste quota:

> I was informed that the Vehicular Bridge Maintenance Company gives out iron wreckage to its employees as payment in kind. According to one of the decrees of the NT these allotments must be stopped, but I request that the scrap iron quotas of the Vehicular Bridge Maintenance Company be raised, because it is obvious that they still have reserves. (UML 1952, Fonds XIX-A-16a, group 257, box 493, document 257/N-3)

Party and enterprise documents suggest that the misappropriation of waste materials and rejects was common and remained a headache for management for a long time. Nitrokémia, a prominent chemical plant, for example, felt the need to regulate the procedure of scrapping and the sale of wastes and rejects every year between 1963 and 1966, due to disciplinary problems, as suggested by the quote below.

> Our firm does not sell waste to private persons, not even to employees, except for those few materials that are mentioned in the first paragraph of our decree and are later detailed.
> . . . shavings, sawdust, hay, and branches. These materials will continue to be sold to our employees following our existing practice. However, in order to prevent crimes against public property, it has become necessary to regulate more strictly the sale of these materials as well. ("The Number 12/1966 decree of the President of Nitrokémia," *Nitro Közlöny* 1966, 2–3)

Workers did not only "steal" waste materials, they created household items out of scrap, which Miklós Haraszti, in his ethnography of a Hungarian factory, called "homers" (*fusizás*), and which he described as the only escape from the alienation of their Taylorized work.

> By making homers we win back the power over the machine and our freedom from the machine; skill is subordinated to a sense of beauty. However insignificant the object, its form of creation is artistic. This is all the more so because (mainly to avoid the reproach of theft) homers are rarely made with expensive, showy or semi-finished materials. They are created out of junk, from useless scraps of iron, from leftovers, and this ensures that their beauty comes first and foremost from the labour itself. (Haraszti 1977, 143)

This practice, as the passage suggests, was considered theft just like other appropriations of waste materials by workers.

The Party did not need to eradicate such practices completely, but only had to hijack workers' ingenuity in finding uses for wastes and stored materials for the purposes of plan fulfillment, and for creating a local, and thus politically valuable, knowledge and control over managers' use of resources. This was also the rhetorical function of the waste bookkeeping system.[14] Having created an account called "Waste materials," in which wastes taken back to storage were recorded, this system aimed at inculcating in economic actors the idea that wastes were useful *for the state*, and that, therefore, they were not to be appropriated for individual uses.

It is also no accident that the most used quote from Lenin in waste reuse propaganda materials was one emphasizing that resources should be shared and used not according to the particular interests of relatives and acquaintances but according to the common interest of the entire society:

> Communism begins where the simple worker starts to think, in a self-sacrificing way even as he copes with hard work, about the increase of labor productivity, about saving *each and every pound of grain, coal, iron*, and other products, even though those will not benefit him, nor his "next of kin" but "those distant ones," that is, the whole society. (Lenin, quoted by Mándi 1951, 15; also in Ember 1952, 26; emphasis in original)

The Party, however, was not only channeling wastes away from workers: with its waste movement rhetoric, it hinted that the role of the individual worker was indispensable. Claims about the movement, such as "there are thousands of ways and possibilities to reuse wastes" and "here ingenuity and creativity are given free rein," suggested that workers had a considerable amount of freedom to innovate and experiment, and that the movement had to rely on such "from-below" or underground initiatives.

Managers not only participated in "misuses of waste" of the kinds mentioned above, but, as journalistic evidence indicates, they even manipulated the concept of waste: they labeled perfectly good-quality goods as waste, so as to sell or trade them.[15] A "muckraking" article by the head of the Control Department in the Ganz-Mávag factory exposed people in leadership positions in the newspaper of the company.

> We were informed that certain people are managing the *"waste materials"* of our factory in an incorrect and unconscionable manner, partly by selling certain materials at an unreasonably low price, and partly by selling as wastes new materials that could still be used in our production. Taking advantage of this laxity, certain employees come forth with massive orders for various materials. *The situation is exacerbated by the fact certain high functionaries also abuse this opportunity and use their high positions to reap various benefits for themselves.* (Pintér 1951, 3; emphasis in original)

It was exactly this commonality of interests between workers and management that the designers of waste politics tried to erode. The constant mobilizing of workers for collecting and reusing wastes infuriated managers, because they viewed such campaigns as bypassing their authority and as legitimating workers' alleged neglect of their normal work tasks. An article in *Szabad Nép* asked the question, "Why was the Gazda movement not developing in the Ganz Wagon Works?" The answer of an operative designer, one of the evaluators of the Gazda proposals in his factory, illustrates the prevailing attitude: "Oh, come on, the innovation fever will just go to people's heads" (*Szabad Nép* 1951d, 5).

Another source of anxiety for managers was the goal of the material conservation and Gazda movements "to integrate the discovered reserves [that is, wastes] into the plan" (No. 102.700/1951 Decree of the Director of the Central Planning Office on the Bolstering of the Material Conservation Movement), as in the following example:

> On the Day of Ideas this month, 21 out of the 32 proposals submitted targeted waste reuse. We recuperated so much wrought iron, otherwise difficult to obtain, that we withdrew our orders for the fourth quarter of this year and the first quarter of next year. (Vasmunkások Szakszervezete 1951, 29)

Finding reuses for waste could be an argument by distributors against giving in to enterprises' demands for more and more materials. This obviously met with managerial resistance. Two months before Gazda became well known, a report appeared in *Szabad Nép* about how the railroads were lagging behind in the coal-saving movement. The article mocked the Minister of Transportation and Post Offices for boasting of 150,000 tons of achieved savings, but retracted the claim as soon as the Central Planning Office decreased the input plans by this amount. The article concluded from the case that "in the struggle for savings on coal use, the railroad operators, simple workers, furnacemen and engine drivers must be relied on much more than before" (*Szabad Nép* 1951e, 5). Another article in the same daily half a year later also reproached management for not searching out and utilizing wastes for plan fulfillment. "Certain plants that are behind in fulfilling their plans often use the excuse that there is no material, when in fact there is waste" ("Százezres érték a hulladék között," *Szabad Nép* 1951, 5).

Discipline and Recycle

The Party's key motivation for such total mobilization around waste was that, as is obvious from my discussion of the material production of waste, most wastes were produced haphazardly, in amounts that were simply incalculable for the center. In this situation, the party-state, whose power depended on its ability to keep resources under central control, and its legitimacy on its ability to redistribute, obviously had to make an effort to have firms produce some knowledge about their wastes. The aim of accumulating such knowledge was not necessarily to reduce the amount of wastes, but to be able to control even these hidden resources and use their existence as an excuse to reduce input quotas for the constantly material-hungry firms—that is, to keep plans even tighter.

Documents indicate that knowledge of waste—its amount, its kinds, its potential uses, and the potential savings of its reuse—was more important than making sure that wastes were economically reused, or at least that the goods thus produced were fulfilling real human needs, and it was even more important than ensuring that they were properly distributed. What an official complained about in an internal report was not the actual uses or squandering of wastes but about the lack of sufficient knowledge.

> The production ministries [meaning the Ministries of Heavy and Light Industries] are not clear themselves how much iron scrap the companies under their management use within the Gazda movement, how much they transfer directly to firms of the local industry [meaning firms in cooperative ownership], and how much they are able to supply the waste-collecting enterprises. (UML 1951, Fonds XIX-A-16a OT, group 25, box 446, no file number)

The politics of waste proved to be a very effective tool for keeping in check workers, management, and private and cooperative producers and merchants. This, however, was not the only goal. The Panopticon of the waste movement allowed an even tighter control not just over wastes but also over primary resources principally needed for the production of productive goods. First of all, transferring wastes "primarily to the local industry and the small producers' cooperatives" relieved the planners of the obligation to support these undesirable forms of ownership with materials. Second, delegating waste reuse to the private and cooperative sector made it possible to reserve productive capacities for the production of "normal," that is, nonrecycled goods.[16] Third, the stipulation that the wastes discovered in factories were supposed to be used "primarily for consumer goods" also allowed channeling even more of the primary resources into the manufacturing of production goods. Finally, "the integration of the discovered reserves [that is, wastes] into the plans" held the lid tight over raw material transfers to the enterprises.

While in all these ways waste became a great excuse for the party-state to extend its control and "recycle" people into useful socialist citizens, the materiality of production and waste also had a significant impact on the emergent social relations and institutions. First of all, if metals had not been so crucial for the Party's plans, the metal scraps lying around in the postwar ruins and those produced by the ever-increasing heavy industries arguably might not have been considered such an important resource. As a result, there might not have been such a fierce struggle for wastes between the state on the one hand and workers, managers, privates, and cooperatives on the other, and the disciplinary aspects of the Gazda movement might have been subordinated to its stated official goals, namely waste reuse. Second, while nonmetal wastes were also registered and collected, waste legislation and institutions might have been more sensitive to their specificities and especially their differences from metal scraps.

Wastes did not simply "fall victim" to the preexisting social institutions and economic logic of state socialism, but rather wastes "bit back," and thus modified human intentions, and so themselves were formative of social relations and organizations. It matters whether state socialism was being built in a world which depended on and cherished above all steel, plastics, or wheat. In the next chapter I will demonstrate just how formative the material agency of production and of wastes has been, through my analysis of the unintended consequences of the metallic waste regime.

four
The Primitive Accumulation of Waste in Metallic Socialism

By the early 1950s, there had evolved a pervasive cult of waste in Hungary. Enterprises registered, collected, and reused their own or other companies' wastes. Workers, managers, cooperatives, women, and students were all enlisted in nationwide waste collection campaigns, and material conservation was hailed as a most noble characteristic of *Homo Sovieticus*. Yet by the early sixties, a new complaint was voiced: not about failures in reuse, as in the fifties, but about the absence of waste dump sites. In 1961, the Executive Committee of the Council of Budapest complained that there was no "regulation concerning the neutralization of waste and garbage of industrial origins" (BFL 1961, 63), and in 1967 authorities called attention to the mounting practice of "depositing [waste] without permits in the capital" (BFL 1967, 13). From the perspective of the enterprises that were doing the illegal dumping, one sees the flip side of the problem: their futile search for landfill sites for their wastes. In the year 1968 alone, for example, the Budapest Chemical Works approached eighteen organizations in search of a dump, in vain.

What was going wrong? Why didn't these companies simply recycle or reuse their by-products? And why couldn't they dispose of their unutilized wastes? These are the questions I will address in this chapter, concluding that the metallic waste model and the waste policies of the 1950s developed unintended consequences whose effects started to be felt less than a decade after their inception. First, the waste movement encouraged the generation of even more wastes, resulting in a hypertrophied waste regime. Second, due to the limitations of the metallic concept of waste, the waste movement led to the accumulation of nonrecyclable wastes, especially chemical wastes. I will discuss this second type of unintended consequence through the case of the above-mentioned chemical plant, the Budapest Chemical Works (BCW).

Hypertrophy

The early state socialist waste concept treated wastes as useful, multifunctional, pliable materials. Nevertheless, as I argued before, the key goal was to make sure these wastes were collected and redistributed; reducing them or making sure they were economically reused remained of secondary importance. This attitude to wastes was very well represented in the design of bookkeeping. Experts in the eighties claimed that "the registry of wastes had been completely fused with the enterprise's material management (with its analytic material bookkeeping), unfortunately so much so that wastes have been entirely inseparable from total material use" (Ladó, Romhányi, and Büchner 1983, 80). This system accepted as real input even those materials that, in reality, were turned into waste during the production process. For example, if in the manufacturing of a dress, six square meters of textile were used, but a half–square meter was dropped during tailoring, then the actual material use to appear in the accounting was not five and a half but six square meters. The half-square-meter piece of waste showed up in one of the material inventory accounts, called "waste materials," but only if this amount of waste was collected and taken back to the stockrooms. As, however, the cleanup and the reentry of waste in the inventory occurred only periodically, and at a pace different from that of the production process, the exact amount of waste generated in each production process could not be determined. Furthermore, wastes that had been simply thrown out, drained, lost, or stolen did not show up on paper. Other waste materials were not fit for storage, such as electricity, water, or steam, or had a small value and ended up under the category of "current productive use" (KSH 1983, 101). Thus, in its effort to register by-products as credits rather than losses, the Hungarian bookkeeping system was inadequately equipped to keep records of production waste.

But if the usefulness of waste was clear, the usefulness of waste reuse was not. This discourse on waste, in fact, turned out to be counterproductive. First, because the reuse of waste materials itself required additional raw materials, energy, and labor, which, along with most products, were all in short supply, the already collected wastes were often left to rust and rot and turned into useless materials. As an evaluation of the Ministry of Mining and Energy put it: "Last year, the absence of materials and coverage for costs necessary for investments, experimentation, implementation or material substitution obstructed the realization of conservation measures" (UML Fonds XIX-A-75, box 1, no document number, 1). A bulletin prepared by one of the trade unions primarily emphasized the additional labor that waste reuse required: "[W]e have to overcome a considerable aversion of certain worker circles to the use of wastes, because production out of waste is naturally more labor-intensive, and requires greater circumspection and care than the use of normal materials" (Department of Wage, Production, and Economics of the Central Council of Hungarian Trade Unions 1953, 7).

As a result, the wastes already collected were left unused, and in the process of storage, they lost their value and turned into garbage. This practice must have become clear to planners, because in 1954 they passed a decree ordering that "[t]hose wastes that are usable within the Gazda movement without melting, breaking, etc. can be stored only in the amount that is sufficient for their processing for 90 days" (No. 2.500-21/1954 decree of the Director of the Central Planning Office).

However, reuse, even when it materialized, did not prevent wastes from becoming trash. These early recycled goods were in many cases not needed, and even chronic shortages could not increase their appeal. As a contemporary brochure said: "[I]t may happen that they produce a good for which there is no demand, when in fact the same waste material could be used for making more important and more sought-after consumption goods" (Bőripari Dolgozók Szakszervezete 1951, 12). Another source put the blame for this on the outmoded mentality of consumers: "[T]he public . . . has aversions to buying products made out of wastes. On this terrain, those employed in commerce have serious agitation work to do" (Department of Wage, Production, and Economics of the Central Council of Hungarian Trade Unions 1953, 7). The Trade Union of Employees of Commerce and Finances, for its part, however, had previously refused this responsibility, and rather had called on a better evaluation of consumer needs and taste:

> [W]ithout a knowledge of the market and due to the ignorance of demand, goods are manufactured out of valuable wastes for which there is no demand.

> One characteristic example of this is the use of leather wastes that are perfectly fit for children's sandals for 60-centimeter-long leather belts, which first of all cannot be used because of their size, and, second, could be made out of plastic and textile wastes as well. . . . By including experts from commerce, we could eliminate the mistake of marketing valueless, often tasteless and useless goods made out of valuable waste materials due to a lack of expert knowledge. (MDP-MSZP 1951, box 5, document 34, 1)

As this advice was not heeded, unsalable recycled goods piled up in such quantities, despite shortages, that in 1959 the National Office of Materials and Prices found it necessary to introduce "Gazda movement prices," a euphemism for discounts.

However, as for the surplus supplies of Gazda movement goods produced before 1959, neither the industrial ministries nor the Ministry of Domestic Trade could calculate and prescribe prices. What decades of economic reform could not carry through later—a market-dependent price system—the Gazda movement achieved by 1959, well before the 1968 economic reforms:

> The industry [in this case the Ministry of Light Industries] cannot responsibly prepare a price calculation, nor has there been a controllable basis for the expenses in the price calculations in previous cases. The establishment of consumer prices is not feasible either; thus, the Ministry of Domestic Trade does not wish to deal with calculating prices for the products of the Gazda movement. . . . *Let this be the object of agreement between the producer and the trade companies.* (UML 1959, Fonds XIX-A-48, document 524.1199/5, Ár-1959; emphasis mine)

Realizing how collected wastes—whether recycled but not sold, or not recycled at all—turned into trash, we can start seeing the truth in a Hungarian anthropologist's evaluation of the socialist effort to reuse waste as a "transformation of waste into garbage at a significant expense" (Dömötör 1980).

Surprisingly, not only did the movement and waste policies fail to reuse wastes, they also strengthened the well-known and already existing tendencies of centrally planned economies toward wasteful production. The approach that wastes are always reusable in an infinite number of ways led to a counterproductive attitude, which Gazda reproachfully caricatured this way: "It does not matter if I produce rejects, since the spoiled product after some modification can still be reused. That's what the Gazda movement is for" (Vasmunkások Szakszervezete 1951, 8).

The concept of waste as useful material and the encouragement of using wastes had the result of relativizing the notion of rejects. As Gazda warned:

> My worry, nevertheless, is that we will hurt the trend towards standardization that has just now started on the entire terrain of industry, and it will teach many plants and their leaders laxity, since [this practice suggests that] if the size does not turn out quite right, it could still be used somewhere. (SZOT 1951, box 5, document 33, 3)

Another document expressed a similar concern:

> With regards to waste reuse, there have been initiatives and results on a smaller or greater scale. These, however, were exhausted in not throwing out but simply setting aside wastes. Such accumulation of waste materials however often had the exact opposite results as the intention behind saving them. These materials were kept so they could be drawn on when necessary. In reality, however, the workers used them for making up for materials they botched. In this sense, of course, this did mean material conservation, but it resulted in the loosening of plan discipline and the distortion of the concept of rejects. (MDP-MSZMP 1952, Fonds 95, group 4, preservation unit 103, no document number, 2)

There were unintended consequences not only from the concept of waste as always useful but also in the tools of early socialist waste politics, such as bonuses and quotas. It is easy to see how these created an added incentive for workers and managers to produce with even higher waste ratios. In response to a 1952 proposal by the Ministry of Local Industries regarding the reuse of wastes, an official of the National Bureau of Materials and Prices weighed in against giving out bonuses for collecting wastes beyond the planned amount because, as he argued, that could lead to passing on good or new materials as wastes so as to secure the bonus (UML 1952, Fonds XIX-A-16-a, box 446, group 25, no document number, 1).

Waste delivery quotas, furthermore, encouraged waste-intensive production; there was an explicit motivation for increased waste generation built into waste laws. The No. 102.700/1951 decree of the Director of the Central Planning Office ordered that "[i]f the workers propose a counter-plan and the [production] conference accepts that, the larger quantity established in the counter-plan will become the quantity the firm is obliged to collect." In other words, such plan targets, once agreed upon by the ministries and enterprises, could only be modified to increase. Furthermore, other laws ensured that waste quotas, just like production quotas, increased from year to year, even in the absence of precise plans. The No. 113.900/1951 decree of the Director of the Central Planning Office on the waste quotas to be delivered in the first quarter of 1952, for example, established an obligatory rate of increase: "To insure the continual collection of wastes until the approval of the 1952 plans for waste reuse, . . . in the first quarter of 1952, the enterprises subject to central planning must deliver 20% more than the quarter of their quotas for 1951." The counterproductive effect of quotas was eventually admitted by central organs:

> In 1956 ministries, and the companies subordinated to them, which generate non-ferrous metals, stopped getting plan quotas [for waste]. To wit, experience showed that it was impossible to prepare technically grounded and correct delivery plan quotas for the deliverers [of waste]. It happened that certain enterprises received quotas that were unrealistically high, which motivated them in the wrong direction, while other firms received loose delivery quotas, which they could fulfill much too easily. (UML 1960, Fonds XIX-A-16-u, box 32/a, topic 5, document 2-00188/1960, 1)

"Motivation in the wrong direction"—that is, the production of wastes for its own sake—in fact reinforced the tendency of centrally planned economies toward wasteful production and a Sisyphean exhaustion of natural resources and the destruction of nature—resource use that produced no or very few benefits in return (Gille 1997).

In sum, the concept of waste as a material useful under any conditions and the tools of the early state socialist waste politics led to (a) the production of even more waste and rejects, (b) their accumulation without use and their subsequent spoilage, and (c) their accumulation as unsalable recycled goods.

The Accumulation of Nonrecyclable Wastes

The negative impacts of early socialist recycling efforts were not restricted to resource squandering. Another unintended consequence had long-term effects. In order for us to understand this consequence, we must appreciate the profound implications of the metallic waste model.

The Chemical Industry as the Inferior Other of Metallurgy

In the previous chapter, I demonstrated the underlying metallic nature of the concept of waste prevalent in early state socialism. If metallurgy and metal-working industries were strategic and played an indispensable representational role in state socialism, other industries—primarily the chemical industry—were considered to be an alien territory for state socialism. Let us review the causes of this ideological hierarchy.

The kind of production processes that characterize the chemical industry did not lend themselves easily to the organization of central planning and the disciplinary organization of production. First of all, chemical production is a continuous process and, as Blauner summarizes,

> chemical processes cannot be subdivided to the extent that the mechanical operations in assembly can be. Chemicals are not discrete units upon which a number of operations can be performed very quickly, but liquids and gases that flow continuously through a series of automatic operations, each of which takes a considerable amount of time. (Blauner 1967, 163)

In the chemical industry, products and semifinished products are produced in large batches, then the production line is reorganized, and another product or semifinished product is produced. Since one batch may take several weeks, no single finished product is produced for weeks or months. For this reason, initially, plans were disaggregated not into monthly targets but into quarterly ones only. However, when the planners tried to break those down into monthly ones to comply with central regulations and to have workers enroll in the work competitions, chaos prevailed. As a trade union report explained:

> This method [breaking up quarterly quotas into monthly ones] is particularly incorrect in chemical industries, where the monthly production program within the quarterly one changes frequently. In case of a change in the program, it may happen that the worker works on an entirely different task than he/she made a pledge for. As a result, the competition only exists on paper. (SZOT 1953, box 12/90, no document number, 2)

It was not only the temporal disaggregation of plans that caused problems, but so did the breakdown of plans into quotas for individuals. In the chemical industry, as Blauner argues, work tasks are less individualized. Workers mostly add or drain materials, check meters, weigh materials, and oversee the otherwise quite automatic chemical processes. Here work cannot be as standardized as in the mechanical process or assembly line industries, because a lot depends on the chemical givens of each unique production process. For the individual worker, this means that s/he has less control over her/his individual performance. Speeding up, looting, or slacking off is difficult. As a result, the socialist work competitions that urged the breakdown of plans into individual workers' quotas and a rivalry among individual employees had a poor prospect for implementation.

> The detailed disaggregation of the plans met with serious obstacles, because they only broke down the plans to shifts. Since in the great majority of the chemical plants the product of each shop goes through various labor processes, it is necessary to break down the plan in such a way that would determine for the individual worker the task per shift, so that the particular final results of each worker in the shop add up to the targeted goal. (SZOT 1953, box 12/90, no document number, 2)

The idea that production is an aggregated total of tasks performed by individual plants, shops, and workers is a characteristic logic of central planning that, in turn, is predicated upon a schematic understanding of mechanical or metallic production models. High-level Party and trade union officials, however, remained stubborn and aggravated technical managers.

> The breakdown of plans in such a way met with a serious resistance by the technical employees; what's more, the enterprise triangle [a body consisting of management, the Party, and trade union officials] in the Budapest Sulfuric Acid Factory could only be persuaded after a several-hours-long debate. (SZOT 1953, box 12/90, no document number, 2)

Indeed, reports indicated that chemical plants were lagging behind in the socialist work competitions. When explaining the poor records of chemical plants in the work competitions, Party officials often referred to the "special situation" of the industry.

> The chemical industry differs from other industries to the extent that, in it, it is not skilled workers [that is, with formal qualifications] that work but, rather, workers with long on-the-job experience. The labor processes are not mechanically visible [sic] processes but chemical processes that take place in a closed system. For this reason, the rationalization of work is more difficult than in those industries which have mechanical processes. (MDP-MSZMP 1951, Fonds 276, group 116, preservation unit 40, no document number, 138)

As a solution, the report suggested organizing the Stakhanovite movement not by individuals but by teams, brigades, and plants, and instead of the criterion of production volume, that innovations and material conservation be considered. A later decree nevertheless strongly pushed for individual quotas and, as a result, a 1954 report still found that "on the terrain of the chemical industry, the organized direction and control of the work competition is not sufficiently held in hand and, as a result, there are not enough steps taken to correct mistakes" (MDP-MSZMP 1954, box 174).

In terms of the planning of material use, chemical plants were also in an ambiguous position, because of the calculability of raw materials but the incalculability of the need for auxiliary materials (catalysts of a chemical reaction that do not become part of the final product). On the one hand, as a contemporary evaluation suggested,

> [b]ecause the use of auxiliary materials cannot be deduced from the chemical equations of the technological process, and their "wear and tear" depends on a lot of different factors, the calculation of material norms requires an even more careful pioneering work that can give [practical] experiences a scientific foundation. (Jávor 1954, 11)

On the other hand, it was also claimed that "[o]n the terrain of raw materials, what makes our [the chemical industry's] situation easier and helps us to recognize our mistakes is the fact that in the chemical industry one can establish what amount of raw materials is theoretically necessary for the production process" (SZOT 1956, box 8, no document number, 2).

However, this was a double-edged sword: the precision of chemical laws could help not only to determine more easily what constitutes a wasteful use of materials (although not the use of auxiliary materials) but also it posed definite limits to thrifty material use. Such confines, in turn, were seen as too strict to allow spectacular achievements in material conservation.

One of the plants in the Chinoin pharmaceutical company also invoked such biological and chemical givens as a reason for failing to fulfill the plans or pledges.

> The Penicillin plant pledged to fulfill its July and August plans by August 20. Unfortunately we could not fulfill them partly for technical reasons, partly for reasons that have to do with work discipline, and partly for reasons of the nature of production. We have overcome the technical obstacles, and there seems to be a definite improvement on the terrain of work discipline. *We know that the biological process influences our production to some extent, but not entirely.* We will strive to manage production in such a way that these factors don't hamper our production. (MDP-MSZMP 1951, Fonds 176/2, group 184, preservation unit 2, no document number, 15; emphasis mine)

Just as chemical processes have a certain material autonomy, the biological ones employed in some parts of the chemical industry, especially pharmaceuticals, did as well.

In the eyes of the authors of some of these reports, however, this technological uniqueness did not absolve the Hungária Chemical Works and Chinoin of their poor record in the Stakhanovite movement. The general cause of such bad performance might be technological, but the concrete cause had to be political. One assessment not only excluded such technological arguments but also identified them as suspect when it alleged that "in the organic and inorganic chemical industry they are avoiding the question under the pretext of various special situations" (MDP-MSZMP 1951, Fonds 276, group 95, box 46, documents 12227 and 30581). A Party report went even further, attacking the political convictions it thought characteristic of the industry, claiming that "there are a lot of fascists and social democrats among the lower-level technical cadres" in these factories (MDP-MSZMP 1951, Fonds 276, group 116, preservation unit 40, no document number, 138).

This political mistrust was partially the result of the uniqueness of the industry and especially its strong reliance on high-level technical and scientific knowledge, and thus of a certain sense of insecurity in the economic and ideological leadership. Put yourself in the shoes of these Party apparatchiks and trade union representatives, whose level of education was rather low. "50% of the cadres in the statistics did not complete the eight-year elementary school," recounted an internal survey, which then suggested to increase the proportion of the technical intelligentsia (MDP-MSZMP 1952, Fonds 95/2, preservation unit 282, no document number). A 1954 report, however, still found only 5.7 percent of intelligentsia among cadres, and even within this group the proportion of the technical intelligentsia represented only 2.8 percent. At the same time, 69.2 percent of the paid Party activists were workers previously employed in factories (MDP-MSZMP 1954, Fonds 95/2, preservation unit 282, no document number). It is quite reasonable to expect that such officials felt intimidated by the kind and level of knowledge that the management of chemical plants required. For them, such production processes remained inscrutable, and thus dangerously out of reach of their control. Suspicion must have been their natural reaction.

This suspicion probably also had a lot to do with a severe mistrust of the class basis of the chemical industry, and of engineers and professionals in general. A 1952 Chemical Workers' Union memorandum warned that "we still have functionaries who loathe technical employees and, generalizing, identify everybody [in the industry] with the technical employees of capitalism" (MDP-MSZMP 1952, box 127, no document number, 4).

The chemical industry thus was seen as an alien territory for the building of communism. The metallic production culture imported from the Soviet Union and the political suspicion toward the chemical industry led to the representation of waste as exclusively metal, or metal-like, often explicitly as steel scrap. This resulted in a waste model that was based on a metonymy in Gudeman's (1986) sense: the schema that planners in early state socialism applied to the economy was steel manufacturing, which was to stand in for the entire economy, turning metal waste into the icon of all wastes. Once the idea took root—that wastes were raw materials that could help fulfill plans faster—it was forcefully applied to all other branches of industry. I will discuss the consequences of this model in the next section.

The Problem of Chemical Wastes

In the previous section I analyzed the alienness of the chemical industry in early state socialism and analyzed the reasons leading to the rejection of the

Chinoin proposal (introduced in chapter 3) to become the model for the material conservation movement. In this section I will examine those elements of the metallic waste model that led to counterproductive outcomes in this branch.

The kind of built-in recycling that characterizes many chemical production processes was not the kind that the Party could show off as novel, and the achievements of chemical wastes were thus not as spectacular. In fact, a trade union representative suggested that there was a confusion about what workers could pass off as new. "The widening of the Gazda movement in the chemical industry creates a problem, because there are a lot of materials that the plants reused before, and they wonder whether this [practice] is a part of the Gazda movement" (SZOT 1951, box 5/34, no document number, 1).

To the extent that the point the Party tried to drive home was that wastes are always useful, the propagandistic value of the kinds of products produced out of chemical by-products was lower than of those made out of metal, textile, or wood. Consider the following quote from Gazda: "What can you use a thousand tons of [scrap] reinforcing iron for? For the ferro-concrete ceilings of 750 two-room apartments, or for covering the iron needs of three buildings as big as the Sport Stadium of Csepel, or, . . . 50,000 bicycles or 64,000 sewing machines, or 160 large, radial drills, or boiler tubes for 300 engines" (Gazda 1951). What would be the rhetorical impact of this claim if we were to replace the recognizably useful goods produced out of metal wastes with products such as acetic acid anhydride, brenzkatechin, or papaverin?

The dominant discourse constructed waste as something useful, and therefore the state's task was to make sure that appropriate use values were assigned to it. By-products were not to be thrown out but to be kept in production and circulated in the economy as long as possible. If technical conditions for the reuse of certain wastes were missing, this was viewed as a temporary problem that rapid technological development and the genius of socialist workers would solve shortly.

There was only one decree, the No. 2.500-21/1954 decree of the Director of the Central Planning Office on the collection and utilization of wastes, that indicated what was to be done with wastes for which no uses had yet been found. It ordered waste generators to

> bring the attention of their superordinate authorities, the Ministry of Light Industries, or other competent organs (such as research institutes) to so-far unutilized wastes, to ask for their advice and opinion and, if a utilization opportunity is available, to organize the collection, utilization or sale. If the

> experiments to find uses for certain wastes in the local industries have been
> successful, the supply boards of the ministries are obliged—on the order of
> the Minister of Light Industries—to have the waste generators complete their
> plan for reusing the wastes in question.

However, the decree still did not give any instructions as to what should happen if the experiments for reuse were not successful: what other institutes or organizations enterprises could turn to for further research, and what practical steps those results entitled them to take. Ultimately, it left the burden of determining utility and economic feasibility, but most importantly, the task of dealing with unusable wastes, on the shoulders of managers.

A key area in which such nonrecyclable wastes piled up was the chemical industry. The chemical industry turns out nondiscrete products, which makes the applicability of Gazda's model difficult. Gazda noted this difference in his talk at a discussion group on the achievements of his movement.

> I must note that in one respect, the workers of the chemical industry are in a
> more difficult situation than, for example, those in the steel or timber industries. The wastes whose reuse possibilities we ponder in the steel industry are
> more tangible than that in the chemical industry. Waste in the chemical
> industry leaves in a gaseous state, which is intangible. (SZOT 1951, box 5,
> document 33, 8)

For Gazda, however, the problem of chemical wastes resided in the technical difficulties of reusing and recycling wastes, and not in the pollution such wastes might cause: "It hadn't occurred even to me when leaving the factory and passing by the gas plant, where we always have to walk carefully to avoid the constantly leaking tar water, how much money must be poured in the Danube annually" (SZOT 1951, box 5, document 33, 8). It is telling of the metallic model that in Gazda's eyes, what poured in the Danube was not polluting materials but money that could have been saved by reusing these materials. Treating by-products as useful apparently precluded the idea that they might not only be useless but harmful as well. As a result, the polluting effects of unutilized wastes remained in the planners' blind spot, leading to severe environmental consequences I will return to.

Another problem created by chemical wastes, as an industry report pointed out, was that the uniqueness of each production process placed limits on its wider applicability: "The chemical industry is a unique case in this regard, because it is difficult to find methods that could be applied in other plants due to the fact that the production processes markedly differ from each other. This is so even within individual industries" (SZOT 1956, box 8, no document number, 5).

In the chemical industry, waste reuse in most cases was, for technical reasons, restricted to recycling—that is, the reuse of materials after some chemical transformation. Gazda's notion that wastes are 100 percent reusable/recyclable was not adaptable to the chemical industry. Metal wastes, in general, could indeed be reused over and over again, and even if they were left to rust they did not constitute a significant source of air or water pollution. To deal with chemical wastes, whose reuse or even recycling was a technically much more thorny problem, and whose accumulation in storage *was* an environmental threat, would have required a more flexible attitude. Problems created by such wastes called for (a) a much more rigorous focus on source reduction, and especially (b) facilities for safe waste treatment and dumping. Source reduction was not prioritized because the metallic waste models suggested endless reusability, and requests for disposal were denied legitimacy because that would have meant renouncing a secondary raw material. Consequently, wastes were not only treated as exclusively useful, but also as always harmless.

As wastes were seen as useful resources that could contribute to the building of state socialism and thus needed to remain under the control of the Party, they were not supposed to be discarded or liquidated. Consequently, enterprise requests for disposal or treatment facilities were denied. One area where this created a lot of problems was, not surprisingly, the chemical industry.

First of all, the by-products of the chemical industry tended to be dangerous to health; second, due to the rapid growth of the chemical industry, such by-products were now being created at an unprecedented rate. The significance of chemical investments grew due to the increase of hydrocarbons among energy and raw material sources, and due to the industrialization of agriculture. Between 1960 and 1970 the chemical industry was made to become the fastest-growing branch. The annual average rate of growth was 13.3 percent, double the average industrial growth rate (Pető and Szakács 1985, 553). As supplying the population with consumer goods received greater political and economic priority after János Kádár took over following the failed 1956 Revolution, the provision of agricultural chemicals became a key area of expansion, actually suppressing growth in other areas of chemical production (Pető and Szakács 1985, 553).

Despite this rapid growth, socialist countries, including Hungary, still needed to import pesticides from capitalist countries. In 1970 the share of domestic production in the use of all pesticides was 39 percent, the share of imports from socialist countries was 13 percent, and the share of capitalist imports was 48 percent (*Vegyiművek* 1971, 1), motivating the Hungarian government to keep increasing pesticide production, and chemical production in general. The slogan "We'll be a country of iron and steel" was replaced with the slogan "Let's chemicalize!"

Struggling outside the Metallic Waste Model

The story of the Budapest Chemical Works (BCW) in particular demonstrates how the wholesale imposition of the metallic waste model on nonmetallic spheres affected waste practices concretely. The company's postwar history demonstrates the negative long-term consequences of the simultaneous growth in chemical product output and the state's ignorance of the special problems chemical wastes created.

The Social Relations of Waste Production

The Budapest Chemical Works was among the most significant chemical plants in Hungary, the successor to Hungária and the Budapest Sulfuric Acid Factory, two firms that excelled already in the interwar period. In 1967, BCW produced one-third of the pesticides (including insecticides, herbicides, and fungicides) and one-fourth of the phosphorous artificial fertilizers used in Hungary. In order to understand BCW's economic and environmental impact, we first need to understand its location in the political map of state enterprises and Party–firm relations.

Partly based on the monthly "mood reports" Party secretaries submitted to the next-higher level of the Party, a hierarchy of firms was established. Enterprises with good political records were those that gave prominence to Party members and officials in the management of the company, or encouraged Party membership, ideological education, and participation in various political campaigns among their employees.[1] Firms with bad political records were those whose management preferred not taking the advice of Party officials in economic decisions about investment or remuneration, or who made promotion decisions based on work performance rather than a good political resume, or those who were less than willing to carry out a witch-hunt for "ideologically unreliable" employees. The managers of such firms were in constant danger of losing their positions, unless they proved themselves irreplaceable in the economic sense. This, however, was all the more difficult because, due to the lack of such managers' political leverage, they encountered difficulties in securing subsidies, credits, or extra funds for social welfare goals.[2]

The Budapest Chemical Works was a firm whose political profile was always looked at with suspicion. Its longtime manager was far too reform-minded: he protected intellectual and professional employees from Stalinist witch-hunts during the fifties; he advocated team-based organization and economic incentives in the early sixties; he successfully fought the idea of his firm building a huge and most likely inefficient replica of a Soviet chemical plant in the seventies. No wonder that he failed to secure the goodwill of Party and ministry officials, consequently depriving BCW of subsidies and loans. Since BCW's management knew that its political performance remained dubious, it had to compensate with its economic performance. The firm was not only a major provider of Hungary's pesticide and fertilizer needs, but, thanks to its ability to overfulfill the plans, it won the "champion factory" title eighteen times between 1948 and 1968. It continued to score high in economic terms even after 1968, when the old indicator of economic performance, plan fulfillment, was replaced with a monetary indicator, and in particular with that of hard currency earnings by exports. As a result, the company's economic success effectively demonstrated its management's irreplaceability.

This success, however, came with its own set of contradictions. In 1967 Hungary, along with many countries, ceased the production of DDT because of its recently discovered harmful effects on public health. Not only had DDT production constituted an important part of BCW's production (7 to 10 percent, according to my rough estimates), it had used as its primary input the main product of one of BCW's plants—chlorine. Since there was no demand for chlorine elsewhere in the country at the time, BCW had to find uses for it, lest a third of its post-DDT productive capacity be idled. Such a setback would have shaken the security of BCW's management, previously maintained by its economic excellence. The solution lay in cooperation with an Austrian firm. In this deal, BCW was to barter tetrachlorobenzene (1,2,4,5-TCB), for the production of which chlorine was needed, with ÖSW, a firm in Linz, for a herbicide the latter produced out of TCB. For the TCB delivered in excess of what ÖSW needed for that year's production, BCW, or, more precisely, the Hungarian state, received hard currency.[3]

The seemingly rather advantageous deal nevertheless had its opponents. A former middle-ranking manager and a foreman raised a concern over the large amount of waste the technology of TCB production entailed: the waste-to-final-product ratio was as high as 45 percent; in fact, a 1969 report claimed it to be 47 percent. This meant that in the first year of production, the company produced almost as much by-product as final product, 700 tons. This is an admittedly high value even among the usually high waste-ratio aromatic compounds (personal interview, Gyula Eifert, Budapest, 1995).

When a former foreman asked a plant manager what would be done with all this waste, the latter indignantly answered, "that is not for you to worry about" (personal interview, Budapest, 1995). Indeed, the waste product (a mixture of paradichlorobenzene, other isomers of TCB, and hexachlorobenzene) turned out to be a major headache for the company—a problem that now, after more than thirty years, is still waiting to be solved.

In this case, waste is not the outcome of material or allocative inefficiencies, but the result of an unequal international division of labor. According to two of my interviewees, both former employees of BCW, Westerners were already trying to get rid of this nasty production process, which generated as much toxic by-product as final product.

> They weren't producing much of TCB in the West because of the large expenses due to waste. We should have sold this [product] at a four-fold price. . . . There they did calculate how much it cost to make the crap disappear. (Personal interview, Budapest, 1995)

Other BCW employees did not confirm this to be the reason for the deal made with Austria, and statistical data on TCB production that could corroborate or disprove this claim are extremely rare and inconsistent. One thing does seem clear, however, from market reports at the end of the sixties. In the first half of 1968, the U.S. Army awarded a three-year contract for the annual production of 30 million pounds of 1,2,4,5-TCB to Delaware Chlorine Products and Sonford Chemical Company. The chemical 1,2,4,5-TCB is an intermediary for Agent Orange, a herbicide the United States used in the Vietnam War for jungle combat. It is possible that some of that amount was contracted out to Austrian firms, either by the U.S. Army directly or by U.S. companies. The former is less likely given that Austria was a neutral country. Some BCW employees claimed in interviews to know that ÖSW's TCB was indeed used for producing Agent Orange, either at ÖSW or by selling it to other companies that manufactured Agent Orange. Another piece of circumstantial evidence that might point in the same direction is Green activists' account that when they first visited the site where the drums of TCB waste were ultimately deposited, they found drums with U.S. markings. After they contacted the U.S. Embassy in Budapest, however, those drums mysteriously disappeared, the activists asserted. Whatever the truth and whatever purpose BCW's TCB product served, it does seem likely that with the U.S. Army's large need, a shortage of TCB productive capacities was created on the world market, and Hungary was there at the right time and right place to occupy this niche. In addition, as it becomes clear from these documents, BCW could sell TCB cheaply. The U.S. Army offered $0.20/pound, while BCW sold to the Austrians at $0.18/ pound. This adds up to a significant difference ($30,870 for the first year), if one considers that in the first year BCW sold or bartered 1,543,500 pound, and that based on this lower price, BCW made a meager profit of $30/ton, that is, $21,000 in the first year.

Indeed, the dollar-generating value of TCB production (that is, how many Forints were invested in producing one dollar of income) was low, as was admitted by managers in archival documents; nevertheless the mentioned pressures felt by BCW and pressures to develop foreign trade, especially barter, overwhelmed the worries about the waste product. Not only did the management keep producing tetrachlorobenzene, it even increased the production volume. The mediator that put the deal together was Chemolimpex, a state-owned company that had a monopoly on the foreign trade of chemical products. Chemolimpex, of course, took its cut, 50 percent, but it was interested in the increase of the sale volume also because of the political value of such deals. By the end of the sixties, Hungary was increasingly opening toward Western markets. Acquiring semifinished products and know-how from the West was advantageous to COMECON and the Soviet Union, in particular, because the member countries could get access to these without having to spend hard currency (Staniszkis 1992). Among such contracts between Hungary and the West, that between BCW and ÖSW was among the first, and, in fact, the very first one involving chemical enterprises (personal interview, Mrs. Miklós Durkó, Budapest, 1996). Obviously, the stakes of fulfilling the contract obligations and renewing them were high.

In addition, BCW was explicitly encouraged to export by a grant it won. The Ministry of Foreign Trade awarded the grant in the form of a tax return to companies who earned one dollar with less than 80 Forints' expenditure, and who committed themselves to expanding their exports to capitalist countries. These grants were to finance technological innovations involved in their export activities, and BCW was among the six firms who received one (MDP-MSZMP 1969, Fonds M-Bp-14, preservation unit 27, no document number, 8).

Therefore, we may appreciate BCW's waste as the outcome of Hungary's precarious balancing of its political alliance (that is, its political dependence on the Soviet Union and chains to COMECON), geopolitical relations (the Cold War, and in particular the U.S. Vietnam War), and Hungary's economic dependence on the West (the need to generate hard currency to access Western goods). Furthermore, this case may be more than simply the result of an unequal international division of labor (exploitative or self-exploitative export price); it might have resulted from a conscious effort of Western countries to hand this waste-intensive production process down to their Eastern European counterparts.[4]

The Imperative of Waste Reuse

Even the more conscientious engineers who cared about the fate of waste products expected that they could quickly find a use for the by-product soon to be generated in the quantities of hundreds, and later thousands, of tons per year. It was not only the official waste credo that maintained such an optimism; the engineers' belief in their own science also helped eliminate the waste problem as a significant worry. Given the excellent fungicide qualities of the by-product (another polymer of TCB), BCW's researchers thought they would eventually find a way to reuse it (personal interview, Emil Valovits, Budapest [by telephone], 1997).

Indeed, they immediately started looking into reuse possibilities. The management commissioned the Gödöllő University of Agricultural Sciences to conduct experiments on the possible uses of the by-product. For a while it seemed that it could be transformed into petachlorofenolate, a fungicide, but the public health authority disapproved of such use, arguing on the basis of toxicological tests that it could endanger the public (BVM 1968). The other option was more successful. The Hungarian State Railways (MÁV) used the by-product as an impregnator for its wooden sleepers, but its needs were too small compared to the amount produced—a one-time order of 150 tons, in the face of 700 tons/year generated initially, and 1,200 tons/year thereafter—and the later switch to concrete sleepers eliminated even this demand.

The president of BCW also urged engineers to reduce the amount of the by-product. Indeed, a proposal dated January 7, 1969 suggested to "start from another raw material in the process of chlorinating, so that the 1,2,4,5-TCB could be produced more economically" (BVM 1969). As suggested by the question marks scribbled on the margin next to the concluding sentence asking for permission to realize this research project, this did not receive the president's approval. Since the raw materials already used, benzene and chlorine, were very cheap—in fact, chlorine was produced in another plant of BCW—another raw material would have increased the production costs significantly. Indeed, no document I found in the company archives mentioned this proposal ever again.

The firm, however, did not restrict its search to reduction and reuse prospects; already in 1968 BCW started looking into the technical possibilities of storing or liquidating the by-product. As is evident from a letter by the president, dated April 4, 1968, the management approached the following institutes and authorities: the National Hydrological Inspectorate, the Central Water Reserve Management Inspectorate, the Ministry of Heavy Industries, a professor from the Geological Department of the Budapest Technical University, the Technical Inspectorate of Mining, various regional Hydrological Directorates, a regional Public Health Inspectorate, the National Company of Oar and Mineral Mines, the Budapest Sanitary Authority, the National Geological Authority, the Mine Shaft-Sinking Company, the Nitrokémia Company, the Scientific and Research Institute of Hydrology, the Geological Institute, the State Forestry and Wildlife Farm of Telek, the National Nature Protection Authority, and the Hungarian Shipping Shareholding Company (BVM 1968). The list is impressive and suggestive.

As one could guess from the list, proposals included storing the waste in drums in abandoned mines or in forests, but the locations recommended would have endangered nearby underground drinking or thermal water sources. Another idea was to incinerate it in a facility run by another chemical plant, Nitrokémia, but it was later ruled that this waste was not incinerable. Finally, dumping into the Black Sea also emerged as a solution. This, after three or four deliveries (500 to 1,000 tons), was stopped personally by a Minister, who probably feared the international political consequences of dumping waste in a neighboring country. It is still a well-kept secret of BCW which country this was.

Realizing the daunting nature of this quest, the management raised the sale price of the TCB. In 1969 1,500,000 Forints, or about 8 percent of the total production cost, was added into the price calculations for waste neutralization—calculated for 1,200 tons of waste annually.

The desperation of BCW's president is palpable in the letter he wrote to the Ministry of Heavy Industries. Interestingly, his desperation is not over pollution and potential public health consequences, but over the potential costs of the environmental consequences (fines and cleanup costs). To get a full understanding of the framing of the problem, let me quote from this letter at greater length.

> At our company, wastes are generated that cannot be processed or neutralized. The generated amount of organic wastes are as follows:
> 1. from the production of 1,2,4,5 TCB, TCB isomers,   800 tons/year
> which is a solid material containing small amounts of water
> 2. by-product with a low humidity level   50 tons/year
>   [here follows a summary of nonorganic wastes]
> Presently we deliver the wastes to various places with the permission of authorities. We cannot always live up to the standards of storage and, as a

result, there are negative consequences. *Last year, for example, we polluted the water of drinking water pumps near a dump site assigned in the village of Gyál, which beyond endangering public health, caused a much too large financial loss to our company.*

For the safe placement of wastes we consider appropriate those low-lying exhausted and abandoned mine shafts whose hydrological environment is not a source of drinking water.

We approached with this proposal of ours the head of the National Hydrological Inspectorate (NHI), comrade Undersecretary Imre Dégen, who ordered the head of the Chief Department of Water Supply and Canalization, comrade Péter Pásztó, to assist our firm in searching out, assigning, and acquiring permits for a waste dump site. The NHI in principle accepted burying the waste in abandoned mines. In this matter, we approached Academy of Sciences Member Ferenc Papp, professor in the Geological Department of the Budapest Technical University. . . .

We suggest that after the concerned mining authorities have assigned the places fit for waste burial proposed by Professor Papp, the Ministry of Heavy Industry (MHI) turn the request for permit in to the NHI.

Since the safe placement of wastes poses problems not just for our company, but for the Hungarian chemical industry as a whole, we also suggest that the MHI call a conference at an appropriate level with the inclusion of the Technical Inspectorate of Mining, the affected enterprises, the NHI's Water Quality Control Department, the Hydrogeological Control Department, the regional Hydrological Directorates, and [NHI's] Water Quality Control Department, the regional Public Health Inspectorate, and of Professor Ferenc Papp.

The solution of the waste disposal problem is a rather urgent task, because the current uncertain and not always professional practice could cause a lot of damage to water management, and impedes production and its development. Solving the problem of waste burial in the proposed manner at the level of the entire chemical industry could guarantee the [planned] rate of development for a long period. (BVM 1968, 1; emphasis mine)

While I found no records in any of the archives of such a conference ever being called, subsequent documents in the archives of BCW indicate that the Ministry of Heavy Industry did reply at least to BCW's concrete proposal. Experts and officials were reported to have made field trips and surveyed various locations for "burial," but they found some of them geologically inappropriate, and others were just not followed up in a way that could be detected from written sources.

Rather, in various upper-management meetings reporting on talks with superordinate offices or scientific institutes on the waste problem, it was repeatedly stated that the primary goal was reuse. After the above surveys, an informal memorandum dated June 12, 1968 exhibited a glimpse of hope for at least a short-term solution until a reuse for TCB could be found:

> I suggest acceptance of the offer of the Mine Shaft-Sinking Company [burial in mine shafts with a ferro-concrete roof], because that would solve our waste placement problem for two years. Then, in the next two years we may find a solution, partly for reuse, since such experiments are being conducted even presently at the Gödöllő University of Agricultural Sciences, and partly for neutralizing it in Fűzfő [incineration], or we could chose both. (BVM 1968)

The hope to find a "burial place" and the hope to find use for the TCB waste both proved ephemeral. Another circumstance that aggravated the situation was that the drums, being piled up on the factory yard, started corroding and leaking. This is indicated by several BCW documents. In 1970, the management decided to transfer its waste drums, at least those still intact, to a newly opened branch plant in the countryside at Hidas, Baranya County, in the southern part of the country. They still did not entirely give up hope on reuse possibilities; as they argued, in a memorandum dated August 17, 1972, this transfer was necessary purely for purposes of storage: "The by-products of tetrachlorobenzene must be stored in drums in our Hidas plant until they are reused" (BVM 1972). Even in 1975, when another possibility appeared for dumping, the primacy of waste reuse was maintained as indicated in a letter by the president on July 14, 1975:

> The National Committee on Nuclear Energy, in cooperation with the Public Health and Epidemiological Authority, is planning to build a waste dump site in the vicinity of Vác for the placement of non-incinerable wastes. There seems to be a possibility for them to receive the TCB wastes for 10–20 years. In the first approach we must correct the misinformation according to which the TCB waste is incinerable. The primary goal continues to be the reuse of wastes. *The possibility mentioned above [dumping] must be maintained only for wastes that cannot be sold.* (BVM 1975; emphasis mine)

The Budapest Chemical Works must not have been alone in seeing its reuse hopes fail and in having its requests for facilitating safe dumping turned down by state authorities. By the sixties, unreusable wastes were piling up on factory premises across the country in such quantities that enterprises were being forced to find illegal ways to get rid of them. Local government officials now started complaining about illegal dumps appearing, both next to dumps managed by councils (local governments) and on territories of closed dumps that had been declared full and were being recultivated. In 1961, a talk given at a conference on the problems of waste treatment in the capital claimed that "the trustworthy deposit of various industrial wastes is unsolved in our country" and complained that the practice of illegal dumping not only ruins the cityscape but incurs additional and superfluous expenses, because when filling up the holes, the norms for height are rarely kept. In order to level the materials down to the necessary height, graders must be used often and several times in the same place. (Országos Közegészségügyi Intézet és Budapest Fővárosi Tanács VB (National Institute of Public Health and the Executive Committee of the Council of Budapest) 1961, 63)

In 1967, the Executive Committee of the Council of Budapest was also forced to admit that there were no appropriate guidelines for enterprises to dispose of their unwanted by-products. "Neither the OÉSZ [National Construction Code] nor the Budapest Code of Urban Planning contains regulations concerning the neutralization of waste and garbage of industrial origins" (Fővárosi Tanács Végrehajtó Bizottsága (Executive Committee of the Council of Budapest) 1967, 3).

Such problems would eventually make the metallic waste regime obsolete, and were often used as a rationale for new ways of approaching the problem of wastes in Hungary.

The Metallic Waste Regime

Let me now summarize my findings and analysis of the early state socialist waste regime. The social relations of waste production are best characterized as a web of power relations among the party-state, enterprise management, workers, and the cooperative and private sectors. The party-state's aim was to keep all resources, including wastes, under central control, and to establish an ethos of discipline necessary for an economy whose success was perceived to be dependent on the fulfillment of taut plans. Workers and managers primarily tried to survive under conditions of simultaneous shortage and strong sanctions associated with a failure to fulfill the plans. In order to survive, however, they needed to have a certain amount of control over the production process and material use. Managers and workers used wastes or manipulated their definition to their own advantage. In order to create yet another check on managers, the party-state mobilized workers in constant work competitions and material and waste reuse campaigns, in the course of which they involuntarily divulged local knowledge and information on the everyday operations of their plants. In the plans of the Party, the role of the private and cooperative sectors was restricted to reusing the wastes of the state-owned machine industries. The owners and managers of the cooperative and private businesses, however, were denied access to certain wastes when those were needed by the state sector or when they managed to profit from their use. In early state socialism, thus, waste became a valuable resource, which as such became the target of fierce political struggles.

The ideal-symbolic production of waste partly reflected these disciplinary goals, but it was partly independent from them. The prevalent cognitive model of waste production and reuse was a metonymical model that supplanted metallurgy for the entire economy. The metallic waste model treated waste as a tangible, discrete material in solid state, which could be reused over and over again, making the production process appear as a closed system in which no material is ever lost. To the extent that this model suggested that all wastes are reusable and useful, it legitimized the state's incessant efforts to create control over their use.

The disciplinary goals of the material conservation and waste reuse movement ultimately contradicted their official goal of waste reuse, leading to a number of unintended consequences. One consequence of the waste reuse movement was the generation of even more wastes, the transformation of already collected wastes into trash, and the accumulation of unsalable recycled goods. Besides contributing to this hypertrophied waste regime, the metallic waste model prevented the emergence of an alternative concept of waste, as not always useful but in fact harmful at times. Instead of allowing chemical plants to safely dispose of or neutralize their nonrecyclable wastes, authorities pushed for reuse and treated dumping and incineration as taboo. This led to the accumulation of these often hazardous wastes on factory yards or in illegal and unsafe dump sites. Ultimately, the regime was only concerned with accumulating wastes and mobilizing them for plan fulfillment, entirely disregarding the economic and ecological consequences.

Part 2

Reform and Reduce
(1975–1984)

"Collect iron and metal, with this, too you defend peace," went at
one time the animating call, which recently has got into cabaret
numbers not just because it testifies to the incomplete knowledge of
materials of its author. Since then it was discovered that the reuse
and collection of secondary raw materials is not primarily a matter of
slogans but of money and interest.

"Kiguberált milliárdok" (Scavenged billions),
Heti Világgazdaság, March 21, 1981

five
The Efficiency Model

Starting in the mid-seventies, the concept of waste went through a radical transformation in Hungary. There were several factors that made the early state socialist concept outmoded: (1) the recognition of the unintended consequences of the early state socialist waste policies; (2) the economic reforms, which created a new discursive environment for waste issues; (3) the post-1956 Kádárist détente, which rendered the disciplinary waste politics of the fifties obsolete; and (4) the successive dramatic price rises in raw materials and energy on the world market.

In this chapter, I will describe a move away from the appreciation of the intrinsic values of waste—that is, from a strict use-value mentality and the metallic concept of waste—again along the three dimensions of the production, the representation, and the politics of waste. In particular, I will analyze (a) the changes and continuities in the production of waste, (b) the monetization of the concept of waste, and (c) the professionalization of waste issues.

Discrediting the Movement Approach to Waste Reuse

In 1964, Hungarian writer Endre Fejes published his novel *Generation of Rust*, which was ultimately translated into more than thirty languages.

The book, whose title literally translates as "rust cemetery" (*Rozsdatemető*), narrates the life of the Hábetler family through the twentieth century, and thus well into socialism, in order to make sense of a murder: János, a son of the first generation covered in the book, kills his brother-in-law in a scrap yard. The ascetically worded chronicle provided a sobering portrait of Hungary's so-called working class, devoid of purpose, prospects, values, and sophistication. Clearly, Fejes hinted, the former petite bourgeoisie and peasantry failed to metamorphose into the high-minded, class-conscious proletariat the officials envisioned. This stratum that socialism failed to "melt down into useful material" (to quote Menzel's fictional character again; see chapter 3) had, according to the last words of the murder victim, found itself on the waste heap of history.

> This regime is kissing *your* forehead, is begging you to please go to college, be doctors, engineers, judges, chief plant managers, chief inspectors, chief military officers, chief god-knows-what, and you have crawled out from your barracks, and keep on living like hamsters. Jazz, dance, "go, Fradi."[1] You are just stuffing your faces, wolfing down cottage cheese noodles, fried fish, burping and slipping into bed, dear comrade Hábetler! (Fejes 1964, 345–46)

Fejes leaves it up to the reader to decide whether they got there on their own or because the Party who officially represented their interests betrayed them. While one of officialdom's highest recognitions of intellectuals, the Attila József Prize, wasn't taken away from the writer, the Party's propagandists opened fire ideologically on the successful volume, and a veritable shoot-out with other intellectuals defending Fejes ensued on the pages of various periodicals.

State socialism as a scrap heap that had such a propensity for producing human as well as material waste became a favored metaphor of artists in the seventies. Ukrainian artist Ilya Kabakov embarked on various projects of assembling collages of mundane, everyday objects and garbage. His installation *The Garbage Man* portrays a communal apartment filled with garbage. Rod Mengham, a biographer of Kabakov, interprets the artist's obsession with waste as a critique of the regime:

> Reversing the order of priorities in a culture whose axis was the process of production, Kabakov began to cultivate an aesthetic in the early 1980s that was organized around waste products, which lavished attention to an obsessive degree on the undervalued, on what was neglected and unwanted. Organizing several of his projects around the preservation of what had been thrown away, around preparing a taxonomy of what would normally pass as formless, Kabakov began to pose questions about the allocation of value in a system of meanings where artistic judgment is conditioned by an ideological imperative. (Mengham n.d., n.p.)

Kabakov himself sees a value in waste itself, and comments on the common habit of retaining everything in state socialism this way: "To deprive ourselves of all this means to part with who we were in the past, and in a certain sense, it means to cease to exist" (quoted in Mengham n.d., n.p.).

In 1976 the internationally renowned Czech writer Bohumil Hrabal (1990) published *Too Loud a Solitude*, the story of a waste-paper compactor who, rather than pulping unwanted or banned books, reads them or gives them away to his friends living on the margins of society. Finally, after his job is given to a more efficient brigade, he commits suicide. Czech director Jiri Menzel's film *The Snowdrop Festival*, based on another of Hrabal's writings, also ends with the death of a lovable and affectionate guy whose shack is crowded with defective objects, such as pairs of two left shoes he could not stand throwing away because "one never knows when they might be needed." Even the circumstances of his death are symbolic. He is hit by a truck as he rides his bike precariously balancing a huge canister of soup in one hand. He dies with a contented smile though: he didn't spill even a drop of the soup.

The theme of the common man finding his calling and following his destiny of saving wastes and recovering past values in garbage is also present in the work of another Czech writer, Ivan Klíma. He makes a distinction between the individual craftsmen sweepers and the mechanized "jerkish" cleaners. The former can carefully separate polluting garbage ("refuse," "soot") from the valuable leftovers of the past, while the latter simply sweep away everything and thus erase the past, while themselves contributing to further soot.

> Thus I moved in my orange vest through the little streets and lanes of my native city which was slowly giving up its spirit, my companions at my sides as witnesses. We were cleaning the town on which refuse had fallen and soot and ashes and poisoned rain and oblivion. We strode along in our vests like flamingoes, like angels of the dying day, sweeping away all rubbish and refuse, angels beyond life, beyond death, beyond our time, beyond all time, scarcely touched by the jerkish. Our speech resembled our age-old brooms, it came from a long way back and it moved along age-old paths. But behind us others are moving up: already the jerkish sweepers are arriving on their beflagged vehicles, pretending that they are completing the great purge, sweeping away all memories of the past, of anything that was great in the past. (Klíma 1991, 58)

> My dear Lída is mistaken when she thinks that sweepers must feel ostracised or humiliated. They might, on the contrary, if they cared about such things, regard themselves as the salt of the earth, as healers of a world in danger of choking. (Klíma 1991, 128)

As we can see, waste in these literary and artistic representations is not portrayed as something inherently negative and dirty; in fact, the quoted authors express a pronounced distaste for methodical orderliness and mechanized cleanliness. Rather, waste appears as a depository of old meanings somehow buried, or slated by the authorities for figurative and literal cleanup. If waste is a depository of history and truth, then Hrabal's, Menzel's, and Klíma's main characters, who all live on the margins of society, are the knowers of truth. Analogous to Georg Lukács's Marxist epistemology, such artists, unknowingly or knowingly and with poking irony, push forth their waste heroes as the identical subject/object. Lukács (1971) found the proletariat to have the knowledge of the Truth, because for the proletariat there is no schism between their immediate experience (as objects of production) and their class consciousness (the understanding of totality). Nancy Hartsock (1987), with a similar materialist logic, argues that inasmuch as women participate not just in production but in the reproduction of men as well, they have insights into both sides of the traditional binaries of mind and body, culture and nature, outside and inside, and, in fact, for them the boundaries are less fixed than for men. Their very involvement in the sexual division of labor renders their stand-point the only angle from which to see totality and "to critique and to work against phallocratic ideology and institutions" (176).

Hrabal's and Klíma's unheroic waste heroes—those dwelling in, working with, and collecting waste—are what the proletariat is for Lukács and what women are for Hartsock. It seems only right that a social order that prided itself on creation and production but which produced so much waste, yet that was so keen on erasing all traces of the past as waste, would give birth to novels in which the protagonists' main activity is not creating and pro-ducing useful things but collecting and/or destroying discarded objects.[2] These are the antiheroes of state socialism; they are the antidotes to the Men of Marble—the Stakhanovite work heroes.[3] In these representations we see not just a society suffused with waste, but the Gazda-type socialist waste hero superseded by the "underground" or oppositional waste hero.

Needless to say, the Party distanced itself not only from these fic-tional characters but also from their real versions—the "hobos" and waste-collecting private "businessmen"—and viewed them with suspicion. Hun-garian newspaper articles in the early seventies continued to express resent-ment toward the way of life such people led, while exhibiting a certain envy for their ability to profit greatly from scavenging and selling wastes:

> What is in the garbage? Is it really the treasures that make the garbage profession attractive? What value can make the scavengers forget about hon-

est work, what do they live on, and why does a cut-throat competition war rage among them? . . .

The legend of the treasures in garbage goes on. There are no treasures. Only a few human wrecks dread that modern garbage incinerators will start operating, and fear the day when the garbage of the capital flies to the sky without their cooperation. (Gömöri 1974, n.p.)

Soon, however, restrictions on waste collection by private businesses were received critically, or at least with a greater sympathy for the victims of such restrictions. A 1981 article pointed out the economic consequences of disciplinary actions: "Leather collectors, who often could not even read and write, although their activities were very useful, were required not only to present a certificate of good character, but also to fill out such complicated forms that most of them just quit the whole thing" (Radio Free Europe 1981, 370).

The disciplinary goals of regulation of waste collection were not only openly questioned in the media but, in the new political atmosphere, also proved obsolete. The Kádárist détente (1956–1988) sought to win the obedience of citizens by means of consumer goods and that of economic actors by means of monetary incentives, rather than outright oppression and disciplinary politics. The mobilization of the population and the politicized approach to waste collection, however, did not disappear. The growth spurts in the prices of raw materials and energy prices in the seventies provided a new rationale for keeping wastes under central control. To encourage enterprises to collect more wastes, social organizations, such as the People's Patriotic Front, the Communist Youth Organization, the Hungarian Alliance of Pioneers, and various Party organs, renewed the mobilization of the population for waste collection.

Such movements, however, were treated with increasing skepticism. Consider the following radio interview with the head of the public relations department of MÉH.

> MÉH: Among the new collection methods are the expansion of the mobile collection system, and other collection methods were elaborated with the county committees of the People's Patriotic Front and introduced in the last year or two. So-called charitable collections have been organized by MÉH, the Hungarian Alliance of Pioneers and many other state and social organizations.
>
> Reporter: My problem is that it is an economic question to recirculate reusable by-products and waste materials into production. *I feel that this is not the task of the People's Patriotic Front. After all, there is no People's Patriotic Front in the U.S., and still I have the impression that reusable wastes are collected in a more organized fashion there.*
>
> MÉH: I agree, but we don't have to go overseas; it's enough to look around

among the neighboring [meaning socialist] countries. There is the GDR, where waste management and the collection of wastes are significantly better organized and more efficient.

Reporter: I am pleased with the theoretical agreement, but I still don't see how the collection of valuable wastes can be transformed into an economical and economically regulated branch. And this is not an issue for the individual enterprise, *even if I debate your attitude that wants to solve economic questions with movements. By the way, the income from the pioneer actions is less than the rewards paid out.* (Radio Free Europe 1979, n.p.; emphasis mine)

While articles in the Party's newspaper and a few other dailies kept talking about the benefits of mobilizing the population for waste collection, economic periodicals started to strike a dissident chord, emphasizing the economic nature of waste reuse. Just like everything else, as the epigraph at the beginning of this part indicates, waste policy also came to be seen as a matter of interests.

With the reevaluation of the role economic calculations should play in socialism, the West ceased to serve as the classic example of market uncertainties and resulting wastefulness. The same article went on to argue the superiority of the West in tackling waste problems by mobilizing economic interests:

> For the next years our goal is to reduce the distance we lag behind the industrially developed countries. That we will really be successful in this is made doubtful by the still existing bureaucratic obstacles and negative attitudes. In Budapest, the district councils failed to secure a place for even just one MÉH site when the old ones closed down due to the construction of new housing projects. These councils, by the way, collect a significant fee from MÉH when it parks a mobile collection center somewhere. Contrary to this, in England, for example, the entrepreneur who organizes the removal of waste gets the money the city would have had to pay for that purpose. ("Kiguberált milliárdok" (Scavenged billions), *Heti Világgazdaság.* March 21, 1981, 28)

The increasing envy of Western rationality and professionalism was palpable. In 1979 journalists even started using the term "recycling." The article that first referred to the English word immediately argued that taking waste as seriously as Western recycling did demanded taking waste collection out of the hands of children:

> We should not underestimate the enthusiasm of the kids collecting paper. But it is incomprehensible that one of the types of "recycling" that is worth hundreds of millions [paper waste] remains a Pioneer[4] cause just as the whole "recycling" affair remains subsidiary. Children on the front line of the cause of the whole economy, children as raw-material miners, and children as the

carriers of a world concept in an economy that calls itself "of all the people" [*össznépi*]. . . . So far only school children and Pioneers fulfill the task, which is a task for the entire economy, and even they do so usually only during vacation. It's as if industry, trade and society hopes to achieve savings by entrusting the collection of hundreds of millions to a grotesque child-crusade. (Bor 1979, n.p.)

Note, however, that even as the politicization of waste issues was increasingly questioned, the usefulness of waste reuse was not. It was not the idea of recycling but rather its existing administrative and amateur methods that were criticized. A high-ranking employee of the company in charge of cleaning public spaces in the capital, who also disparaged children's involvement, put forth a nuanced evaluation of the problem: "The greatest problem in Hungary is not the collection but the reuse of wastes. What we need in order to move forward is investments on the order of billions and not the pledges of Pioneers" ("Kiguberált milliárdok" (Scavenged billions), *Heti Világgazdaság.* March 21, 1981, 28).[5]

Rationalizing Waste Production and Reuse

The idea that wastes are useful and that their reuse is imperative and beneficial thus still prevailed. While Gazda's name was long-forgotten— there was no mention of him in the media and propaganda materials or textbooks after 1959—the concept of waste as useful material did not disappear. In fact, most waste institutions remained intact, and waste collecting campaigns became permanent rituals of social life. A quote from a 1971 conference dealing with wastes practically plagiarized Gazda's exclamation from twenty years before: "In the last year, for example, 310,000 tons of the indispensable raw material of the Siemens-Martin steel production were collected. From this much iron scrap, 10,000 km train tracks or 62,000 D-4 type tractors could be manufactured" (*Komárom D. L.* 1971, n.p.).

Slowly, however, the unintended consequences of the early state socialist waste policies, such as increased generation of waste and the spread of illegal waste dumps, were acknowledged. Furthermore, the easily accessible waste reserves, such as those found among the ruins of the war and those lying around the yards of factories, as well as the enthusiasm of workers and youth troops exploring and collecting wastes in their free time, were exhausted (Dömötör 1980).

A key factor in the change, however, was no doubt the economic reforms, which created a new discursive environment for the waste policies. From the end of the sixties, but more pronouncedly from the seventies,

Hungary, preceding other socialist countries, implemented several major reforms in the management of the economy. Hungarian economists started proposing reforms already in the sixties, and indeed a series of new policies, collectively labeled the New Economic Mechanism, was introduced in 1968. These reforms experimented with giving enterprises more freedom in production, in remuneration, and in conducting foreign trade. The administrative sanctions associated with a failure to fulfill plans were replaced by monetary incentives, and the success of enterprises was measured more in the profits they made than in percentages of plan fulfillment. These reforms made the enterprises' budget constraints harder, which supposedly had a beneficial impact on material efficiency and thus on the amount of waste generated.[6] According to a 1975 survey by the Central Commission of People's Control (CCPC), the new economic management, technological development, and the increasing verticality of manufacturing indeed decreased the amount of generated waste (UML 1975, Fonds XIX-A-16-a, topic 134, document SZH 595/D/75). There is however no data provided by the authors, or to be found elsewhere, to corroborate this.

To the contrary, in the seventies and eighties, Hungarian journalists still found ample examples of old, wasteful uses of materials in industry; and, comparing the weight of the products produced in Hungary to those produced in the West, they drew a rather negative balance. Other evidence also suggests continuity in the material production of waste. If we look at the region as a whole, reforms did not seem to affect material and energy intensity. In terms of energy use, for example, Stanislaw Gomulka and Jacek Rostowski found that, in industry, the "energy-efficiency gap" between state socialist and Western capitalist countries actually grew after reforms and price adjustments; and that in the former, the rate of improvement in energy efficiency even fell after the mid-1970s (Gomulka and Rostowski 1988).

Not only did the reforms fail to attenuate the wastefulness of production, they also failed to increase waste reuse. First, the stricter quality requirements and the new efficiency criteria advocated by the reformers did not dovetail well with the low quality of wastes (Dömötör, 1980). Raising their reliability as raw materials would have required more thorough selection and various forms of treatment prior to processing. Second, financial tools did not make enterprises open to the use of waste materials, nor did the calculative ethos of the reforms extend to waste issues. A political aspect of the economic reforms was that the state turned to financial motivation to promote its economic goals. Since it would have cost enterprises more to increase their use of waste, waste policy was doomed to irrelevance. The survey of CCPC found that

> [t]he [higher] price for waste materials [set to encourage waste reuse] did not motivate the great majority of the sellers [of waste] to better use their possibilities. The income from selling wastes constituted only an insignificant amount of the profit. . . .
>
> Typically, most enterprises surveyed did not even make economic calculations. In the absence of calculations, exact evaluation cannot be made, but the aggregated experiences from the survey indicate that the expenditures [on waste collection] are not covered by the prices. In certain cases we found significant losses from sales. (UML 1975, Fonds XIX-A-16-a, topic 134, document SZH 595/D/75, 12)

Therefore, the material production of waste remained basically unchanged. In fact, with regards to waste reuse, the CCPC report on the country's waste management in 1975 argued that the situation had worsened:

> Theoretically, 85% of used tires can be collected for reuse in the future. In 1960 our country was still in a leading position; we collected about 32% of the collectible amount, when the world average was 22%. By 1973 this [latter] proportion grew to 46%; here however it decreased to 3%. (UML 1975, Fonds XIX-A-16-a, topic 134, document SZH 595/D/75, n.p.)

Let us note, however, the novelty of the language of the CCPC survey. This was the first time official documents approached waste issues with concepts such as "profit" and "losses from sales." It was exactly the tension between the spirit of the reforms and the old approach to waste production and reuse that allowed a new waste discourse to emerge, and eventually to gain dominance after 1975. This discourse aimed to rationalize waste production: first, by transforming the waste issue from a political into an economic task; and second, by reducing the amount of generated waste. Let me first attend to the latter.

The price explosions of raw materials and energy in the seventies and Hungary's heavy reliance on such imports from the West led to a debt crisis. In order to avoid the rescheduling of debts, the Party voted for stringent austerity measures. Aiding this course were several government programs promoting innovation, energy, and material conservation; among them was the 1981 Waste and Secondary Raw Material Management Program, then the next year's Economical Material Use and Technological Modernization Program. The first emphasized innovation in waste reuse; the second aimed at source reduction.

The purpose of the 1981 waste reuse program, according to an official of the National Office of Environmental and Nature Protection, was "to approach the level of the industrially developed countries in terms of material use [that is, conservation]" (Horváth 1985, 4). They hoped to achieve this by doubling the proportion of waste in all materials used in production and increasing the collection of scrap iron, nonferrous metals, textiles, paper, rubber, and glass. Indeed, the amount of collected wastes increased considerably. Between 1981 and 1986, the collection of iron and nonferrous metals increased by 30 percent, and that of paper waste by 20 percent. MÉH invested in numerous facilities preparing waste for reuse (compresses, crushers, and selecting equipment), with a capacity totaling 500,000 tons per year.

Observers often stated that the reuse of wastes was not nearly as successful as their collection, but by 1987 more than half of the total waste amount generated was claimed to be reused. The progress in the field of plastic wastes was especially spectacular: their reuse increased by 200 percent, to 20 percent of the total generated (NÉTI 1987, 6). While the program did not achieve its stated goal of substantially increasing the portion of secondary raw materials among industrial inputs (KSH 1988), it turned out to be quite successful in finding uses for potentially dangerous wastes. Before the implementation of the 1981 Waste and Secondary Raw Material Management Program, 17 to 18 percent of hazardous wastes were reused or recycled (Tudományos Ismeretterjesztő Társulat 1980), while in 1982 the figure was 21 percent and in 1986, 29 percent (Árvai 1990).[7]

Efforts to reuse wastes were not new. But how did the need to reduce the amount of waste emerge? Reducing waste was consistent with reform efforts to rationalize economic management, expressed in a language of rationalization of resource use and management efficiency. Already as early as 1975, an article in the Party's daily argued that

> it has been proved that it is not necessarily automatic for the amount of waste to increase parallel to the increase in production. With careful material management, the amount of waste can be reduced in the case of the same product. That is, if production is organized based on appropriate calculations, the waste per product can be reduced. (Sólyom 1975, n.p.)

The exhaustion of usual resources of growth was just as important in bringing about the change as the increases in fuel prices on the world market. It was no longer possible to achieve growth simply by channeling more labor power into industry, both from agriculture and from formerly unemployed groups; by opening more mines; by building more factories; or by cultivating more land. The extensive path of development based on quantitative growth had reached its limits. The new, intensive form of development that economic policymakers argued Hungary was embarking on in the second half of the sixties meant to use the same amount of resources with greater efficiency. Similarly, collecting and reusing more and more wastes by mobilizing more and more people for such tasks had also reached its limits; and, as I showed in chapter 4, there were counter-productive effects. The approach to waste problems, therefore, also had to change: to have better results, it became necessary not only to keep collecting and reusing wastes but also to reduce the amount produced.

While the 1982 Economical Material Use and Technological Modern-ization Program did not directly address wastes, in practice its implementation was intertwined with that of the 1981 Waste and Secondary Raw Material Management Program. In fact, these two programs were commonly referred to as the "expenditure reduction programs," and evaluations of the success of the 1982 program included waste reuse.

Two officials who participated in the implementation of the Waste and Secondary Raw Material Management Program and the Economical Material Use and Technological Modernization Program emphasized the significance and solid results of these programs, such as the actual achievements in lowering the specific use of materials and, in general, directing the attention of engineers to economical material use (personal interview, László Kovács, Budapest, 1996; personal interview, Árpád Bakonyi, Budapest, 1996).

One of them, however, also admitted that such quantification of this success was debatable. Expressing savings in material use in terms of prices was misleading when prices contained varying amount of subsidies, but calculating savings in use value was not less problematic. After all, statisticians could not reliably aggregate tons, meters, and joules (personal interview, László Kovács, Budapest, 1996). As a result, evaluating the "expenditure reduction programs" remains difficult to this day. In the next chapter, I will analyze the effects and contradictions of these campaigns.

One thing however should be mentioned here. Perhaps efforts to reduce wastes could have been more successful if, first, the social relations of waste production, analyzed in chapter 3, had been transformed radically. Rather than, for example, overhauling the relationship between the state and the enterprises, and thus achieving source reduction, these government programs simply added the criterion of efficiency to the definition of "successful performance," just as they had complemented production quotas with waste delivery quotas in the fifties. Former officials I interviewed pointed out that a certain voluntarist or quota mentality still prevailed (personal interview, László Kovács, Budapest, 1996; personal interview, Árpád Bakonyi, Budapest, 1996). For example, there were targets both for source reduction and for the rate of wastes among industrial inputs. That is, the programs prescribed the annual rate by which material intensity had to decrease. "It was written down that the specific use of materials had to be reduced by 5% per year. You can easily calculate how many years it would have taken for cars to be made out of thin air," one of the officials then in charge argued humorously (personal interview, Árpád Bakonyi, Budapest, 1996). Another problem appeared when such reductions were achieved at great cost, only to realize that the product, whose material content they had cut, as a result did not conform to the standards enforced by international agencies Hungary had just joined. This was the case with certain specialized containers whose walls were made thinner in an effort to cut down on material use; this move, however, precluded their use in international traffic (personal interview, László Kovács, Budapest, 1996).

In sum, it was in theory a positive development to concentrate on waste reduction, and the waste programs of the early eighties were quite effective. Nevertheless, the social relations of waste production of the fifties remained fundamentally intact, and it was primarily this continuity that prevented the conservation programs from transcending the existing instruments of central planning.

The Monetized Concept of Waste

While the systemic forms of waste production persisted, the representation of waste changed considerably. Let me first describe the process by which the political or movement approach to waste collection and reuse was eroded.

The Efficiency Model

The discourse embodied in the 1981 Waste and Secondary Raw Material Management Program still operated with a notion of waste as useful, but the usefulness of waste was now understood differently. The utility of wastes was now seen not in use value but rather in monetary terms: waste was a cost of production. The merit of waste reduction and waste reuse, therefore, resided in decreasing this cost. Consider the differences in emphasis in the following claim of propaganda material from 1951 and the description of the 1981 Waste and Secondary Raw Material Management Program quoted thereafter:

[O]ur Party has now been keeping the cause of material savings on the agenda for a long time, but especially since the Congress. The leaders of our Party have already emphasized many times that this is *not simply to be talked about as one tool of decreasing production costs, but primarily as the basic condition for fulfilling the plans* in many industries. (Ember 1952, 27; emphasis mine)

The more rational management of material resources received a priority among the economic policy goals of the Sixth Five-Year Plan. The program announced chronologically as the second among the austerity programs wished to achieve an increased substitution of primary raw materials with wastes, and the exploration and mobilization of economic reserves hidden in the recycling of secondary raw materials. *It treated waste utilization as an activity reducing expenditures, by which the per unit material costs could be reduced* in relation to all costs of production. (KSH 1988, 10; emphasis mine)

The difference from the early state socialist waste policies was repeatedly stated quite explicitly.

The elderly and the middle-aged still remember the "Collect iron and metal . . ." period. Such generalities in waste reuse are useless, both from a movement and a technological aspect. It is a waste of time to encourage people to do anything just in general; to gain their readiness to help it is necessary to name the goals precisely and determine objectives that they find attractive. . . . Because today it is not enough just to collect waste. Waste is not a secondary raw material for industry in all cases, but only after sufficient preparation. (Mónus 1983, 12)

While increasing emphasis was indeed placed on reuse rather than just collection, those responsible for realizing the program did not entirely give up on the mobilization of the population for collecting some wastes, primarily paper and metal. "Now we will finally have at our disposal the desired billions for each task [collection and reuse], although the National Bureau of Materials and Prices did not wish to renounce the cooperation of students, retired people, and in general that of the population" ("Kiguberált milliárdok" (Scavenged billions), *Heti Világgazdaság* 1981, 28).

This time, however, the mobilization of the population did not exclude the utilization of economic tools. Among these were price increases for wastes, which made the collection and resale of wastes more worthwhile; and the new opportunity for firms to calculate the prices of their recycled products as if they had used new raw materials for them, which was supposed to encourage them to use wastes. Reusing wastes now became the object of cost-benefit analyses, and funds were established to motivate firms to apply waste-conscious technologies. Credits and loans were not granted automatically—applicants had to promise a profit rate of 14 percent. The state financed at least two-thirds of the costs of the reuse facilities, firms were exempted from taxes on such investments, and 25 percent of the interest on loans borrowed for such purposes was remitted. In addition to firms, individuals involved in waste collection (teachers coordinating children's waste collection, or concierges of apartment houses) were also entitled to special monetary rewards. Since teachers and concierges had previously been denied payment for such assistance on moral grounds, this new attitude was a sign that collecting waste for monetary compensation was no longer considered illegal or a kind of private employment, but rather real work that needed to be acknowledged and financially motivated.

From 1985 the monopoly position of waste collection companies was ended: any firm could now buy waste from any other, as long as it did so for its own use. Central authorities hoped in this way to shorten the road to waste reuse, and to incite competition that was supposed to increase the quality of waste offered for sale.

Parallel to this change in the concept of waste, the relationship between enterprises and the state also went through a transformation. Instead of centrally calculated waste quotas, enterprises were now free to decide which wastes they wanted to reuse, sell, treat, or dump, and they were to be motivated by the above-mentioned financial incentives. As a corollary, the agents changed as well. While in the early state socialist period it was workers who were encouraged to redesign products and technologies and to invent waste reuse possibilities, now such tasks were transferred to professionals with economic and engineering expertise. Rather than consisting of small but ingenious adjustments on the existing product design and labor process, waste reduction and waste reuse now became subject to cost-benefit analysis, and were considered possible only after implementing high-tech innovations and large-scale modernization. For example, the Hungária Plastic Processing Company bought a license to implement a new production process to reuse its wastes; other modernization included new facilities for reusing tires and for recovering metals from dross, and the construction of a new plant to extract straw from cellulose (Remetei 1986). By 1986, 133 facilities had been established and 26 modernization projects completed in the framework of the program.

The relationship between scientific research institutes and enterprises and among enterprises also became more direct. For example, in 1977 an association was formed to collect and use wastes and by-products for manufacturing fodder. The main intellectual leader of the association was the Keszthely University of Agricultural Sciences, but it had contacts with the University of Veterinary Science as well. Other similar initiatives abounded, judging by the number of articles reporting on them. The Hungarian Alliance of Technical and Scientific Associations (MTESZ), a national organization that united various groups of technical intelligentsia, announced a competition for material conservation proposals, and a good number of those awarded were based on waste reuse.

The new attitude to science and the change in the preferred agency is palpable in the official discourse, as this quote in one of these articles illustrates:

> No conservation program detailed for all the products of our economy can be made centrally. This can only be a task for enterprises: for those managers, technical-economic experts, and members of brigades who participate in the manufacturing of products.
>
> Therefore the "mine" is in the heads. The material conservation competitions of MTESZ, like exploratory drill shafts, show that this source is rich. (Kozma 1982, n.p.)

Let us now look more closely at the role of the intelligentsia in bringing about this discursive change.

The Professionalization of Waste Issues

The technical intelligentsia played an indispensable role in bringing the question of industrial wastes to the forefront in Hungary, and as early as 1976 they started demanding that state authorities solve this problem in cooperation with enterprises and experts. These were primarily engineers, hydrologists, and geologists affiliated with one or another member group of MTESZ. In order to understand the change in the politics of waste, let us review the change in the role of intellectuals in economic management and environmental claims making.

In the first period of state socialism, the Party's ideological suspicions about intellectuals' class origins and sympathies led to the marginalization of engineers and economists who had environmental expertise. Because of their very pragmatic involvement in industry, these intellectuals saw a lot, probably a lot more than was evident to laypersons, and they tried to blow the whistle when they were appalled by what they saw. However, their suggestions had to be justified on the basis of their contribution to plan fulfillment if they were to get a green light from Party and state officials. I interviewed several engineers who had designed environmental facilities or policies or had written studies on the subject, and they suggested they knew of the many urban environmental problems but found that their "expert" opinions didn't go very far in the face of the agendas of bureaucrats or political figures. One of them who worked in the Waste Water Department of the National Main Water Administration still recalled with resentment that when his department had started administrative proceedings against a particular offender based on emissions standards established in 1961,

> the penalty was canceled if the plant proved that it had no money to pay it, or if the Party secretary of the plant was on good terms with the director [of the Water Administration]. [Or] the Party secretary of the County just had to call over and the director ended the proceedings of the Waste Water Department. As a result, it was exactly the large enterprises [those with the most significant emissions] which were let off, because these were the ones that had the highest contacts. (Personal interview, Ferenc Kelemen, Budapest, 1997)

If this engineer found himself to be successful—as, for example, in one instance in which he persuaded a firm manager to build a new waste-water treatment facility (that he also helped design)—it was not because of his expertise but rather because of his contacts in ministries and other offices. When he had such resources, as he put it, the "whimper of the 'technical ones' found open ears"[8] (personal interview, Ferenc Kelemen, Budapest, 1997).

While the technical intelligentsia's contacts in various sectors of the economy and various decision-making places, and the information accumulated from these various channels positioned them particularly well to push authorities to take ameliorative steps, the justification of such steps still needed a certain rhetoric until the end of the seventies. Experts found that complaints about industry waste causing health problems and air and water pollution were not nearly as effective in themselves as they were when couched in terms of their implications for fulfilling the plan or for industrial development in general. As one of the engineers described the prevalent view on industrial waste and emission,

> they started dealing with waste problems more seriously in the case of those water resources that were mostly important for industry. . . . [The concern was] to achieve a water quality that would not cause trouble for industry, and it was of secondary importance that it wouldn't cause trouble for people. (Personal interview, Ferenc Kelemen, Budapest, 1997)

A Party secretary of Budapest's Ninth District complaining about the pollution caused by BCW, for example, did not find it sufficient to claim that the red ore dust was "exceptionally harmful to health"; he had to put special emphasis on the damage the air pollution caused to other factories, whose machines were corroded by the dust and gas emissions of BCW (personal interview, Ferenc Kelemen, Budapest, 1997). Remember that

BCW itself, when asking for help from the state in solving its waste problems, similarly argued that

> [t]he solution of the waste disposal problem is a rather urgent task, because the current uncertain and not always professional practice could cause a lot of damage to water management and impedes production and its development. Solving the problem of waste burial in the proposed manner at the level of the entire chemical industry could guarantee the [planned] rate of development for a long period. (MDP-MSZMP 1968, 1)

Later, as a cautious political liberalization proceeded, as the economy was increasingly reliant on knowledge-based industries—such as the chemical industries and electronics—and as the reforms placed increasing emphasis on expertise in the management of the economy, the freedom and leverage of intellectuals with technical and scientific training increased considerably.[9] As a result, by the late seventies and early eighties, claims on purely ecological grounds became more and more acceptable. When asked about the causes of a new, environmentally more sensitive attitude that took hold in the eighties, one of the three reasons provided by an engineer interviewee was the fact that the "relationship between the 'technical ones' and politics changed"—that is, that scientific arguments gained more acceptance (personal interview, Ferenc Kelemen, Budapest, 1997).

Most studies done on industrial waste problems in the seventies and eighties were done on the initiative, within the framework, and with the support of the Alliance of Technical and Scientific Associations (MTESZ), the above-mentioned national organization that united various groups of technical intelligentsia. The genesis of the first national waste-dump register, also initiated and completed by MTESZ in 1983, further indicates the importance of professional contacts for gathering data and making claims. When I asked the director and designer of this project how the idea occurred to him, he responded that everywhere in the country engineer acquaintances mentioned their waste disposal problems to MTESZ members, until finally there were so many complaints and requests from so many enterprises that MTESZ leaders decided to carry out a survey that would compare the location of existing waste dumps with the location of geologically safe soils (personal interview, Miklós Kassai, Pécs, 1996). They managed to get state funding for the survey and to get it incorporated into the plans of the Hungarian Geological Institute (MÁFI). Having found that about half of the existing dumps were established in dangerous soils, where the disposed wastes could reach and pollute groundwater, their next task was to draw up plans to relocate the inappropriately sited dumps. The Budapest Chemical Works' landfill in Garé, the southern Hungarian village whose name in 2006 is still the emblem of Hungary's toxic waste conundrums, was a prototype of these "scientifically sited" dumps. Before analyzing the consequences of the professionalization of waste issues in the next chapter, let me first make theoretical sense out of the efficiency waste regime.

Socialist Ecological Modernization?

The novelty of the efficiency regime can be summarily captured in the following list:

(1) waste policy objectives are achieved by economic means, by financially motivating waste producers and traders;
(2) the key goal is to reduce waste and thus to cut down on production costs; and
(3) the state cooperates with producers rather than only commanding them, and in this cooperation scientific expertise has a distinguished and ever more significant role.

Social scientists noticed a similar transformation in the West in the 1980s, and termed it *industrial ecology* when referring to micro-level, and *ecological modernization* when referring to macro-level changes.

In the past few years, industrial ecology has emerged as a new approach to resolving Western countries' environmental problems. Its proponents have argued that, given sufficient freedom, business is capable of integrating environmental concerns into the production process, and of self-monitoring its environmental impact, with the help of such tools as voluntarily assumed environmental quality standards, green accounting, and ecodesign, among others. As a result, industry's relationship with the state and with regulation becomes more active, horizontal, and cooperative. As Robert Socolow says:

> In industrial ecology, industry becomes a policy-maker, not a policy-taker. Industry demonstrates that environmental objectives are no longer alien, to be resisted and then accommodated reluctantly. Rather, *these objectives are part of the fabric of production*, like worker safety and consumer satisfaction. (Socolow 1994, 13; emphasis mine)

Or, in the words of Robert M. White, the president of the National Academy of Engineering, "the objective of industrial ecology is to understand better how we can integrate environmental concerns into our economic activities" (White 1994, v).

Many debate whether this trend is real or whether it is simply clever public relations on the part of corporations trying to limit the punitive effect of environmental regulations. Proponents of ecological moderniza- tion theory, however, whose focus is broader than the individual firm, also agree that a transition in environmental discourse and practice has begun in these countries, with the Netherlands and Japan leading the way (Hajer 1995; Mol 1995; Spaargaren and Mol 1992). Their argument is that while before, environmental protection was primarily focused on how to "safely" displace hazards from production, and while environmental politics con- centrated on the distribution of hazards, now the intention is to keep the problem of emissions and wastes within the sphere of production, and solve it there. It is in production that emissions can be reduced or prevented, and it is in production that by-products can be reused or recycled. Such an internalization of environmental externalities is now seen as consistent with efforts to increase efficiency and even as inducive to technological innovation. For these authors, acknowledging that an actual change has occurred does not necessarily mean endorsing it. Hajer is especially critical of the technocratic tendencies in the West's present path of ecological modernization. With that qualification, let me put forth the provocative argument that socialist Hungary's efficiency regime was also an attempt at ecological modernization.

First of all, I would propose that the principles and policy tools of the efficiency regime are consistent with the objectives of ecological modern- ization and industrial ecology. What are the common elements in Western ecological modernization and the efficiency regime in Hungary? (1) From the mid-seventies, Hungarian policies framed wastes as both an economic and an environmental problem, and waste reduction and reuse programs played an integral role in the government's response to the price rises in energy and raw materials of the early seventies. (2) Beyond the integration of economic goals with environmental ones, the emphasis on prevention of Hungarian policies in the efficiency regime also constitutes a key charac- teristic of the Western ecological modernization discourse. (3) Both ap- proaches rely on economic and engineering expertise and technological innovation to achieve these goals. (4) Finally, both encourage the coopera- tion of the state and the enterprise in working out the concrete objectives and tools of environmental policies.

The comparison may upset the belief of some in state socialism's irra- tionality and inability to modernize. I am, however, not proposing that the socialist version of ecological modernization was an entirely homegrown project. Rather, the experts who started playing an increasingly significant role in defining environmental problems and devising solutions to them were definitely aware of new monitoring and policy tools consistent with ecological modernization. The tools of regulation that I will detail in chapter 6, such as material flow charts and material balances, while certainly not alien to the state's penchant for planning in use value, were informed by the ever-intensifying professional dialogue Hungarian engineers had established with their Western counterparts. In a way, the heritage of the metallic model proved to be a fertile soil for the seeds of Western ecological modernization, creating the unique waste regime based on the efficiency model. This model still viewed waste as something useful, but its utility was no longer determined by political considerations. At the same time, some of its tools, such as five-year targets for waste reduction and for a certain elevated ratio of recycled materials in the overall material input, demonstrated the stubbornness of a central planning mentality.

The unique historical context of ecological modernization, however, resulted in its having an effect quite opposite of the one in the West. It actually led to the legitimation of an end-of-pipe solution, namely landfilling. This was for two reasons. First, professionals had long demanded legal dumps, and now that their voice was heard, they prevailed. Second, when the choice between recycling and dumping came to be subordinated to cost-benefit analysis, in many cases the latter appeared as the rational solution. Nevertheless, the historical insistence on recycling (that is, the insistence on the positive value of waste) still produced a reluctance to allow the latter (dumping). In the next chapter I will analyze the unintended consequences of this legacy.

six
The Limits of Efficiency

On Highway 58 going south from Pécs, Hungary's fifth-largest city, until recently there was a large sign painted on a wall with the ditty: "Waste is not garbage, MÉH will take it and pay for it."[1] Just about ten kilometers from this billboard oozes Hungary's most notorious toxic waste dump, filled with the wastes of BCW that MÉH could not take and that the reform-inspired expenditure reduction programs could not diminish.

In this chapter I will describe the contradictions and limits of the efficiency model and its implementation. I will concentrate on BCW's failure to reduce the tetrachlorobenzene waste, in the framework of the new waste reduction campaigns, and on the effect of professionalization on the fate of this by-product.

The Ineffectiveness of the Efficiency Model

While there is no evidence of the Gazda movement existing past 1959, its legacy lived on in sporadic waste collection campaigns that continued into the seventies.

Even after several waves of economic reforms since 1968, achieving economic goals such as waste reduction in the early eighties was still predicated on the fifties' and sixties' model of plan fulfillment. The government's expenditure reduction programs of 1981 and 1982 defined the country's waste problems as problems with efficiency: too much use of materials and thus too much waste in relation to the useful final products. One of my interviewees, who was in charge of implementing the economic rationalization campaigns spawned by these programs at the Budapest Chemical Works, described them as follows. The central planners had a general objective of material conservation, such as the percentage by which their specific material or energy use was to be cut. Enterprises then made pledges about how much they could decrease their material and energy use. After the campaign period, enterprises competed with each other on the basis of their actual achievements. According to articles in the company's newspaper and interviews with former employees, BCW performed successfully in the expenditure reduction programs.

Initially, such conservation campaigns were still announced with the slogan of thriftiness and concentrated on the negligence of employees. Their most common goals were to reduce water and energy consumed in the public spaces of the plant, such as the locker room and the restaurant, and to rationalize the use of new work clothes and shoes. From the mid-seventies, however, the conservation campaigns finally started concentrating on reducing the wastes and losses of the actual production processes, and even made it possible for brigades to pledge to cut the by-product-to-product ratio by a certain percentage, as in the case of the dichlorinoetudin production. The source of production waste, however, was often still seen in minor flaws of the production technology, such as leaking pipes or too-tight openings on containers, as a result of which herbicides were easily spilled in the process of packaging. To the extent that waste was seen as an accident, the campaigns of the late seventies still invoked workers' alertness and sensitivity to such problems.

Articles in the BCW publication *Vegyiművek* (Chemical Works) indicate a certain resistance to overgeneralized conservation efforts. In a few instances they contrast such campaigns with professionalism and the good reputation of the company. A 1979 article with the title "Is It Worth Being Thrifty Just to Lose Money at It?" disclosed the huge losses BCW suffered because one of its final products was shipped off in overused drums that leaked their contents ("Megéri takarékoskodni, csakhogy veszítsünk rajta?" 1979). The article claimed that if the drums had been scrapped, the company could have avoided the lawsuits brought by customers. The management, however, failed to heed warnings implied by this case, because in 1983 the manager of the TCB production plant proudly announced a conservation method: storing the TCB by-product in used drums rather than in new ones, resulting in a savings of almost 2 million Forints ("Az önköltséget vizsgálták két üzemcsoport gyakorlatában" (Production costs examined in the practice of two plants), *Vegyiművek*, June 20, 1983). This practice later led to the early corrosion of the drums and to the leakage of their contents. The environmental consequences of this "prudent" conservation action, which I'll discuss in the next chapters, are still felt today.

The unique production process of the chemical industry was also brought up as demanding a special form of material conservation. An article from 1981 posed the question about the methods of material conservation in BCW this way: "In the chemical industry no material can be 'scrimped' on in making a certain product. Still, how can you use the materials handed to you more sparingly?" The answer of the manager of the plant where TCB was produced was: "We achieve material conservation *not by reducing the ingredients of final products*—our lab after all guarantees the prescribed quality by strict tests during production— but by cutting the losses during production, storage, and transportation" (N. Gy. 1981, 1; emphasis mine). He claimed to have saved about five million Forints in materials this way. Whether the manager would have listed packaging final products in used drums among these methods is not known, but by framing savings on packaging materials as material conservation in the chemical industry, he certainly legitimized that practice. While these conservation campaigns probably did cut down on incidental losses, they were unlikely to have significant impact on the volume of the by-product, which was in large part determined by chemical processes, and was routinely, rather than accidentally, produced. In sum, the waste reduction campaigns in the chemical industry tended to exclude exactly those materials that were the most toxic.

How is it possible then that chemical companies excelled in improving material efficiency? As one of the former officials in charge of the implementation of the expenditure reduction programs pointed out, it was much easier to demonstrate a significant decrease in the specific use of materials in material-intensive industries. In the chemical industry, material expenses tended to account for a much greater share of the total production costs than in other industries; therefore, even a small amount of relative change amounted to great improvement in absolute numbers.

Another way BCW could excel in material conservation competitions, according to a former employee, was by adding more auxiliary materials, such as thinners, to the final product. This way, they increased the overall volume of the final product without using more raw materials, though augmenting the use of auxiliary materials. Such modifications did not cause problems for customers as long as the concentration remained in the range prescribed in the product specifications (personal interview, Gyula Eifert, Budapest, 1995). It is easy to see, however, that cutting down on specific material use in this way did not affect the amount of production wastes, which tended to be generated before the auxiliary materials were added to the final product.

Thus BCW could show excellent results on paper in the material conservation efforts, while in practice the beneficial environmental effects were rather insignificant. My point is not to blame managers or other individuals for concentrating on cutting down on packaging expenses or on incidental losses and wastes. My point is rather that the material conservation campaigns imposed on BCW necessarily materialized in contingent methods that not only failed to bring substantial results but even could prove counterproductive. Because of the previously discussed nature of chemical production, the range within which source reduction or cutting material expenses was possible was much narrower in the chemical industry than in other industries. Cutting down on incidental losses, on water or energy use in public use areas, or on packaging materials did very little to reduce the volume, let alone the toxicity, of those by-products that were systemically generated in the main production process.

This is not to say that material conservation plans materialized solely in disciplinary conservation campaigns or in efforts that rarely went beyond minor adjustments. In the case of TCB production, BCW did experiment with technological ways to reduce waste, although the actual goal of such modernization was more to increase the plant's capacity and alleviate workers' physical efforts. At the end of 1972, the technology of TCB production was transformed into a partially automated process, which led to a more efficient use of materials in chlorination. Employees' answers to my questions about the proportion of the final product in the overall output volume achieved in this way were evasive, but one of them admitted that in order to raise the proportion above 60 percent, they would have had to distill the residual compounds, which however would have required additional and rather expensive facilities (personal interview, Zoltán Balla, Budapest, 1995). There was no trace of such investments ever being considered either in my interviews or in written records. So by 1981, BCW had done everything within the realm of waste reduction that was economically feasible, short of ceasing production.

While the government's Waste and Secondary Raw Material Management Program and the Economical Material Use and Technological Modernization Program were meant to encourage exactly such investments, archives and documents at BCW show little impact of these programs beyond an increase in the number of articles that focused on conservation and thriftiness, and especially on the incentives that environmental fines created for modernization. After 1981 there was only one innovation mentioned concretely in the TCB-producing plant that was called an environmental investment. In 1983 the oxygen analyzer on the centrifuge was modernized, but how this was beneficial for the environment was not discussed.

Not only did waste-conscious modernization fail to materialize in BCW as a result of the two government programs but also, to the extent that both programs were meant to spur exports and earnings in hard currency, they left early state socialism's emphasis on growth intact. Concretely, in the case of BCW, the problems caused by the absence of substantial conservation methods were exacerbated by the constant growth of TCB production. Already in 1972 an article acknowledged that "since production increases, so does the by-product, and the placement of closed drums poses greater and greater difficulties" (*Vegyiművek* 1972, 3). In sum, while no source-reducing modernization was implemented, the production of TCB increased, and the volume of the toxic by-product kept increasing. By the time BCW finally stopped producing TCB in 1987, the accumulated by-product amounted to 17,500 tons in over 60,000 drums.

In sum, the expenditure reduction campaigns failed to produce results tangible in terms of the volume or proportion of the TCB by-product. Moreover, the reforms' emphasis on hard currency earnings and growth even worsened BCW's waste situation. Rather than reducing or discontinuing TCB production, BCW kept producing TCB in increasing quantities.

Dumping as the Consequence of the Efficiency Model

The professionalization of waste issues and the monetization of the concept of waste had further unintended consequences. As the waste that BCW could neither decrease nor reuse was piling up, a professional approach to the problem emerged to supplant the officially prioritized one. Its solution was dumping.

By the mid-seventies, newspaper accounts about illegal and dangerous disposal practices started to appear. Previously such accounts had remained classified, or at least inaccessible to the public. These accounts were preceded by, and must owe their legitimacy to, the already mentioned 1975 survey by the Central Commission of People's Control. The report, while mostly dedicated to waste reuse, also argued that "[p]lanning on the level of the national economy and of branches must be extended beyond the consideration of sources, domestic use and exports [of wastes] to the realistic possibilities of liquidation (UML 1975, Fonds XIX-A-16-a, topic 134, document SZH 595/D/75, 1–2).

What allowed the relaxation of the view that waste is always useful, and what led to the notion that it can be dumped or liquidated? One factor was the slow breakdown of the metallic concept of waste, and more precisely the idea that metal wastes can and should always be reused or recycled. By 1983 the new paradigm was crystallized in explicit claims about the erosion of the metallic model:

> Waste is not a secondary raw material for industry *in all cases*, only after sufficient preparation. *Metallurgy does not need iron scrap in general*, but well-prepared, easy-to-feed, smaller, less rusty and sufficiently dense bales, since with today's technology [only] the reuse of these is economical. (Mónus 1983, 12; emphasis mine)

Abandoning the old "recycle always and under any condition" attitude was specifically propelled by an oversupply in iron scrap, which appeared first in 1971. This situation resulted in part from the absence of sorting and waste preparation facilities. Initially, officials felt that iron scrap should continue to be collected, even though MÉH was increasingly reluctant to keep buying it.

> It is a fact that there is an oversupply in iron scrap in the country. But it is also a fact that the interministerial committee established by the Ministry of Metallurgy and Engineering and several high authorities took the determined stance last winter that the iron scrap accumulated at the enterprises and plants must be taken over [by MÉH].
>
> It is not our task to decide what should be done with the superfluous iron waste, but it is certain that the present complete confusion brings no result. Unless those responsible have in mind the solution suggested to one of our plants: "just dump the whole lot in the Sajó" [a river in the northeast of Hungary]. (Pusztai 1972, n.p.)

It was in the seventies that the export of iron scrap was first allowed, albeit amid much debate about whether Hungary, so poor in iron ore, should indeed renounce this important material.

The oversupply later became permanent due to technological change. By the end of the eighties, the Siemens-Martin technology was abandoned everywhere in the country, and the new converter-based technology required much less, and much more carefully selected, iron scrap (NÉTI 1987). Iron scrap accumulated in such quantities on MÉH sites that an article on the subject even started with reversing the age-old slogan: "Don't collect iron and metal" (v. a. 1988).

Another factor that made waste dumping and liquidation more acceptable was the monetization of the concept of waste itself. As the reuse of wastes became subordinated to cost-benefit analysis, dumping emerged as a legitimate way to deal with nonreusable wastes, or wastes whose reuse was noneconomical. This connection was made for the first time in 1975:

> [I]t is a mistake to view production waste as an inherent harm and loss, and as a necessary bad. There is no doubt that production on a large scale results in wastes in the case of any kind of product. But deciding what to do with this large amount of waste is a question of economic calculation. It is possible that the most profitable [course of action] is to liquidate a part of the waste material, but it could happen that the better solution is to export this "by-product" of production, or to return it to the process of domestic production after professional treatment. (Sólyom 1975, n.p.)

The first articles in the media that dealt specifically with the problem of hazardous industrial wastes appeared in the fall of 1976. In particular a report on a conference organized by the Hungarian Hydrological Association raised this question in a novel way. As if talking expressly about BCW's experience of being left alone in solving its reuse and disposal problems, one contributor suggested that

> [w]e must not view waste deposition as the internal affair of individual enterprises and institutions, industrial, agricultural plants, health organizations, research institutes, etc., but as a primary public affair; that is, we must urge a cooperative solution of the tasks. Hungarian experts are striving to solve the problem of waste neutralization together with the concerned authorities. (környei 1976, 5)

Other participants warned about the dangers of existing practices, and blamed those on the absence of a consistent central supervision:

> [S]ince at present unified supervision over the neutralization of industrial wastes in our country is practiced by no authority, the plants just get rid of the hazardous wastes that are a big burden for them. From open-air burning to dumping in forbidden locations all solutions occur. . . . (környei 1976, 5)

Some also warned that an increasing number of settlements failed to satisfy their drinking water needs from local resources due to the pollution of groundwater. In sum, professionalization legitimized not only an explicitly environmental mode of thinking, as I described in the previous chapter, but also helped legitimize dumping, by calling for it to be done in a systematic, supervised manner.

Let us see how monetization and professionalization affected the solution BCW found for its long-standing waste problem. As more and more companies found themselves in need of a legitimate dump site, and as the new reform attitude indirectly legitimated disposal, BCW's chances for finding a site increased. By this time, some stories were reported on in the media as well, and they brought the necessity of safe dumping into the forefront. The case of one slaughterhouse is indeed indicative of a situation in which central authorities were already becoming sufficiently sensitive to the environmental and public health consequences of illegal waste dumping to stop the practice, but in which the technological conditions to deal with these wastes were still lacking.

> "You can't imagine how much trouble we [quoting the president of the slaughterhouse/meatpacking company] have had with this for years." Until August 1974, the Sárvár Plant of the Animal Protein Fodder Producing Company bought the waste from us for 20–40 Fillérs per kilo. But on August 29 we received this letter:
>
> "We regret to inform you that from today we are unable to process the waste generated in the meatpacking plants due to a lack of capacity created by the extreme increase of slaughterhouse wastes."
>
> "What could we have done," Imre Monori, the president of the meatpacking plant throws up his arms. "We buried it, but KÖJÁL (the public health authority) *prohibited* it. Then we approached the turf plant of the city, asking them to take it away even for free. In the end, we paid 100 Forints per shipment. . . ." (Elek 1976, n.p.; emphasis in original)

In 1978, BCW was invited to cooperate in establishing a waste disposal site in Garé, a village in Baranya County, southern Hungary. Its partners were factories from Pécs, the county seat—the Pécs Tannery and the Pécs Meatpacking Plant. The management could now legitimize its decision to dump with a reference to cost-benefit analysis. The memorandum dated January 23, 1978 announcing the creation of the site claimed that "we must continue searching out reuse possibilities, and a contest with this objective must be announced. All proposals that would pay the half of the unit transportation costs from Budapest to Hidas [site of a BCW branch plant, near Garé] to the reuser may be accepted" (BVM 1978).

The Effect of Professionalization on Waste Distribution

Why couldn't BCW store its waste in its yard or elsewhere in Budapest? This question leads us to consider the state's interests and authority in assigning land uses—that is, in regional development. For on-site storage, the amount of the waste was obviously prohibitive; but permits for a dump or for a temporary storage site in Budapest would have been rejected even if BCW had requested them. This was due to a new direction in regional development policies that from the mid-1960s prohibited the siting of new industries in the capital, and called for relocating many of the existing plants to the countryside. The rationale behind this prohibition was to alleviate overcrowding and to improve the quality of air in Budapest.[2]

Interestingly, it was exactly such a relocation project that allowed BCW to transfer its glue plant to a former briquette plant in Hidas in 1970.[3] However, the drums' corrosion and their imminent leakage made it clear that this was only a temporary solution. The company was, therefore, relieved to be invited as a partner in establishing a waste dump site in the nearby village of Garé in 1978.

Let's look at the local antecedents of this dump. In the 1970s, Pécs was struggling with the same environmental problems challenging Budapest. In addition to facing serious air pollution, its local factories produced unwanted wastes, which were being dumped on municipal waste sites on the outskirts of the city. In 1976, local water authorities reported an impending danger to the city's drinking water sources caused by one of these dumps. Simultaneously, plans were being drawn up for a hiking and picnic ground in the same location that "could make possible active weekday or weekend recreation, useful leisure activities, and the protection of health for the urban population" (BML 1976, 1).

As a result, the dumping permission for two of Pécs's most significant firms, the Pécs Tannery and the regional subsidiary of a nationwide meatpacking enterprise, was withdrawn even before a new dump was sited and established. As the city government strove to distribute more environmental public goods (clean water and a greenbelt) to its constituency, the two enterprises were faced with the problem of finding a new location for their wastes. They turned to the local seat of the Hungarian State Geological Institute (MÁFI).

By this time, MÁFI had already completed the so-called pollution vulnerability maps of the entire region of Southern Transdanubia (the southwest of Hungary), initiated by its forward-looking director in 1974, as mentioned above. It could thus point scientifically to those areas where a bed of clay would protect the groundwater from contamination. By the fall of 1977, MÁFI found the right spot for disposal, in the vicinity of Garé, and acquired the approval of the local public health authorities.

The same year, BCW also commissioned MÁFI to search out a place for the TCB by-product. The company originally asked for locations of appropriate clay pits both near Budapest and near Hidas. The institute mediated between BCW and the two Pécs firms, and the result was an arrangement in which BCW paid all the costs of the new road leading to the disposal site from the highway in return for a dumping permit in the same location. Many other companies who also got wind of the siting in Garé sent in their requests for dump sites to the council of Baranya County, but they were turned down one after another. The request of the Furniture Manufacturing Company of Szekszárd in neighboring Tolna County was turned down, specifically with the argument that Baranya County was only willing to receive wastes produced on its own territory. Amid such strong competition for dump sites, BCW could win only by offering substantial financial support, and by presenting the TCB waste as having been produced locally— that is, in its Hidas plant, ostentatiously called the Hidas Chemical Works in many documents.

Now that we understand how BCW got its waste into Baranya County, let's see what made Garé a very likely choice as a dump site, and why MÁFI had prepared the vulnerability maps. The economic contribution of Southern Transdanubia, and Baranya County in particular, to the establishment of a modern industrialized society was primarily seen in its rich source of ores and minerals, especially uranium and coal. As a report on the county's geological research put it, "[t]he industry of our county is commonly known to be of an extractive nature; therefore, it is necessary to analyze the situation and the experience of geological research" (BML 1978, Fonds 1, group I, preservation unit 8, no document number, 1). The Southern Transdanubian Department was the largest among the regional departments of MÁFI; in fact, it was authorized to do a follow-up test for uranium on test drills done anywhere in the country (BML 1978, Fonds 1, group 1, preservation unit 8, no document number, 7). This department therefore accumulated a vast amount of geological data and, because of Baranya's geological potentials, it accumulated a huge amount of data about the soil conditions in Baranya in particular. It was thus very likely that the kind of soil (clay) whose impermeability made it look appropriate for a hazardous waste dump was most likely to be found in Baranya County, as well. This is despite previous suggestions by the Hydrological Association that regional dumps should be established in "valueless territories with low population density" (környei 1976, 5).

Baranya surely had many "valueless" territories but its settlement density was the largest in the country. If the region did not exactly have a low population density, it *was* perceived as a "valueless territory." The minutes from a meeting between such representatives of the Pécs Tannery and officials concluded that "the assignment of the territory for disposing the waste does not interfere with the County's developmental interests" (Executive Committee of the Council of Baranya County 1978). The area around Garé certainly had no industrial potential, since the region's close vicinity to Tito's Yugoslavia had discouraged planners from industrializing it in the fifties and sixties. Its agricultural potential was also minimal, because the region's characteristically hilly plots were not suited to mechanized cultivation. On the land where the dump was to be established, the value of the produce grown had been, in the words of the present mayor, former member of the local council and longtime resident of the village, "practically zero." Obviously, this was important not just from the state's or the county's point of view, but also from the standpoint of the enterprises, which could therefore acquire the land very cheaply.[4]

Garé and its vicinity easily fulfilled not only the criterion of economic insignificance but also that of political insignificance. Its rapidly aging peasant population and the large ratio of ethnic minorities, primarily Croats, Germans, and Romani (otherwise known as Gypsies), coupled with the retirement of old village leaders in the seventies and lack of replacement for them since, eroded the political clout of residents, leaving them ill-equipped to defend themselves from the centralizing efforts of socialist regional development.[5] Garé found its agricultural cooperative merged with that of Szalánta in 1974, which justified the administrative fusion of the two villages in 1976. This implied the closure of Garé's council and the use of joint budgets for the sole benefit of the superordinate village, Szalánta. Two years later the joint council issued the permits for the new dump. With this Garé made a smooth transition from being a figurative wasteland to a literal one.

According to one source, the authenticity of which I cannot judge, the president of the joint council protested the idea of the dump site but was threatened. In the reminiscences of one of the members of the joint council, who was a Garéan, this decision-making process was experienced as a rather predetermined process:

> At that time I was a member of the council, and they were coming here from I don't know what organs to try to persuade us that there was no soil anywhere in the country that had such impermeability, which is the most appropriate for this purpose. Of course we didn't believe it, we never agreed to have such a site here. Once after a council meeting, I talked to the president of the council, and she said, we discussed this last night [presumably with her

representing the council vis-à-vis the tannery and county officials] and we didn't accept this, but today it was already in the *Közlöny*[6] that the national organs arranged it all and that [the dump] will be here in Garé.

The gentlemen (then still comrades) in the delegation always told us that this would be a concrete bunker [as opposed to sitting in the open air, exposed to the elements], and the material would be dropped in through a trap-door, and they said that they would deliver [waste] from the slaughter-house, we never even heard about a Budapest firm, only about the tannery [in Pécs]. (Personal interview, Anonymous, Garé, 1996)

Many claim that the money Szalánta received in return for permitting the siting was used for building its new road. In addition to the carrot-and-stick method, certain informal relations also must have been essential in making the deal. This is indicated by the fact that Garé and Szalánta were switched to the district of Pécs just for the short period (from April 1, 1977 to December 31, 1978)[7] in which the decision on the permits was made (not just for BCW but for the other two firms in Pécs), rather than leaving them under the jurisdiction of the Siklós district, where they had always been.

The Consequences of Professionalization

For BCW, which gave voice to professionals even when the Party suppressed experts, professionalization mostly meant more freedom to continue to look for solutions consistent with its engineers' ideas. It was exactly professionalization that legitimized BCW's choice to dump its wastes in Garé, even though, as it was soon found out, this was neither a geologically sound choice, nor was the realization of the dump up to scientific standards —even those of the early eighties. As a result the barrels started corroding quickly and this not only resulted in a constant foul odor but also the contents eventually finding their way into the groundwater. This lack of professionalism is counterintuitive, first because science was supposed to prevent all this; and, second, because professionalization also meant an increased legitimacy for explicitly environmental claims. The only way we can resolve this seeming contradiction is if we revisit what professionalization actually meant and what environmental claims were made in favor of Garé's dump.

To wit, Garé's dump *was* the consequence of explicit environmental action. Those ameliorative steps that were reluctantly taken at the end of the seventies by the state under pressure from experts, such as eliminating threats to the safety of drinking water or establishing more greenbelts, tended to concentrate on urban environments. Why? First of all, experts stepping forward with environmental claims were a lot more likely to be urbanites themselves, therefore they were more exposed to and more familiar with urban and industrial environmental problems than with rural ones. Second, if environmental problems initially had to be dressed up as impediments to plan fulfillment and industrial growth in order to be heard, then, clearly, urbanites living near factories had a discursive advantage over residents living in agricultural areas. Third, the technical intelligentsia's services and contacts, so crucial in making claims, were inaccessible for rural villagers. In sum, both the "software" (information and discourse) and the "hardware" (contacts, institutional positions) of environmental claims making placed rural residents at a disadvantage.[8]

Budapest's and Pécs's leaders took measures to ensure safe drinking water and clean air for their constituencies, while endangering and polluting the same for disempowered villagers. Budapest protected its air quality by prohibiting the siting of new industries in the capital, and strongly encouraging the relocation of existing ones to the countryside; and Pécs's leaders revoked the dumping permits from the meatpacking plant and the tannery even before a new location was found, in order to keep drinking water safe and to create greenbelts. In contrast, Garé received the by-products of urban "environmental protection," despite desperate attempts by its powerless leaders to prevent the dumping.

> The Meatpacking Plant, the Tannery and the Hidas Chemical Works dump their filth and slurry here if they want to. It seems like there is no appeal against this. The population and the council both took steps, but these somehow did not achieve anything. The bosses decide, and the village smells the stink. That's just how it is. ("The Chronicle of the Village of Bosta," BML 1979)[9]

That Garé could not defend itself was therefore not the result of the state's ignorance of environmental problems, but rather of social and spatial inequalities in environmental claims making. That the site was assigned to Garé in the first place was the consequence of the socialist state's principles of regional development, its ethnic politics, the accumulation of scientific knowledge on the region's soil conditions, and the economic power of BCW in convincing county officials to accept its TCB waste as locally produced and in making Szalánta accept the deal. Garé's dump was not an illegal dump. Garé's dump was not simply assigned on the whim of the party-state. Garé was scientifically sited, and, as such, its dump was an intellectual product—the fruit of an alliance among professionals (geologists, hydrologists, soil scientists, and public health experts), the management of three state enterprises, and county-level officials. The fact that this deal was made practically without the central authorities, that it was made despite the protest of the village leadership, and that it was legitimated with a scientific façade testifies not to a totalitarian practice, but rather to a technocratic environmental politics. Public control over disposal was surely minimal, but not entirely absent: it was absent only for those living next to the dump. In 1981, Garé formed an environmental committee under the tutelage of a party-controlled civil organization, the People's Patriotic Front, but for many years it remained entirely powerless in the face of this technocratic alliance.

The Limitations of Dumping

According to high-ranking employees of BCW, at the time the Garé dump was established it was hailed by authorities as a model facility to be followed in other parts of the country. I, however, found no evidence of its existence in the media until 1983, except for a passing mention in 1981 in the newspaper of BCW. It is nevertheless certain that Garé was among the first professionally assigned hazardous waste storage sites, if not the very first one, and since disposal problems were occurring with increasing frequency, it is quite possible that decision makers looked forward with high expectations to the opening of the Garé site.

Indeed, the draft of a 1978 internal report by a committee of the Council of Baranya County on the county's environmental state of affairs mentioned the dump site as an environmental protection facility, as the "reassuring deposition of these wastes" (BML 1978, file number 31.234). Furthermore, the document makes it clear that, despite the original intention to create a temporary storage site, county officials viewed Garé from the beginning as a dump site to be developed so that it could accept other wastes from the county, and not only for a limited period but in the long run: "under preparation is a 10-square-kilometer territory in the vicinity of Garé and Szalánta, which *in the first period* would receive the wastes of the Pécs Tannery, the Hidas Chemical Works [*sic!*], and the Meatpacking and Animal Trading Companies" (BML 1978, file 31.234; emphasis mine). A 1979 report by the county's public health authority was even more explicit: "The central waste dump site of the County will also be established on the same territory. The enterprises will have their own dump sites [within the County site] where they can deposit their wastes for 15–20 years" (BML 1979, group 20E4, microfilm roll 96, file 31.488).

It is clear from these and other documents and from the story of how BCW acquired the permit to dump in Garé that the siting of hazardous wastes, and even the definition of hazardous wastes, was unregulated. The absence of coherent regulation allowed the investors, builders, and officials to water down the original technical prescriptions for the dump's design and operation. As a result, the dump had a lot of problems from the beginning, such as missing structural and infrastructural features and the absence of fences and constant supervision, creating a public health hazard.

Such regulatory chaos was to end in 1981. That is when the Decree on Hazardous Wastes (56/1981 [XI. 18]) was finally put into effect. This decree defined hazardous wastes and regulated their elimination for the first time in Hungary, and it marked the beginning of the official framing of waste problems as environmental concerns. This law laid the basis for two practical measures on the terrain of hazardous wastes over the next couple of years. First of all, the law obliged enterprises to prepare material balances and material flow charts that allowed the agencies responsible for the execution of the decree to acquire a relatively clear picture of the type and amount of hazardous wastes a company generated, and to then proceed to check on the practices of treatment and disposal (see fig. 6.1). The second practical measure was establishing the technical parameters for the kind of controlled and professional hazardous waste treatment that the Decree on Hazardous Wastes prescribed. This obviously implied at least a limited legitimization of waste disposal. Many companies, however, first saw the revocation of permits for existing disposal and incineration methods, which did not conform to the 1981 hazardous waste decree. A widely publicized case was that of Vác, where for decades pharmaceutical wastes had been stored and periodically (four or five times a year) incinerated in the open air. In 1981, public health authorities ordered the companies involved to stop the practice, but without having guaranteed the concrete conditions (administrative, technical, financial) of legal dumping previously.

Indeed, reluctance to dump continued: just like Garé, other, soon-to-follow dumps were never intended as final waste disposal sites. The new legal facilities were called storage sites, and even the 1981 decree on hazardous wastes only talked about "temporary storage sites" (*ideiglenes hulladéktároló*) and not "disposal sites" (*hulladéklerakó*). Why was this distinction repeatedly made? Because the state hoped that in more prosperous future years the firms would be able to finance the reuse of wastes stored in such temporary dumps (personal interview, Krisztoforosz Szterjopulosz, Budapest, 1996; personal interview, Attila Takáts, Budapest, 1996). As a study from 1982 put it, "[a] presently indeterminable portion of hazardous wastes are stored by enterprises on their own territories, thinking of the future possibilities of reuse" (Olessák 1982, 42). This practice partially

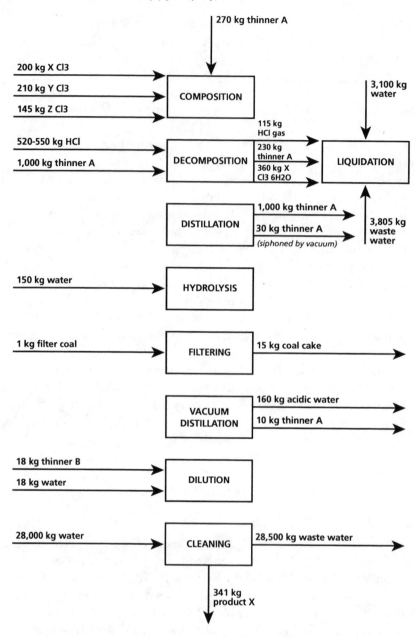

Source: Ladó, Romhányi, Büchner 1983

FIGURE 6.1. Material flow chart for Product X. Source: Ladó, Romhányi, Büchner, 1983.

reflected the staying power of the now residual metallic waste model, according to which one should never give up on finding reuse possibilities even in the most hopeless cases.

Another source of this foot-dragging in disposal siting was increasingly the political stakes involved:

> There are cases of enterprises wanting to build disposal sites for themselves, but they have been waiting in vain for a permit for years, even though there are only three years left until the deadline for establishing such dumps. But the realization [of these plans] is stalling because, for example, the county councils are late in assigning the territories suitable for storing hazardous wastes. The consideration of the countless geological and meteorological aspects is not easy *nor is taking the responsibility for designating a territory for burying toxins.* (Radio Free Europe 1983, 1474; emphasis mine)

Indeed, containing the waste problem was beginning to mean containing it politically. The cardinal question for the next waste regime that took hold at the end of the eighties was the issue of local self-determination in terms of environmental quality, and in general that of democratic participation in environmental decision making.

Temporary storage sites, however, while perhaps politically less risky, were technologically inappropriate for long-term use and for large amounts of waste. As those more prosperous years when the hazardous wastes stored could be reused failed to materialize, the dumps designed for temporary use turned into long-term wastelands harboring ecological time bombs. The BCW dump is simply the most notorious among them. In Garé, by the early eighties, the drums containing the TCB waste had started to corrode or even explode in the heat of the summer, causing a constant foul odor. Test drills later demonstrated that their contents had leaked into the ground, endangering the groundwater and the nearby spring. Villagers soon began to voice suspicions about the mysterious deaths of domestic animals and increased cancers in the village, and environmental authorities themselves acknowledged the dangers of the dump when they suggested such emergency measures as covering and, later, repacking the drums.

The lack of certain knowledge about the dump and the lack of any contact with BCW or any responsible authority that could explain to Garéans what was going on, coupled with the tangible but mysterious signs—the animal deaths, the sicknesses, and the odor—made villagers desperate. To make sense out of the smell and the slowly leaking pieces of information about the dump and its dangers, the villagers conjured up an absent Other. When animals died, BCW had killed them; when red snow fell, BCW had colored it; when Szalánta got a new road, BCW had paid for it; when trees dried out, BCW had desiccated them; when fruits tasted bad, BCW's poison had spoiled them; when the candle went out in the basement, BCW's gases had put it out. Despite the increasing certainty that it was not safe, and despite the village's obvious if ineffective resentment, the dump was not ordered to be closed but rather to be upgraded to a permanent dump site. What's more, a 1982 plan for a network of regional waste treatment facilities, which initially consisted of eight dump sites and five incinerators, assigned it as one of the new regional dumping centers for hazardous wastes.

In the efficiency waste regime that became dominant in Hungary in the mid-seventies, the social relations of waste production from the metallic waste regime persisted. The representation and the politics of waste, however, were radically transformed. Wastes now were not slated to be collected and reused under any conditions, but rather were primarily to be reduced, because in this way production costs could be decreased. Instead of conceptualizing waste as use value, the efficiency model took a pragmatic approach: it subordinated the reuse or recycling of waste to cost-benefit analysis. This, and the concomitant professionalization of waste issues, legitimated waste dumping, a taboo in the fifties and sixties. But the metallic waste model, even though now a residual representation, still obstructed permanent waste disposal and promoted the establishment of temporary sites. While the establishment of these temporary disposal sites was now based on scientific considerations, this in itself was not a guarantee either for public control over siting or for environmentally safe operation of the sites. As the state of the economy worsened, the hopes to ever reuse the thus-stored wastes melted away, and the temporary dumps metamorphosed into long-term wastelands and environmental disaster areas.

Part 3

Privatize and Incinerate

(1985–present)

[Czech writer visiting the president of the Ford company]: I wanted to know how he removed all those cars from the world once they'd reached the end of their service. He replied that this was no problem. Anything that was manufactured could vanish without trace, it was merely a technical problem. And he smiled at the thought of a totally empty, cleansed world.

quoted in Ivan Klíma, *Love and Garbage*

seven
The Chemical Model

It was 1988, and I felt weird. Here I was, at my second demonstration against the construction of a dam on the riparian border of Hungary and Czechoslovakia,[1] feeling righteous and, since I was surrounded by hundreds of others, quite strong as well. Yet, when I looked around, all I saw were women and children. As this was a women's march, men were only encouraging us from the sidelines. We were also chanting slogans about the future of humans and nature, and we were carrying symbolic representations of human victims and the threatened body of the nation. In one of the posters, a huge dredger was menacingly extending its arm toward the beautiful Danube bend; another featured the dam as a vampire. Victimhood was the primary mode of subjectivity in various Hungarian environmental protests of the 1980s. Indeed, the political symbolism of the protests could not have been more different from that of early state socialism. In the 1950s, political posters featured humans as masculine workers with hard, fit, metallic bodies; by contrast, the 1980s movements, which hovered in the ever-shifting border zone between the official and the illegal, displayed images of mothers and children and sick, mutilated, or dead human bodies. While the athletic bodies of socialist realism sported unisex overalls and proudly wore the soot on their faces, the human images of the fledgling environmental movements draped themselves in black and wore dust or gas masks. The proletarian and peasant heroes of Stalinism assumed active poses and looked into the future with great anticipation; the costumed figures at environmental protests were passive, silent, and pretended to be sick, disabled, or dead (Harper 1999; Lipschutz and Mayer 1996). Such were the images of a new discourse of the body at the end of state socialism.

By the 1980s, we knew there were enough things to fear in our air, water, and soil. And we felt scientists, who could tell us what those things were, were our natural allies. These experts, for their part, grew increasingly bold and loud in demanding the legalization of toxic waste dumps and incinerators. For them, waste surely held no positive meaning; rather, it was inherently useless and harmful.

By the mid-eighties, the previously latent and suppressed chemical model of waste had replaced the efficiency model and the residual metallic model. The ascendance of the chemical model to hegemony was rooted in two key phenomena: first, in the increasing professionalization of economic management and the significance of knowledge-based industries in keeping the economy afloat; and second, in the increasing politicization of environmental issues.

As the professional intelligentsia increased its importance in economic management, its cry for a way to deal with nonrecyclable and nonreusable wastes became louder and less suppressed. At a 1981 conference on the liquidation of hazardous wastes, a high-ranking official of the Ministry of Industry, a chemical engineer himself, posed the question: "Why is it that the Budapest chemical plants and the world-famous Hungarian pharmaceutical industry still do not have a modern incinerator that could guarantee the legal air quality standards?" (Szász 1981, 6). In his narrative, the chemical and especially the pharmaceutical industries appeared as pioneers that already in the seventies strove to establish safe incineration practices, but whose requests for permits for a safe incinerator in Budapest were repeatedly turned down by one authority or another. The reasons usually had to do with the local councils' contrary interest in a certain path of economic development for the proposed location. He criticized the 1981 hazardous waste decree for only punishing the enterprises but not establishing the technical conditions to comply with the law, a theme repeated in my interviews with engineers and managers. This way, the blame for illegal dumping was pushed back to the state:

> One thing is certain: until the chemical plants and plants applying chemical technologies have no possibility to have their wastes incinerated or them-

selves incinerate them in modern facilities, the danger will always remain that they will choose an undesirable way of making materials disappear. (Szász 1981, 6)

Experts at this conference called for a compromise to replace the simple prohibition of dumping or storage, including the prohibition by the county councils.

> We had to choose between two bads: we either incinerate or contaminate the water, because it was impossible to choose "neither this, nor that." All right, but then what should we do? A decree ordered Chinoin to transport its waste away from Vác, but it turned out that, of the nineteen counties of the country, none gave permission for storage. (Nuridsány 1981, 58)

From the perspective of the chemical industry, waste reuse, recycling, and source reduction through modernization were insufficient. These were all partial solutions, mostly because the processes underlying chemical production are irreversible, and usually only a small amount of the products and by-products can be regained or reused. In the chemical model, production is not a closed cycle in the sense that all materials produced can be recirculated into production. As I detailed in the previous chapter, the reduction of by-products also meets greater difficulties than in other industries. Finally, these mostly hazardous substances require immediate and safe handling.

In the chemical waste model, wastes appear as negative and harmful and they are best kept away from production and people. They are to be liquidated by dumping or incineration. This model was once again a model based on metonymy: the chemical industry's waste model was made to be the general waste model that applied to the whole economy. In the chemical industry, as I demonstrated in chapters 3 and 4, the precision required for controlled chemical reactions and the time of chemical and biological processes imposed strict limits on how much human ingenuity and stronger, more metallic bodies could improve on the efficiency or speed of production. Most importantly, however, the type of body present in the background of the chemical model is not a working body but rather a consuming body—a body that consumes, willingly or unwillingly, the products and by-products of the chemical industry.[2] The key concern is not so much with controlling production but with controlling consumption—that of products and by-products.

The acknowledgment of the seemingly obvious fact that bodies don't just produce but also consume literally revolutionized thinking about wastes. As the fog of omnipresent censorship slowly lifted, the effects of decades of illegal dumping of chemical wastes came to light, Western ecological and public health information crept through the Iron Curtain, and details of the Chernobyl nuclear power plant were revealed piece by piece. In the representations of these cases, bodies lost their metallic strength and their immunity to natural laws and were rather portrayed as frail, vulnerable, and sickly. The public became sufficiently primed for a different way of dealing with wastes, one that emphasized protection from and thus the safe disposal of harmful wastes—not their collection and reuse.

This new approach resulted in the politicization of environmental issues. This was not the politicization of waste in the fifties' sense of making waste collection a political obligation of workers, but rather an increase in questioning the legitimacy of the Party's leadership due to environmental problems.

As dumping was legitimized and as legislation acknowledged the environmental hazards involved in dumping and established the dumpers' legal liability, siting waste treatment facilities became a delicate affair. This was palpable already at the previously mentioned conference, where a contributor pointed out that "[t]he present situation in Vác [regarding Chinoin's waste storage; see quote above] is not only an economic question but a very serious political question as well. That's why the government also examined the issue and directed comrade Borbándi, Vice-Premier, to take the necessary steps" (Szász 1981, 6). This time the representatives of the chemical industry had a stake in defining such issues as political—that is, as questioning the Party's legitimacy—because that way they could cajole the state's assistance if not intervention into cases where siting met repeated obstacles. Remember, fifteen years earlier BCW was unsuccessful in framing its waste disposal problems as political to thus get state assistance to solve them (see chapter 4). But in the early eighties, the chemical industry managed to put the issue on the agenda of various state authorities. The conclusion of the conference claimed it was a serious achievement that "a common language is beginning to be spoken by industry, social organizations, and authorities" (Horváth 1981, 59).

The state now shifted its efforts to assisting in the siting of waste treatment facilities. In 1985, the Party's daily broke the news about the construction of the country's first modern hazardous waste incinerator, at Dorog, twenty kilometers west of Budapest; and the news of the siting of other incinerators and dumps followed. In 1986 a new hazardous waste dump was opened in Eger; in 1987 Rudabánya found itself assigned as the location of a new incinerator; a new temporary hazardous waste storage facility with a capacity of 10,000 tons was sited in Hernádkércs (Borsod County), to be operated by the local agricultural cooperative; and the same year, plans were announced to build a hazardous waste storage site in Szőreg (Csongrád County). In 1988, the Lábatlan cement kiln announced plans to incinerate pharmaceutical wastes; the same year, Szolnok, Békés, Csongrád, and Bács-Kiskun Counties cooperated to establish a storage site in Kétpó, which was later to be developed into a complex waste treatment and disposal site; and the state assigned Ófalu (Baranya County) as the country's first nuclear waste dump site.

While legitimating waste disposal and incineration, solutions consistent with the chemical model also created their own resistance. Most of these facilities—those of the incinerators in Dorog and Lábatlan, and those of the dumps in Szőreg, Ófalu, and Aszód—met with the opposition of the local population, and, unlike in the case of Garé a decade earlier, their protest was not silenced in the media. These cases indicate a radical transformation in the relation between the state and civil society, and are in stark contrast with Garé's case. The case of Ófalu is especially illustrative in this respect. In 1987 the Hungarian state started geological testing for the country's first nuclear waste dump site in Ófalu, a small village about twenty kilometers from Garé. The village was economically, ethnically, and administratively in the same position that Garé had been in 1978,[3] yet within a year the villagers, supported by scientists and the media, forced the state to withdraw, and by the spring of 1990 the plans were abandoned (Juhász, Vári, and Tölgyesi 1993; Reich 1990).

The year 1985 also marked the first public protests against waste imports from the West. In 1985 the news broke that the Austrian city of Graz was planning to store municipal waste in western Hungary without the knowledge of Hungarian environmental authorities (B. Sz. 1985; Ferenczi 1985). In 1986, the same authorities stopped a similar scheme, in which the city of Vienna was to deliver contaminated soil—containing hazardous waste from the construction of its subway—to Hungary for dumping (Mélykúti 1986). Finally, the Gabcikovo-Nagymaros dam also evoked claims of ecocolonization, because it would have been built by an Austrian company.

Besides the ever-widening application of waste dumping and incineration, there were other, more general reasons behind the politicization of waste issues. In the second half of the 1980s, the cause of the environment became practically the only relatively safe avenue for expressing political dissent. The relative success of publicizing resistance to the Gabcikovo-Nagymaros dam made it possible for other smaller and lesser-known environmental groups to survive. Environmental protection became the only area where initiatives from below did not face an automatic and immediate coercive reaction by the state.

This was for the following reasons:

(a) State representatives thought the call of these movements for better science and more professional economic management harmonized rather well with the reform discourse of the Party, and, therefore, they thought they were integratable into their reform initiatives.[4]

(b) After the Helsinki process[5] took off, but especially after the Danube Movement received the Right Livelihood Award in 1985,[6] the leadership's image in the West would have suffered greatly if it had clamped down on environmentalists. The country's reliance on Western loans having increased considerably, this image grew ever more important.

(c) In some cases, environmental claims enjoyed the backing of urban municipal governments, which used the threat of leaking environmental secrets to cajole extra funds out of the state (Szirmai 1999). While the party-state viewed environmentalism as co-optable and containable within its overall technocratically oriented reform policies, the "Greens"—reform economists, scientists, activists, and, to some extent, local governments—started recognizing the "sacred cow" status of environmentalism. They increasingly used environmental claims as a "Trojan horse"—green on the outside but filled with market liberalism and democratic demands on the inside.[7] In general, the sense of impending political crisis, which was sharpened by the nuclear accident in Chernobyl, made representatives of the state a lot more attentive and flexible on issues that had previously been taboo (Pickvance 1996).

The emergence of the chemical model was initially a positive development, to the extent that it forced the state to acknowledge environmental claims for what they were, rather than viewing them as simply impediments to production; and to the extent that it facilitated a cautious opening of the state to those making environmental claims. The issue of waste distribution was no longer a taboo: not only were dumping and incineration legitimate ways to deal with wastes, it also became increasingly possible to question the siting of dumps and incinerators. The successes of the fledgling civil society in environmental politics made the few years between 1985 and 1990 appear as the years of optimism, namely, a time when a belief that a democratic *and* environment-friendly society could still be created. Garé too had reasons to be hopeful.

Garé's Hopes in the 1980s

By the early 1980s, the toxic waste drums adjoining Garé's woods had corroded (see figs. 7.1 and 7.2), letting the contents leak and causing a

FIGURE 7.1. The drums of tetrachlorobenzene in Garé's dump, 1995. Because of the corrosion of the original drums, the material had to be repacked in larger drums, which, however, also corroded as seen in this picture. Photo by author.

noxious, stinging odor that became especially unbearable in the heat of the summer. Residents claimed they knew that the smell was coming from the waste dump, but it was not until 1990 that they found out that there were dangerous materials stored there. Even without exact knowledge, or perhaps precisely because of the uncertainty, residents were worried about the dump. Two residents I interviewed claimed to know that the dump was established on a spring that was artificially blocked for this purpose. A local teacher even sent an article about this to *Búvár*, a naturalist magazine; and a middle-aged woman, who was concerned about the effect on residents' drinking water, took a water sample to the public health authorities in Pécs around 1985 or 1986 to find out if it was safe to drink. However, as she recalled ten years later, when they found out that the sample was from Garé, they told her that they would not release the results.

By the second half of the eighties, several companies were transporting waste to Garé, some in return for a payment to the Pécs Tannery, and some without the knowledge of the firms who owned the dump. Villagers knew about such illegal deliveries from acquaintances or from being themselves employed by the transportation companies involved. One Garéan claimed that even the police dumped tear gas there. Of course nobody would ever admit to illegal dumping, aptly supporting the proverb one of the villagers

FIGURE 7.2. The house in Garé no one would buy, 1995. It was "on the market" for at least eight years. Photo by author.

acquainted me with, when asked about the culprits: "Shit and stink have no owner." The Environmental Protection Committee founded by Garéans in 1981 was meant to solve this problem, as its primary goal was to "report unintended uses of the dump to the health authority" ("The Chronicle of the Village of Garé," BML 1981). The modesty of the committee's objectives—there was certainly no mention of eliminating the dump—was probably due to the fact that it had to operate under the auspices of the People's Patriotic Front, a toothless umbrella organization of the Party (see chapter 5). Nevertheless we must not underestimate its significance as one of the first, if not the first, rural environmental organizations in state socialist Hungary.

After the passage of the 1981 hazardous waste decree, surveillance over the dump increased. In 1983 tests were made to determine the exact composition of BCW's waste. Later the same year, BCW was ordered to cover the drums and to repackage the contents of the corroded ones. In 1986 the regional environmental authority conducted a field survey that led to a substantial fine of almost two million Forints levied against BCW for polluting the environment.

Partly as a result of all these legal and technical actions, by 1987 Garéans, and especially the village's new doctor, had acquired a surprising technical competence in matters of dumps and incinerators, and formulated their own proposals for a solution. They suggested incinerating the drums in a cement kiln elsewhere, or transferring them to a newly established and modern toxic waste dump site in Pest County, just outside Budapest. They achieved the termination of BCW's TCB production in 1987, and their pressure forced representatives of BCW, the Pécs Tannery, the meatpacking plant, and various departments in the council of Baranya County to sit down and negotiate in 1988. Finally, the committee successfully initiated a criminal investigation against BCW the same year for endangering the environment. With all this attention and increased leverage, Garéans became optimists: this was seemingly the beginning of two-way communication between their village and the state.

The fledgling environmental initiatives in the second half of the 1980s, in sum, proved successful in elevating disposal problems into public discourse, resisting various dump sites, and holding producers responsible for their wastes. The efforts of these movement seedlings still relied on expert knowledge; and professionals, in turn, assisted them as relatively safe outlets for expressing political dissent. The alliance between expertise and demands for transparency, coupled with the thrifty material culture still prevalent in Hungary in the middle of the 1980s, created favorable conditions for an environmentally friendly postsocialist transition. Even though scientific expertise came to play an increasingly significant role in defining and finding solutions to environmental problems, professionals tended to use their knowledge not against but rather in the defense of lay citizens. In the 1980s science was mobilized not against environmentalists but rather to support them; in fact, many activists were themselves professionals. Thus expertise and democratization went hand in hand. This alliance was broken soon after the collapse of state socialism. Let me review the paradigm shift that precipitated this split.

Right around 1989, two models circulated in public discourse about how to reconcile economic with environmental reforms in the former socialist bloc: the economic rationalism and the environmental modernization paradigms. The initially stronger expectation was that liberalization would automatically improve the state of the natural environment. "The Best Earth Day Present: Freedom," the title of an article in the *Wall Street Journal* in 1990 (Solomon 1990), was a most succinct expression of the prevalent hopes for Eastern Europe's environmental redemption after 1989. After listing some of the most infamous cases of environmental destruction in former socialist countries, the author summed up the bright future awaiting postsocialist citizens: "[n]ow all this [environmental pollution] is being swept away by democracy and economic rationality" (Solomon 1990, A14). That marketization and democratization would automatically turn environmental matters for the better has been argued implicitly or explicitly for decades, both by the Western scholarly literature on the environmental crisis of existing socialism (Goldman 1972; Taga 1976), and by reform economists within state socialist countries (Szlávik 1991; Veress 1982; see also DeBardeleben 1985). While the economic argument blamed the socialist state for suppressing the market, thereby preventing it from motivating production units to use natural resources more sparingly and with greater care, the political argument blamed it for monopolizing knowledge and denying accountability for pollution it allegedly caused single-handedly. With the problem constructed as being due to a result of too much state intervention, the only logical solution seemed to be the liberation of both markets and citizens. This is the assumption that informs what I might call, adopting Dryzek's (1997) terminology, the "economic rationalism discourse."

This was counterposed by the path of ecological modernization I defined in chapter 5. Many activists and experts hoped that Eastern Europe, enjoying the Veblenesque advantage of latecomers, could draw lessons from the mistakes of Western capitalism and build an economic system in which environmental concerns were integrated from the beginning, instead of being saved for later as add-on features. Taking this ecological modernization course would require a more active role for the state, or at least a more direct relationship between industry and government, than the economic rationalism discourse sees as necessary. These expectations were later shared by decision makers, some Western agencies, and aid foundations. For example, the White Paper of 1995, addressing the conditions for the accession of former socialist countries to the European Union, declared that

> environmental policy and the internal market are mutually supportive. The EU Treaty aims at sustainable growth and high levels of environmental protection and that environmental requirements be integrated into the definition and implementation of other policies. An integrated approach to allow a more sustainable path of social and economic development is not only vital for the environment itself, but also for the long-term success of the internal market. (European Union 1995, quoted in Klarer and Francis 1997, 39)

To the extent that the integration of economic with environmental policies has become an officially accepted and advocated approach to improving the state of the environment in Eastern Europe, the ecological modernization discourse seems to have won. Its principles appear in various

Western-written pieces of advice, such as the Environmental Action Programme for Central and Eastern Europe presented at the Environment Ministers' Conference in Lucerne in 1993, and in a series of reports by the Swiss Federal Department of Foreign Affairs prepared for the Hungarian Ministry of Environmental Protection and Regional Development in the first half of the nineties. In sum, the European Union has seemed to represent the path of ecological modernization. Let us review what this meant concretely in terms of waste issues.

Ecological Modernization in the European Union's Waste Policies

Even before the collapse of state socialism, it was an officially sanctioned strategy to strengthen Hungary's economic relations with what was then still called "the European Community." One of the first acts by the new government in 1990 was to apply for EU membership. In 1993 in Copenhagen, the conditions for former socialist countries to join was laid down. This conditionality included not only the establishment of a Western-style democracy and market economy, but also the adoption of all EU case law (exceeding 80,000 pages by the spring of 2003) into the countries' legislation, even before the enlargement was voted upon either in the candidate countries or in the existing countries of the European Union. Among these requirements, those concerning environmental regulations were summarized in the Environmental *Acquis Communautaire.* Since this conditionality exerted an important impact not only on the legislative framework of Hungary in the 1990s but also on the nature of the European Union's presence in Hungary's environmental practices, it is essential to contextualize the European Union's policies and interests in the specific area of waste problems.

The European Community first started to elevate environmental concerns to communal legislative actions in 1973 when it passed what came to be known as its First Environmental Action Program (EAP). It is these general programs that define the direction and tasks of environmental legislation in the period to come (ranging from four to nine years). Most legislation is passed in the form of directives written and proposed by the European Commission, then examined by the European Parliament and the Council of the European Union.

The first piece of legislation concentrating on wastes was the Framework Directive on Waste (75/442/EEC) passed in 1975. The ways in which this directive has been amended and modified by numerous subsequent directives illustrate very clearly the changes in ways of thinking about environmental problems, which in turn expressed the public's changing environmental concerns. Initially, most of the European Union's waste policies remained in a remedial paradigm, tackling environmental problems post facto through end-of-pipe technologies. Such technologies with regards to waste primarily included landfilling and incineration. These regulations included the above-mentioned first EU directive on waste, the Waste Oils Directive (75/439/EEC); the Hazardous Waste Directive (78/319/EEC, later replaced by 91/689/EEC); the Titanium Dioxide Directives (78/176/EEC, 82/883/EEC); the Sewage Sludge Used in Agriculture Directive (86/278/EEC); and the Municipal Waste Incineration Directives (89/369/EEC and 89/429/EEC). While in 1981 the Council issued a Recommendation concerning the reuse of waste paper, it was not until 1989, five years after the Brundtland Report coined the concept of sustainable development, that the Community Strategy for Waste Management established waste prevention as a top priority (Gervais n.d.). It is from this time that we can speak of an accepted "waste management hierarchy" (in order of priority):

    (1) minimization;
    (2) reuse (without chemical transformation of waste's material);
    (3) material recovery (recycling);
    (4) energy recovery (some forms of incineration); and
    (5) final disposal (landfill, incineration).

Finally, in 1993, the Fifth EAP, called *Towards Sustainability*, made several steps toward what came to be known as Integrated Product Policy, the title of a White Paper from 2002. The essence of these newer sets of regulations was to integrate environmental and economic policies; that is, to incorporate environmental concerns into economic planning and technological innovation from the beginning rather than saving them as add-on, expandable features. It is in this spirit that numerous waste-related rules were passed in the last ten years. Some of these established economic incentives, such as ecotaxes (for example, the compulsory minimum tax rate on mineral oil introduced in 1993), while others laid down the principles of environmental certification, giving birth to the ecolabel and audit systems, such as EMAS (Environmental Management System) (Council Regulation No. 1836/93). Yet another group of regulations focused on defining the duties of producers and consumers, aiming for a full (cradle-to-grave) responsibility for products, most recently in the areas of packaging waste (94/62/EC), electrical and electronic equipment (2002/96/EC and 2003/108/EC), and vehicles (2000/53/EC).[8]

As a result of these changes in environmental paradigms, the principles of present EU waste legislation are the following (often referred to as "the five Ps"):

(1) The Prevention Principle: top priority should be given to waste prevention and minimization.

(2) The Proximity Principle: waste should be disposed of as close as possible to where it is generated.

(3) The Producer Responsibility Principle: waste producers should bear cradle-to-grave responsibility for any damage caused by the waste they generate.

(4) The Polluter Pays Principle: polluters should bear the costs of safe management and disposal.

(5) The Precautionary Principle: waste management strategies should not take risks even if the causal relation between waste and damage is not fully proved.

Other global forces and discourses, however, encouraged the economic rationalism approach: the rise of a global waste incineration industry, and the neoliberal globalization discourse of supranational financial institutions, such as the World Bank, the IMF, and the OECD.

The Global Waste Incineration Industry

Even according to U.S. experts and industry officials, it has been difficult to obtain reliable statistics on even one country's waste treatment facilities (Repa 2001), yet it is necessary that we at least appreciate the magnitude of waste treatment and incineration. The world produces an estimated 338 million tons of hazardous waste per year. Experts maintain that between 180 and 250 million tons are generated by the United States, 30 to 45 million tons by European OECD counties, 25 to 30 million tons by the former Soviet Union, and about 6 million tons by Central and Eastern Europe. We also produce increasing amounts of wastes. For example, just the European OECD countries add an additional 3 percent, that is, about 9 million tons, to their annual industrial waste output each year. Most hazardous wastes are still landfilled: in the European OECD countries this proportion is about 70 percent, while 10 percent is recovered, 10 percent treated, and 8 percent incinerated (Stanners and Bourdeau 1995). Due to rising public resistance to landfilling and subsequent tightening of environmental regulation, there was a major shift toward incineration of hazardous wastes in the 1980s. (This is also the trend for municipal waste [Gandy 1994], of which 19 percent in OECD countries is incinerated [Stanners and Bourdeau 1995].) In the United States, the quantity of hazardous waste burned increased by at least 20 percent just in 1988–1989 (Costner and Thornton 1993). Individual records of chemical plants also suggest a turn toward incineration.

The initial increase in incinerator capacity led to a falling rate of price increases for incineration relative to that for other waste treatment methods, primarily landfilling, which provided further incentive for those responsible for wastes to burn them. Incineration became a highly profitable business. With charges of $1,500 (US) for burning one ton of hazardous waste, a medium-sized facility (50,000 tons/year) could earn its investment costs (construction and equipment, about $50–$60 million) within a year. In 1988 in the United States, revenues from the manufacture and sale of incineration equipment were estimated "at $1.6 billion, while income from 'incineration services' was estimated at $370 million" (Costner and Thornton 1993). Between 1977 and 1988 the growth in each sector's revenue averaged more than 30 percent per year, while projected growth through 1993 was 20 percent per year for each (Costner and Thornton 1993). A 1995 waste industry periodical summarized the "bright future for incineration" both domestically and internationally thus:

> Incinerator construction remains a large business for US-based companies, according to a recent survey of incinerator construction executives.
>
> In spite of public resistance and regulatory challenges, $2 billion was spent to construct or purchase new incinerators in 1994. In addition, $500 million was spent to upgrade incineration equipment.
>
> The future of the incineration industry is bright, according to 15 executives who participated in the study sponsored by Future Technology Surveys Inc., Lilburn, Ga. New incinerator markets, for example, have been forecasted to reach $3 billion in 1999 and owners are expected to spend an additional $2 billion to upgrade and modernize incineration equipment.
>
> International opportunities have helped spur market growth. While approximately 30 percent of US incineration firms' revenues come from international sales, exports may account for as much as 50 percent of sales in 1999. (Miller 1995)

Costs, however, are not universal: rather, they depend on the stringency of emissions standards in individual countries—hence the geographical element to the mentioned tug-of-war between the waste incinerator business and environmental regulation. Wastes are transported for treatment to those countries that have the loosest emissions standards, until the regulations in the country or region "catch up" with those of others.[9] The gap in regulatory standards is also a key cause of hazardous waste exports from Western Europe to developing countries and to Eastern Europe.[10] The flip side of capital's increasing mobility is the increasing mobility of hazardous waste.

Waste incineration, despite the alleged constant increase in its safety, is still a menace to public health and the environment. Incinerators simply decrease the volume of waste (some only by 60 percent), but whether they actually reduce its toxicity is dependent on the composition of the burned wastes. Incineration itself generates waste products (for example, bottom ash and fly ash), which are still considered toxic and thus have to be screened from the air and landfilled. Incinerator emissions of dioxins and furans, the most toxic substances ever known, account for 80 percent of all such emissions in industrialized countries. Health impacts of incineration have triggered resistance to incinerators in Western countries, forcing the state to raise emissions standards, but ultimately also making it practically impossible to site new facilities.[11] Western investors, increasingly unable to sell their incinerator technologies in the saturated and environmentally more conscious Western markets, seized on the excellent opportunity to expand to an Eastern Europe that had opened up to the West at just the right time.

Whether incinerators could find a new market in Hungary, or in Eastern Europe as a whole, depended a great deal on the regulatory environment. This is where the type of capitalism that abutted postsocialist countries in the late 1980s and early 1990s played a major role. To be sure, this was not the welfare capitalism of Western Europe that many Hungarians associated with the European Union; rather, this capitalism was one in which the role of the state was radically curtailed, and in which state-owned resources were privatized and prices liberalized in the name of increasing efficiency and a greater ability to compete on the world market (McMichael 1996). This new neoliberal agenda led to the uncritical and little-regulated admission of Western incinerator companies into Hungary. Let us review the effects on waste practices in detail.

Privatizing Production

Western assistance in economic recovery and the postsocialist countries' participation in the world market were resolutely conditioned upon privatization, the liberalization of prices, and the elimination of subsidies—that is, on a profound de-etatization. The European Union, while an emblem of regulated markets and welfare capitalism, demanded that postsocialist countries eager to join it implement an economic order in which markets operated unfettered by the state. The 1993 Copenhagen Criteria put the conditions this way:

> Membership requires that the candidate country has achieved stability of institutions guaranteeing democracy, the rule of law, human rights and re-

spect for and protection of minorities, the existence of a *functioning market economy as well as the capacity to cope with competitive pressure and market forces within the Union.* Membership presupposes the candidate's ability to take on the obligations of membership including *adherence to the aims of* political, *economic and monetary union.*[12] (emphasis mine)

Let us now review the effects of economic liberalization on waste practices. The privatization of the almost forty-year-old state waste collection company, MÉH, for one, imposed radical limits on the scope of its activity —that is, the range of waste materials it collected and its circle of suppliers. As for other companies, their privatization often relieved new owners from old as well as new environmental liabilities. Initially, the privatization regulations did not even address the question of environmental liabilities: then, until 1992, the privatization agency provided the new owner with a guarantee that it would clean up whatever environmental damage was later discovered. In one case the amount of this guarantee was equal to the sale price of the firm, reducing the privatization income of the state to zero (Állami Vagyonügynökség 1993).[13] In addition, the amount and the time limit of this guarantee were usually based not on an independent expert assessment but rather on a bargain between seller and buyer. It was only in 1992 that a law (§35 of the LIV. Law) prescribed the obligation of to-be-privatized firms to prepare a plan for repairing environmental damages done in the past. This, however, was not effective with partial privatizations. In these deals, usually the most profitable and cleanest plants or departments were privatized, while those with deficits and environmental problems were left in the hands of the state, thus leaving the cleanup costs to those units that could least afford to pay them (Állami Vagyonügynökség 1993).

The social relations of waste production, of course, went through great changes, especially after the massive privatizations. Yet, these changes did not necessarily signal the immediate advance of the social relations known from Western capitalism. Many sociologists called attention to the survival or the reproduction of old types of horizontal, and often informal, relations and barter (Burawoy and Krotov 1992). Different authors attached different values to these nonmarket-type horizontal relations. While some viewed them as a sign of the unreformability of old production relations, others viewed them as quite promising. Stark and Bruszt (1998) showed that cross-ownership was not only a way for firms to survive in a volatile economic situation by diversifying their assets, but also a form of entrepreneurship that was conducive to innovation. However, the economic benefits of these novel organizational forms should not conceal the fact that they further muddled environmental liability. The mushrooming of phantom waste-dumping firms in the immediate chaotic aftermath of the collapse of the state, for example, created serious havoc. This had much to do with an emaciated state as well.

Reducing State Capacity and Oversight

The restructuring and reduction of various offices or departments in the state apparatus were inevitable during the radical transformations begun in 1989; however, the pattern of departments slated for the most drastic reductions suggests that state capacity was intentionally dismantled and left undeveloped in waste policy areas. The Waste Department of the Ministry of Environmental Protection and Regional Development went through a series of reorganizations and reductions whose final balance indicates that it was the hardest hit among the departments of the Environmental Ministry. A high-ranking official there suggested that the evisceration of this department under the pretexts of rationalization and the so-called integrated approach to environmental protection was encouraged by the industrial lobby.

> This is because there are a lot of problems with industrial wastes, whose solution requires a lot of money. The interest of various groups is to acquire shares of the waste [treatment/disposal/incineration] market. But they only want the money from it without following the regulations. For permits, they have been going to the boss [rather than going through the required channels]. [Some] waste professionals in the ministry stood in the way of these intentions, so they had to be gotten rid of. (Personal interview with Anonymous official of Environmental Ministry, Budapest, 1997)

Private ownership of productive capacities, furthermore, made state monitoring increasingly difficult. Invoking the right to private property and production secrets, firms stopped reporting production and emissions data, as an official of the Ministry of Industry complained (personal interview, Anonymous, Budapest, 1996). The waste policies of the eighties had established a system of monitoring that obliged firms to prepare material flow charts and material balances. This reporting requirement made the evaluation of enterprises' waste activities relatively easy and transparent. The obligation to prepare material flow charts was rescinded in 1992; and even the circle of firms obliged to prepare material balances—a device much easier to manipulate—was severely limited, while exemptions from this obligation became easy to acquire (personal interview with Gábor Romhányi, Budapest, 1995; personal interview with Attila Takáts, Budapest, 1996).

The liberal transition paradigm looked at every state expenditure with suspicion. Environmental expenditures were no exception. Under the conditions of economic crisis and with the elimination of loans, the principal idea of industrial ecology and ecological modernization—that waste problems should be tackled in production through better product design and environmentally friendlier technologies—could not be enforced. The government program for waste reduction and reuse initiated in 1981 was abandoned, and the motivational system of credits and subsidies was subsequently eliminated under the pretext of normativity (that is, the principle of equal treatment of all companies) (Bakonyi 1991; Dworák 1991). Some experts pointed out a missed opportunity in 1989 to implement new economic tools.

> With the introduction of the new tax system, there would have been a possibility, besides the previous direct subsidies, to establish a system of subsidies and regulation based on tax preferences (and naturally, extra taxes) similarly to all developed countries, where such a system was successfully applied. The circle of tax preferences encouraging environmental . . . and waste management activities, however, was finally drawn so narrowly and in such an unfortunate manner that in the case of waste reuse, for example, it functions as an actual counter-incentive. Just as with taxes, there was a failure to apply other economic regulative tools (loans, interests, etc.) to such ends as well. (Takáts 1990)

Such a failure compelled some others to call for renewed and increased state funding for environmental purposes (Kindler 1994).

Obviously, amid a shortage of capital, the elimination of state subsidies, and strong pressures to invest in technologies with fast turnover, those environmental investments that required substantial initial capital and had slow turnover—such as waste sorting and waste storage capacities, as well as technologies for the reuse of certain wastes—did not materialize (Székely 1991). The change was palpable already in 1991:

> At present, the state foregoes the reuse and the neutralization of those wastes which might be more profitable but have slow turnover. These materials, by increasing the amount of hazardous wastes, cause damage, pollute the environment, and later will lead to serious problems in the whole economy. (Dworák 1991, 26)

The radical reorganization of various state agencies and the end of state funding for environmental purposes generated counterproductive effects. The MTESZ survey of existing dumps initiated in 1983 (described in chapter 5) now came to a halt, and there was no comparable data collected on waste sites until 2001. As one of the initiators of the survey put it, "the change in the political system stopped this process; the second stage, such as test drills and [verification] did not materialize; the pool of experts was replaced, and ideas were forgotten. It was if we had lost several years from our lives" (personal interview, Miklós Kassai, Pécs, 1996).

Legislation

The legislative area is perhaps the most telling of the direction of changes. While the number of laws enacted by the Hungarian Parliament in 1992 was so high that it entered the *Guinness Book of Records*, the Environmental Ministry failed to put forward a new, comprehensive environmental act (Bochniarz and Kerekes 1994). According to activists and others involved in the drafting, this was a conscious delaying tactic of the industrial lobby,[14] whose primary interests lay in a privatization process that would not be held back by ecological considerations, as well as in institutional arrangements in which environmental issues would be merely an add-on feature.[15] "The Parliamentary Committee on Environmental Protection became increasingly frustrated with the impasse, and finally decided to commission an independent draft," which even the minister supported (Sajó 1994, 38). Even so, the Comprehensive Act was not passed until 1995.

Even as comprehensive legislation was held up, older regulations were withdrawn. Most importantly, the decades-old system of deposits on packaging was eliminated. Riding on the wave of suddenly open markets and consumer desires formerly suppressed, Western corporations, such as Coca-Cola, brought in goods whose packaging was nonrecyclable, whose collection was no longer organized, and on which there was no longer a deposit. This was not an exclusively Hungarian phenomenon. As Péter Kaderják says:

> With respect to deposit-refund systems, the common experience of the CEECs [Central and Eastern European countries] is rather that during the period of transition formerly well-performing systems have been partly destroyed (for example, deposit-refund systems on bottles or car batteries). (Kaderják 1997, 169)

The globalization discourse that favored privatization and getting the state out of the economy thus had a devastating effect on Hungary's existing waste policies. Let us see how this discourse, coupled with the pressures by the global waste incineration industry, affected Garé's fate.

An "Entrepreneurial Solution"

Liberalization had unique effects on both Garé and the Budapest Chemical Works. Privatization and democratization quickly led to the undoing of centralized regional development projects: after 1989 villages fused in the seventies eagerly reclaimed their autonomy and severed ties with their formerly superordinate villages. Undoing the political ties, however, was one thing; undoing the harm such centralization projects had done was another.

By the end of the 1980s, the transformation of Garé into a figurative and literal wasteland seemed complete if not irreversible. The village's own businesses and bank closed; Garé lost its veterinarian; those working in the joined cooperative suffered from discriminatory treatment; new houses had not been built for decades; and after 1989 even the bus service was reduced, which increased the isolation of the village and rendered outside employment ever more difficult for residents.

Agriculture, the region's traditional livelihood, would have been the logical choice to regain economic strength. However, it was one thing to gain independence and another to reverse the effects of long-standing, oppressive centralization measures. It was one thing to get BCW to admit its fault, and another to eliminate the effects of decades-long dumping. Because of centralization, younger generations had mostly fled the village by the end of state socialism. As village leaders explained to me, Garé's population had changed; there was no hope for developing agriculture on a private small-scale basis, because nobody had domestic animals or machines to cultivate the land, the elderly were not capable of working enough, and the remaining youth did not have enough experience. Indeed, most people I talked to who had owned land before collectivization left their plot in, or rented it back to, the cooperative. Even those who tried to make a living from agriculture suffered the effects of the publicization of Garé's dump: they complained that no one would buy their produce on the market if they found out its origins. It seemed that Garé was doomed to an eternal wasteland status.

In addition, the collapse of the socialist order and the disintegration of the state quickly crushed the hopes that had started to build in Garéans at the end of the 1980s that they might negotiate the cleanup of the dump. The state could do little to force BCW to clean up, but there was a vague plan in 1988 to build an incinerator in Garé. Neither Szalánta nor Garé approved of such a solution, and with the collapse of the regime, this project was scratched. Further diminishing the pressure on BCW to clean up, already in December 1989 the central police office of Baranya County ended the aforementioned criminal investigation, due to a general amnesty. The still-joint council of Szalánta had appealed with no success against the amnesty. While in 1990 BCW received an order to eliminate the dump by December 31, 1997, an order to conduct surveys, and deadlines for turning in cleanup plans, the radical disarray or at least the momentary opaqueness of the legal system favored BCW's stalling tactics. Indeed, BCW did little to comply with any of these orders.

For BCW, the economically most favorable resolution for the environmental crisis was to build an incinerator that would burn the wastes dumped in Garé. The company had few financial resources to "just" pay the cleanup costs; but burning others' wastes in such a facility could not only cover these expenses but eventually could even be profitable. Obviously BCW did not want to spend money on cleanup if it indeed was going to build an incinerator; and it could not build an incinerator until it was privatized and thus could acquire some additional capital. However, its original plan to establish an incinerator near its Hidas branch plant failed due to the resistance of villagers and the costs of compensation for the houses that would have been demolished. That was when BCW's equally desperate former victim, Garé, rushed to its rescue. A year after Garé announced its autonomy from Szalánta based on a referendum, the village leadership approached BCW and invited it to build the incinerator at the dump's location. The company accepted.

This invitation confirmed BCW's plan to clean up by incineration and, most likely, had a significant impact on its privatization. By mid-1992, BCW had its assets' value assessed and was all ready for privatization, the actual form of which was still unknown. The management had to decide which pattern of privatization to follow: the common practice of leaving the dirtiest and least profitable departments and plants in state ownership by letting its Hidas branch plant take the dump, or else the path of claiming liability for Garé and using it as a springboard for a new, privately owned, profit-oriented waste treatment facility. According to the previously mentioned 1992 privatization law, the value of assets of a firm to be privatized was decreased by the amount of environmental cleanup costs; in Garé's case this reached 2.6 billion Forints, while BCW's assets were valued at over 4 billion Forints. The fact that BCW decided to keep the dump even though doing so meant a substantial decrease in the value of its assets indicates that the incinerator, by then already past the initial stages of planning, was looked at as a factor that could increase the firm's profit-making potential and thus its overall commercial value. Finally, BCW, fully owning the dump, became a private shareholding company at the end of 1992. With this, the state ceased to be the owner of the waste dumped in Garé.

Garéans had by then lost all their faith in the state's ability to solve their problem; for them, BCW's path of "entrepreneurial solutions" seemed the most effective and the most beneficial. However, neither the village nor BCW had the needed capital to build an incinerator. This is where EU-constituent incinerator companies came to the rescue.

The Budapest Chemical Works and the Ministry of Industry announced a bid for the incinerator project, which was won by the French state firm EMC Services. Then BCW formed a joint venture with EMC (Entreprise Minière et Chimique), called Hungaropec.[16] The interests of Garé and BCW now became the same. While during the seventies and most of the eighties neither the state nor the Budapest Chemical Works wanted to "own" the waste as a problem or as a liability, after 1989 the ownership of the waste as a resource became hotly contested. Who—which village, which firm, which country—would get to profit from burning the wastes, rather than who should clean them up, became the primary source of contention. Taking responsibility for the wastes dumped in Garé amid building a society that was supposed to be democratic, transparent, and just was not only necessary but also economically expedient. The landfill now served as a justification for establishing a profit-oriented waste treatment facility; and with this, BCW's oozing herbicide by-products metamorphosed into a resource.

That this turn in Garé's story was not the only fruit of the alliance between neoliberal globalization and the waste incineration industry is indicated by various data. A high-ranking official in the Hungarian environmental ministry, who wished to remain anonymous, described the resulting attitude of waste treatment businesses to me this way:

> Westerners think we don't have environmental impact assessment requirements. Then they find out through their tiny consultant firms what [regulations] we have, and they are shocked that they don't receive the permits and that the ministry is not negotiating with them. They think they can just bring whatever they want wherever they want. They think they can bring us fake pearls! (Personal interview, Anonymous official of Environmental Ministry, Budapest, 1997)

The result was a stampede, not only in Hungary, but in the entire region. Between 1988 and 1996, there was an estimated 18 million tons minimum of annual incinerator capacity planned to be built in Russia, the Baltics, Hungary, Poland, the Czech Republic, and Slovakia, with about 93 percent of these capacities offered for export by Western countries.[17] Put another way, there were about 187 proposed facilities in the region, with 10 in Hungary.[18]

In the next chapter I analyze the political and environmental implications of this synergy.

eight

"Building a Castle out of Shit"

The Wastelands of the New Europe

Somehow we never manage to make use of free monies. To wit, we would have received 66 billion Forints [about $300 million] from the [European] Union, of which we so far have managed to use 3.7 billion, that is, four percent of the funds. For example, we will throw six billion out the window by the end of the year if we don't find locations for two regional waste dumps, one in northeastern Pest [County], and one on the northern shore of Lake Balaton. And it does seem like we won't succeed. To wit, in Pest County, the residents of Püspökszilágy, Sződ, Kosd és Kartal so far have said, "no and no, they want no stinking garbage heaps." Because Hungarians fear for their nests—they associate garbage with putrid dung heaps. They are not moved by illegal waste dumps, on which things that rot are rotting, but if they can vote, then a sudden sense of responsibility erupts from them, and they become Greens. And all this because they don't believe that if the dumps are completed they will conform to the strictest environmental standards, and that the multiple [layers of] insulation will ensure that nothing will ever come out of them. ([spider] 2003)

The above quote is only the most colloquially worded opinion of many in the Hungarian media on the never-ending struggle of villages to avoid becoming hosts to toxic waste facilities since the early 1990s. The usual cast of these stories consists of, on the one hand, irrational and stupid villagers, who are seen as having dirty habits and blamed as the reason the country cannot get the money it deserves and so badly needs in order to develop; and on the other hand, the benevolent and generous European Union with high environmental standards. As for the Greens, they are lumped together with the backward and renegade villagers, rather than with progressive Europe. By the time this report was written in 2003, the Greens had long ceased to be the agents of progress and conscience, the heroes who had much to do with the collapse of state socialism. In this chapter, in addition to calling attention to the paradoxes and environmental consequences of the chemical regime, I will also explain how this change in the Greens' role happened in Hungary. First let us review the consequences of privatization in Garé.

Incineration and the Taboo of Waste Production

Ending the state's ownership of BCW's waste was unfortunate for two reasons. First of all, it became harder to justify using state funds (such as the Environmental Protection Fund) to clean up Garé's dump, even though that might have been the quicker solution. Second, with this development, the earlier plan to build a state-owned incinerator in Garé irreversibly lost its rationale. To the extent that, in contrast to state-owned facilities that are run as public utility companies, privatized and profit-oriented incinerators strive to operate at the fullest possible capacity, the choice of entrepreneurial solutions is likely to have significant environmental impacts. The pressure to run an incinerator at maximum capacity not only intensifies the environmental burden of the facility but also has the effect of expanding the circle of "wastes to be liquidated by incineration." This, in turn, weakens even further efforts to reduce and recycle wastes.

Such a tendency could already be detected in the siting controversy of Hungaropec—the joint venture that would have built the incinerator in Garé. The TCB waste and the contaminated soil could have been incinerated in two years if these wastes were burned alone. Hungaropec, knowing that BCW would not be able to pay for the incineration in two years, expected to burn other wastes simultaneously with the TCB waste; but even in this case, five years would have been sufficient to eliminate the drums. Afterwards, Hungaropec would have had to scramble to find enough wastes to run its 17,000 tons of annual capacity at the highest possible utilization rate.

Anticipating that the low volume of regionally available wastes needing incineration could be an argument against its planned incinerator, Hungaropec commissioned a private firm to carry out a survey among waste producers in Baranya to estimate the demand. Hungaropec, however, treated this information confidentially; and since it kept changing its mind, at least publicly, about whether it would liquidate only halogenic wastes (chlorine-containing compounds) or also take on other wastes that do not require high-temperature incineration, it was difficult to determine just what would be burned in its facility and where that waste would come from. This raised suspicions that France or other Western countries would export their wastes to Garé for incineration.

As another part of the tactic to prove that there was sufficient regional or domestic need for its incinerator, Hungaropec publicly warned about the toxicity of the tannery wastes deposited in Garé. The representatives of the tannery, however, claimed that they had no intention of using incineration, partly for financial reasons and partly because the toxicity of these chrome-containing materials was lower than that of the likely by-product of their incineration. Furthermore, they argued that the wastes they had dumped in Garé, or at least some of them, did not fall into the category of the most hazardous toxic wastes that require special treatment.

The point is not who is right in theory; after all, even experts disagree about whether this type of waste is hazardous, incinerable, and to be liquidated by incineration. The point, rather, is that in practice, it is economic interests that define the boundaries of these categories. Profit-oriented incineration does not so much eliminate wastes as produce them. Public discourse that concentrates exclusively on waste distribution does not so much achieve cleanup as produce spaces to be cleaned up.

Privatization and the hegemony of the chemical model had the combined effect of making waste production a nonissue for public discourse. In Garé's case nobody, not even the Greens, talked about halting the delivery of more wastes to the dump, and nobody called for attempting to reuse the wastes of any of the three companies. Greens, active in the case, were not even against incineration in general; at most, they were against establishing new incinerator capacities in otherwise relatively intact environments, and against importing wastes for incineration. Some of them, moreover, would even favor another incinerator planned in Kökény, just a few kilometers from Garé (as shown in fig. 8.2).[1]

It could be said that in Garé's case the focus was necessarily on incineration rather than on waste production, because what was at issue was the liquidation of wastes that already existed. In 1987 BCW, if not the other companies, had already stopped producing the wastes deposited there.

FIGURE 8.1. Map of Hungary and Eastern Europe showing location of Pécs.

However, by focusing the debate solely on this particular incinerator, the question of whether Hungary should establish more incinerators did not even emerge. To the extent that environmental impact assessments and public hearings must concentrate on one concrete investment, extralocal impacts, such as the effect of an increased incinerator capacity on the country's waste practices, are necessarily ignored. This however is not the only shortcoming of the newly established democratic institutions of environmental politics.

Cleanup versus Incineration

Since the system of obligatory and publicly available environmental impact assessments and public hearings is put in motion by the investor, and since as such, they are limited to the discussion of one concrete solution,[2] these seemingly democratic institutions cannot present actual choices to the residents whose opinions they are meant to solicit and respect. The only choice residents have is to agree or disagree with the proposed facility. Because of this limited choice, even citizens or groups otherwise open to some aspects of the proposal have no other choice than to vote against it. In Garé's case, all the surrounding villages voted against the incinerator, and these opposing viewpoints have not gotten closer since the debate started in 1991.

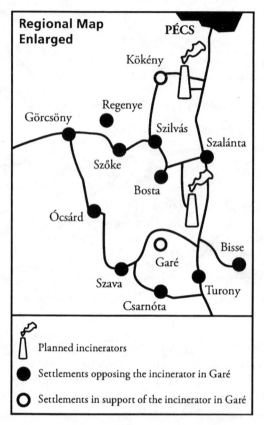

Regional Map Enlarged

PÉCS

Kökény

Regenye

Görcsöny

Szilvás

Szalánta

Szőke

Bosta

Ócsárd

Garé

Bisse

Szava

Turony

Csarnóta

Planned incinerators

Settlements opposing the incinerator in Garé

Settlements in support of the incinerator in Garé

FIGURE 8.2. Map showing the attitude of villages to the incinerator planned by the Budapest Chemical Works. Modified from *Heti Világgazdaság*, February 6, 1993.

In order to understand Garé's position, it is important to review what economic benefits would have accrued to the village had the incinerator been built there. Garéans felt that if they wanted to survive and get rid of their village's role as a literal *and* figurative wasteland, they simply had no choice other than what their opponents called "building a castle out of shit."[3]

Let's see what this castle would have looked like. Garé, like any other settlement after 1990, received funds from the state based on its population size, which had to be spent on maintaining infrastructure and institutions, such as schools or clubs, and organizing local events. This amount, which already included personal income taxes paid by local residents, was about 7.2 million Forints (about $48,000 US) per year.[4] For health services Garé received 2.9 million Forints ($19,300 US) from social security funds, and it raised about 2.3 million Forints ($15,300 US) from interests, rent, and service fees.[5] Thus the basic annual budget of the village was about 12.4 million Forints ($82,700 US), compared to which the amount that Hungaropec offered Garé in return for the land use permit (80 million Forints [$530,000 US]—that is, over six years' budget) certainly appealed to the local elite and residents. In 1994, Garé's government requested an advance of 40 percent of that amount, partly for infrastructure development and partly to cover the investment costs of local waterworks. While some of the development was postponed, the village government distributed 2.6 million Forints ($17,300 US) in aid to individual households just before the 1994 November elections, producing accusations of vote-buying.

If supporting the cause of the incinerator seemed financially advantageous even before starting construction, the long-term benefits promised to be even greater after incineration actually started. Garé would receive shares from the profit, there would be new houses built as well as new infrastructural developments, and construction promised an ample demand for physical labor that would be recruited from the village's unemployed. It was also hoped that these developments as well as lowered or canceled local taxes would spur local entrepreneurial activity.

The village's elite benefited greatly from the cooperation with Hungaropec. First of all, they used the compensation for maintaining their political power; secondly, as villagers told me, they retained some of this new income for themselves by giving local development contracts, paid for by the compensation, to "their people." They also influenced the geographical location of the incinerator in such a way that Hungaropec would have to buy the land from them. The village's increased leverage over other villages and its government's strong bargaining position with a Western company enabled the elite to silence dissent and successfully diminish public control over issues other than the incinerator as well. No wonder that those villagers who fell outside of the circle of beneficiaries complained about abuses that were, according to them, unheard-of under socialism.

If Garé searched in the realm of novel economic activities for a viable economic road, Szalánta seemed a lot closer to an idealized path of transition that relied on the development of more traditional economic activities, primarily agriculture. Szalánta's rate of individual entrepreneurs was barely higher (8 percent of the population) than Garé's (7 percent), but entrepreneurs in Garé tended to be less able to make a living from agriculture (4.5 percent as against 7 percent in Szalánta). In Garé, only 29 percent of the employed worked in agriculture, while in Szalánta 37 percent did. The latter figures put Garé at second from the bottom in the district, while Szalánta was at the top.[6] These local visions of the region's future strongly influenced the position of villages in the public hearings about the incinerators.

Because of its limited focus, the system of public hearings sidetracked negotiations in the 1990s. No longer were the method and the schedule of the cleanup at stake; instead, the question of who should benefit from the cleanup became the primary point on the agenda. If the incinerator in Garé were to materialize, BCW, Hungaropec, and Garé would profit. If, however, the rival incinerator in Kökény were to become a reality, Biomed (the company that would have built it), the county as an investor in the Kökény facility, and, possibly, other surrounding villages would have benefited economically. Building both incinerators not only would mean a greater strain on the environment but also, because of the lack of wastes available regionally, it would make little economic sense. If neither of the facilities in Baranya were built, leaving the waste to be burned in Dorog (the existing incinerator near Budapest), that could benefit the French operator of the Dorog incinerator and also prolong its monopoly, in which case the chemical industry would have to keep paying high prices for having its wastes taken care of. Such were the calculations one heard at various public forums or read in various documents and articles.

In this fierce struggle, waste was transformed from a liability into a commodity whose ownership would make possible and justify a profit-making venture. No wonder that this struggle went on for a decade. In 1995, the Court of Baranya County ruled against the establishment of Hungaropec's incinerator, though years passed before a decision was made about what company would remove the barrels from the Garé dump site. In 2000, the barrels were transported to Germany for incineration, but the incinerator there sent them back, arguing that they contained compounds it had no permit to burn. Finally, the TCB waste was transferred for elimination to the Dorog incinerator. This didn't result in a definitive solution, however.

First, Dorog's residents protested the burning of this unknown type of toxic waste, especially since, environmental groups claimed, the incinerator failed to keep its emissions to the allowed maximum. To the implied criticism that the facility was not the safe high-tech incinerator it was made out to be, an official from the company retorted, "They [residents and Greens] should be looking at the sulfur and the carbon monoxide coming from the local coking plant or from the chimney on every house" (Simons

1993, A8). In the summer of 2004, the incinerator leaked a huge amount of toxic waste into the soil, contaminating local drinking water sources. Residents of surrounding settlements could not drink tap water for two weeks, and the company is now facing not only a huge fine but also an ever-louder demand that the incinerator be shut down. Obviously, it was naive to assume that by incinerating BCW's waste, everything would be fine: the wastes might have been removed but the by-products of their burning could easily spread rather than being localized.

Even as three Western waste incinerator firms were fighting for their turf—a share of the Hungarian waste business—accession to EU membership seemed to offer an alternative to the kind of dragged-out tug-of-war between the pro- and anti-incinerator forces we have seen in Garé. But just as the EU-constituent waste incinerator businesses represent a different Europe from that of the Sixth Environmental Programme aimed at waste prevention, so did different actors in the Garé controversy each appeal to different meanings of Europeanness.

Heading to Europe: The Re- and Degeneration of Local Politics

The novelty of the triumvirate uniting Garé, BCW, and Hungaropec resides not so much in its unlikelihood (a victim with its victimizer; that is, a village with its polluter) as in its example of direct, unmediated relations between a small, disempowered village and a relatively powerful Western company. It is a stark contrast to the past, in which the state held the remote control for Garé's life.

After 1990, the residents of Garé could reach BCW for comment without having to go through Szalánta or other extralocal representatives; and the company, the formerly absent cause of their miseries, suddenly materialized: it was brought near to them, and sat down to negotiate with them. Since then, the company's presence has been made permanent by an office maintained for its French joint venture, Hungaropec, in the town hall. Adding further weight to its presence, Hungaropec organized exhibitions with the aim of popularizing the idea of the incinerator, and published a locally circulated (in ten villages) paper whose title, *Between Ourselves*, expressed rather clearly the intent of BCW and Hungaropec to portray themselves as "one of the villagers."[7] The void created by the state's disappearance from Garé's life, both in financial and administrative terms, was quickly filled by global forces and discourses that the new elite successfully utilized in its own interests under the slogan of cleanup. Such a

FIGURE 8.3. Hungaropec brochure: Information on the incinerator planned in Garé, 1993, Budapest, Burston-Marsteller. Published with the permission of Burston-Marsteller.

direct connection between local and global could not have emerged under socialism, as the state's umbrella shielded localities from global weather, rain or shine.

The state's disappearance from the redistribution of waste not only opened up the space for new structural arrangements and local-global relations, but also made new discursive strategies necessary. This is what I analyze next.

The Incinerator Industry's Europe

If Garé and BCW wanted to successfully deploy the global incinerator industry in their own survival struggles, they first had to sell the idea of "cleanup via incineration" to authorities; and, most importantly, to those villages which now, thanks to democratization, had a say in such investments. Interestingly, the pro-incinerator language applied in the West (that it would bring jobs, tax revenue, improved infrastructure) was much less utilized than a custom-fitted discourse about Garé's insertion into the bloodstream of Europe. The public relations campaign thus drafted a cognitive map[8] that located Hungary and Garé in particular ways vis-à-vis Western Europe. The best visual representation of this cognitive map is the photo on the cover page of the brochure of Hungaropec Ltd. (Hungaropec 1993) (see fig. 8.3). In the top portion there is a close-up of the problem: the barrels, their image filling the outline of the map of the district. In the bottom, partially superimposed on the upper photo, there is a square-shaped, bird's-eye view of one of Entreprise Minière et Chimique's (EMC) reference plants: the incinerator in Saint Vulbas, France. You could not find a more didactic illustration for the story that the Budapest Chemical Works wanted to tell, which went like this: "We have a global solution for a local problem."

The narrative part of the eight-page brochure elaborates on this visually suggested title: the first paragraph talks about the "present situation," the second about the "experiences from abroad," and the third draws the obvious conclusion that the solution consists in the application of experiences from abroad to the present (local) situation. The first paragraph eliminates the history of and agency behind the dump, and it underestimates the ecological dangers, thereby wiping out any remaining traces of the past controversy between Garé and BCW.

> In the vicinity of Garé, there was a significant amount of industrial waste deposited in accordance with the designated location and prescriptions of the authorities. The long-term presence of these wastes *may endanger* the soil, the flora and fauna, agricultural production, the ground- and drinking

water supplies, and, indirectly, people's health. For this reason it is justified and necessary to eliminate and neutralize the wastes stored here, and to re-establish the cleanliness of the environment in the long run. (Hungaropec 1993, 1; emphasis mine)

The next paragraph, anticipating the reader's sense of lack, imaginatively substitutes global histories for the missing local history, and immediately suggests the progressive nature of the solution to be offered in the third paragraph.

Hungary, like her eastern neighbors, was characterized by the dumping of the hazardous by-products of industry, that is by "sweeping the problem under the rug" due to the incorrect industrial policy of the past decades, while in Western European countries with a developed industry and with an ever higher concern about the environment the *most widely accepted solution* has become the *utilization* of industrial wastes *by incineration,* which is already applied in numerous densely populated areas of Western Europe (Switzerland, the Ruhr, the vicinity of Lyon, Strasbourg, etc.). (Hungaropec 1993, 1; emphasis mine)

The third paragraph establishes two unsupported claims: that incineration of the wastes in Garé is the only technologically rational solution, and that the solution must be "entrepreneurial" (Hungaropec 1993, 1).[9] Then the last sentence concludes by saying that Hungaropec Ltd. offers a solution that satisfies both of the above requirements of rationality—the technological and the economical.

In the East/West dichotomy applied in Hungaropec's cognitive map, the "East" becomes synonymous with the past: it is a wasteland that produces so much waste that it threatens its people with "suffocating in garbage" (as expressed by one of the impact study authors), but it is not even credited with having a developed industry. All the East has is an "incorrect industrial policy," industrial by-products (the two thus tacitly connected in a causal relation), and authorities that designate locations and prescribe the technological parameters of waste treatment. What emerges from this distribution of roles is more than just the invitation to the European road, the staple of postcommunist ideology: it implicitly constructs BCW as a victim at the hands of socialist state authorities when dumping, and as a hero when burning the waste it produced, by thus taking Garé into Europe. Indeed, Hungaropec literally took villagers, environmentalists, and journalists for a visit to reference plants in Western Europe in 1993. Individual and collective autobiographies centering around such a passage from victim to hero have been the key source of moral and political capital in Central and Eastern Europe after 1989 (Verdery 1996).

The Other Europe: The Green Perspective

Building moral capital on either side of the Garé incinerator case was a critical strategy. In the reconstruction of the village's independent leadership, and in taking the dump business and, with it, the village's fate into residents' own hands, Garé's collective memory was crucial. Garé could be deprived of all of its past resources and its clean environment, but it could never be deprived of the collective memory of its "good old days." Two churches that are landmarks in Garé served as constant reminders by helping to maintain the villagers' sense of pride, especially vis-à-vis Szalánta, which never had a church, and whose residents were forced to come to Garé for weddings, baptisms, funeral services, and religious holidays. The mistreatment Garéans suffered while under the thumb of Szalánta had always been a key ingredient of this collective memory. In the ensuing conflict about plans to clean up, village leaders cleverly mobilized this collective memory.

The incinerator was viewed by most Garéans as a deserved revenge against Szalánta. Since administration was in Szalánta's hands at the time the permit was issued for the dump, and since it was Szalánta that reaped all of its benefits,[10] Garéans saw Szalánta's residents, more or less collectively, as responsible for the present situation. As a consequence, Garéans believed Szalántans had no moral right to have a say in the decision about the incinerator. Szalánta, however, was quite successful in presenting itself as the guardian of the district's physical and moral health. In doing so it was also able to redefine its leading role in the region, which had been shaken first by the 1990 decentralization and then by Hungaropec's plan to build the incinerator, which would make Garé the most powerful economic settlement in the district.

In resisting the incinerator, local villages, under the leadership of Szalánta, mobilized surrounding towns whose existence hangs on urban and thermal-water tourism and wine production, and whose reputation could easily be ruined by the incinerator. They recruited a competing Swiss-Hungarian joint venture and a French incinerator in Dorog into their ranks by positing them as alternatives to the incinerator in Garé.[11] In addition, they formed an alliance with Hungarian Greens, who provided the villages with information, contacts, suggestions for action, equipment, and publicity.

There were two environmentalist entities active in the case. One, advocating against the incinerator starting in 1989, was the main Green group in the nearby town, the Green Circle of Pécs. The Green Alternative

Party (GAP), based in Budapest, was established in 1993, and for them, the Garé case was a formative issue. Szalánta needed their resources—contacts, information, techniques of political action—and in return, the GAP needed Garé as a salient issue, which it could rally around to generate needed publicity before the 1994 elections. Both Green Circle and the GAP suggested various alternatives to the Garé incinerator. The one that seemed to have the most support from the villagers involved burning the barrels in the already existing incinerator in Dorog; other residents and environmentalists were ready to go along with a mobile incinerator, which could be disassembled and moved elsewhere after cleanup was completed; still others talked about trying the biodegradation method; and a few people, such as the members of Green Circle, might have even preferred the Swiss-Hungarian incinerator planned nearby, for reasons I will clarify later.

Both Green organizations cultivated extensive relations with foreign environmental movements and organizations. Several of their members had been to the 1992 Rio Summit, and they often traveled to meetings in other countries, as well as inviting environmentalists from abroad. Green Circle and GAP asked for information and assistance from Greens in other countries, including the Green fraction of the European Parliament and Greenpeace. The fraction provided them with updates on the incinerator policy of the European Community (about to become the European Union), and it arranged a showing of a Greenpeace video on incinerators in a number of the villages in the area. Green Circle received U.S. Peace Corps volunteers who enriched the group's technical repertoire and made grants with English-language applications more accessible; one of these, a Dutch grant, was used specifically for organizing around Garé. The Austrian Greens were often invited by both environmental organizations to talk on the Garé incinerator, both as experts and as fellow countrypersons of ÖSW (the partner of BCW in the TCB contract). The Hungarian affiliate of a U.S. nonprofit environmental law consulting agency, the Environmental Management and Law Association (EMLA), has been managing without charge several of the lawsuits that have emerged from this case, and has kept the Green alliance up-to-date on the legal tactics used by foreign corporations against environmental activists. In sum, the anti-incinerator agents have been very successful in inserting themselves into and benefiting from the international environmental movement, which is a key pillar of what some call "global civil society" (Lipschutz and Mayer 1996).[12]

As mentioned in the previous chapter, under state socialism, environmental issues functioned as a relatively safe terrain for expressing political dissent, and in many countries (especially in Hungary and Lithuania) the environmental movements were instrumental in bringing down the system. While these fledgling groups and initiatives were certainly informed by Western environmental movements, they developed without much concrete assistance until the late 1980s. After 1989, even though environmentalism was losing its appeal as a political agenda in Eastern Europe, various Western agencies became more active in building cooperation and providing help in many forms to postsocialist environmental organizations (Lipschutz and Mayer 1996).

However, it is not only funds, people, and information that cross borders in this green(ing) civil society, but also discourses. The Green alliance thus drew on one mainstream global environmental discourse—NIMBY-ism[13]—and other less mainstream, but still global, discourses, namely those of ecological colonization and environmental racism. The charge of environmental racism was raised in two contexts. First, it was made in relation to the entire district, if not the whole county, which has an ethnically very heterogeneous population of primarily Croats, Germans, and Romanis. Second, this argument was made more forcefully with respect to Bosta, the village that was the second closest after Garé to the dump and the proposed incinerator. Bosta has a population that is 80 percent Romani, and it had been one of the most disadvantaged villages in the county; it had also been previously economically and administratively fused with Szalánta. Initially, Bosta took Garé's side in the incinerator-siting debate, but when in 1994 the present mayor took her seat, a referendum quickly revealed that the large majority of Bosta's residents opposed the incinerator.

The Greens' insistent efforts to educate Bosta's residents and administration played a major role in this change; however, the economic and social pressure by Szalánta also affected the outcome of the referendum. During the past decades, Bosta's livelihood had grown so dependent on this larger village that the prospect of Szalánta severing these links because of Bosta's decision to support the incinerator had a strong influence on Bosta's residents. They recounted to me confrontations with acquaintances from Szalánta, as well as Szalántans' refusal to continue lending agricultural machines to them. The racist undertones of the 1995 social-economic impact assessment study ordered by Hungaropec (part of the environmental impact assessment study), which Bosta's residents found disgraceful, provided further cement for Bosta's renewed alliance with its former superordinate.

The social-economic impact assessment study of the Garé incinerator was used to try to scare the small villages around Garé into approving the incinerator. The authors of the study tried to scare their populations by saying that they had consistently decreased since 1949, and that they would be "Gypsified" (*elcigányosodnak*) unless there was a boost to their economic development, such as the incinerator. The analysis ignored ongoing Gypsy inmigration, and thus suggested that Bosta, as well as other villages, were approaching extinction. Then, the report brought Romanis back into the analysis, not as a population that could keep the village alive but as yet another force rushing the village to its demise. The deceptive language and misuse of statistics were powerfully confronted in the 1995 Bosta public hearing. The villagers said that, first, eight new families had moved in since last year; second, that it was not their fault that they had not developed and grown; and third, that they were all one people, that is, Hungarian, whether Gypsy or not. While the impact study viewed the incinerator as a way to "keep Gypsies out" of the district, the Romani Civil Rights Foundation, a national human rights group, thought it was exactly the already large ratio of the Romani population that attracted such investments.

In addition to positioning the Garé case on the national map of economic and ethnic relations with claims about ecological colonization and environmental racism, the Greens also used a global cognitive map—but this offered quite a different picture of the West from that of the pro-incinerator map. First of all, Greens took great pains to discredit the expert systems in Hungaropec's references, such as the European Commission/European Union and the Basel Convention (an international treaty on the import and export of hazardous waste adopted in 1989); instead, the Greens exposed the experts as players in the toxic waste export game. The Greens argued that, however high the environmental standards it held for itself, the European Union encouraged the transfer of waste-to-energy facilities to the eastern half of Europe. They also noted that the Basel Convention simply required that toxic wastes be imported and exported with the mutual agreement of both countries, which, they implied, was not likely to be an obstacle in BCW's case.

The villagers and some Greens had an especially poor opinion of France, partly because of its alleged competition with the famous Villányi wine produced nearby, and also because of France's bad historical record vis-à-vis Hungary.

> We have not received anything especially good from the French since Rákóczi's war of independence.[14] So I feel that not until they regain their credit [can we believe them], since so far they only lent a hand to the severing of two-thirds of our country's territory.[15] So now let them leave at least our air for us, and let us live in peace in this country in a manner suitable to a Hungarian. (Speaker at the Baranya County public hearing on the Garé incinerator, Pécs, June 1996)

What about the Greens' image of the East or the state socialist past? Opponents of the incinerator tried to expose Hungaropec and BCW as not a break with, but rather a continuation of socialism. Greens liked to point out that the decision to have a permanent dump in Garé was made under socialism. As one pamphlet said, "a decision made by the State Committee of Planning in 1980 cannot be realized against the will of the region's taxpaying citizens" (Pécsi Zöld Kör n.d., 4). They also saw a parallel between the process of decision making about the waste dump and that about the incinerator. "Once already, there was a bad decision made without us, let's not let another bad decision be made again. . . . I hope . . . we can make a decision based on consensus" (Pécsi Zöld Kör n.d., 5).

Democracy and especially local autonomy are the key arguments of the Greens in the debate; in fact, this is the only positive connotation of "Europe" they acknowledge. This value preference is so strong that it may even take precedence over their environmental principles. Some Greens, for example, would have welcomed the rival Swiss-Hungarian incinerator in nearby Kökény because it would be built from local capital, at least partially, and would incinerate only local (countywide) wastes. One activist stressed to me that the head of the reference plant for this incinerator in Switzerland was a lot "more open and more democratic" in his dealings with the local population than was the leader of Garé and the managements of BCW and Hungaropec (personal interview, Anonymous environmental activist, Pécs, 1996).

Locals were also listening closely to the undertone of Hungaropec's self-praise, which celebrated industrialization. As a participant in the Szalánta public hearing exclaimed, "Socialism is over, and it's not clear that we should be a chemical superpower." This was a tacit reference to the mentioned Hungarian Communist "amen" of the 1960s, "Let's chemicalize!" which, in turn, came after the fall of the 1950s prophecy "We will be the country of iron and steel." Most Hungarian Greens do not reject industrialization in itself, but they do so when it is planned in primarily agricultural areas and otherwise still relatively clean natural environments. They saw Garé's incinerator as the implicit continuation of socialist regional development policy which preferred distributing industry more or less equally on the territory of the country in the name of spatial and social equality.[16]

In sum, the Greens' cognitive map had an opposite gridline: rather than taking us to that paradise-like Europe, Western firms were bringing Europe to the local backyards. But this Europe was different—it was a regressive and even criminal force. For the opponents of the incinerator, Western European firms were not exporting solutions to local problems but rather their

FIGURE 8.4. Poster by Hulladék Munkaszövetsék, 1994, portraying a pig pulling a cart from which piles of Coca-Cola have spilled. "We are going to Europe, we are taking all we have."

wastes and *their* local problems—lack of domestic demand for their waste treatment technologies—and thus were making these problems global. According to the Greens, becoming European or Western—in the dictionary of agents like EMC and Hungaropec—meant, rather than cleaning up, importing waste in the form of Western, high waste-ratio consumer goods and in the form of actual waste to be treated in state-of-the-art Western facilities. Hungarians might tacitly agree that they live in a wasteland in need of a cleanup; but, by accepting Western waste so as to run the incinerator facilities bought from the West for the benefit of Western investors, they would really end up as "the cesspool of Europe," as one local doctor put it, and thus reinforce their wasteland image. This Catch-22, endorsing development via waste treatment and joining Europe via waste incineration, was thus exposed by Greens as a false transition consciousness.

Is it any clearer at the national level what Europeanization will mean? More importantly, will EU membership prevent impasses such as Garé's? In order to answer such questions I must review how EU accession has influenced Hungary's waste policies.

Europeanizing Hungary's Waste Policies

What changes were needed in order to meet EU requirements? In order to understand Hungary's harmonization tasks, we need to know what characterized the country's waste situation and how it differed from that of the European Union on the eve of the accession, at the new millennium.[17]

I will now proceed to quote the available waste statistics for pre-accession Hungary—as found in the National Waste Management Plan (NWMP) of 2000—with the caveat that, as I pointed out in chapter 1 for waste statistics in general, the categorizations employed are fuzzy and relations between them are unclear; in sum, they are less than fully reliable.[18] Hungary produced roughly 70 million tons of waste per year, with 28 million tons being biomass.[19] Of the nonbiomass waste, roughly 70 percent was production waste and 6 percent municipal waste (with municipal liquid waste roughly 11 percent). Five percent of all wastes (roughly 3.4 million tons, that is, 8 percent of nonbiomass waste) were classified as hazardous.[20] In comparison, the European Union's municipal waste ratio without liquid waste was 14 percent, which meant that in Hungary, the share of municipal solid waste was considerably lower than that in the European Union. This reflected not so much a "lower developmental stage," as is commonly implied, but a state socialist past in which consumption was shunned and economic growth was forced, even if it meant high waste-ratio production and thus high levels of industrial waste. High waste ratios did not constitute a problem for a social order that ruthlessly pursued 100 percent recyclability.

The rate of recycling for municipal solid waste in Hungary was 3 percent, compared to the European Union's average 15 percent. The existing (measured around the turn of the millennium) rates of recycling in former socialist countries were similar to several EU members' rates (such as those of Ireland and Portugal), but in general were lower than average rates for the EC as a whole in the 1980s. In contrast to this difference in municipal waste data, the recycling rate for hazardous wastes was 20 percent in Hungary as compared to 8 percent in the European Union. Given that dumping and incinerating hazardous waste was environmentally more risky then recycling it, one would have expected policymakers to welcome this "difference" and, instead of slating all existing policy tools for elimination, to study what allowed Hungary to surpass the allegedly environmentally more progressive European Union in this regard.

Out of the country's 3,000 municipalities, 2,700 had landfills. As was often pointed out, there was a dump in practically every village, though this included "the smallest ditch" (personal interview, Hilda Farkas, Environmental Ministry official, Budapest, 2003). There were 665 registered and municipally run landfills for municipal waste, of which only 15 percent met the existing technological standards. In addition, however, there were also 620 smaller dump sites, not registered and most likely not fulfilling safety requirements.

There was also just one modern hazardous waste landfill, in Aszód, which only took wastes for final (rather than temporary) disposal, 10,000 tons per year. Its overall capacity was 300,000 tons, which was not expected to be filled until about 2020. There was one major hazardous waste incinerator in the country, in Dorog, with a capacity of 25,000 tons per year, and there were some minor incinerators, and some recently built and some older cement kilns, which added up to an overall capacity of 85,000 tons for hazardous waste incineration.

Therefore, assuming no import or export of hazardous wastes, Hungary could not incinerate more than 3 percent of its hazardous wastes. The overall amount of waste actually incinerated cannot be ascertained from the available data, because in the NWMP it is lumped together with other types of elimination, such as the desiccation of liquid municipal waste. While the Environmental Ministry official in charge of the database was unable to clarify this amount (personal interview, Hilda Farkas, Environmental Ministry official, Budapest, 2003), according to my estimates from the available data, the ratio of incineration for all wastes was unlikely to be more than 11 percent. Compared to the practice of many EU countries that incinerated as much as a quarter of their *total* wastes and had dozens of incinerators, Hungary's rates seem very low.[21]

On average, according to the European Environment Agency's report of 1999, accession countries had higher per capita industrial waste ratios than EU members, the reverse of the municipal waste-ratio difference noted above. These aggregate averages however do not allow extrapolation to Hungary. Its industrial waste per $1,000 of GDP was 72 kilograms, which can be said to be in the middle range of Western European EU countries, and well below Finland's 118 kilograms and the Czech Republic's staggering 288 kilograms. Similarly, and even more unambiguously, with 490 kilograms of municipal wastes per capita, Hungary seems to belong more to the West than to the East (should we insist on such characterizations). Its municipal waste per capita was higher than other candidate countries we have data for, and even higher than that of some EU members.

In sum, the areas in which Hungary's waste situation seems to have been significantly and structurally different from the European Union's prior to accession are: (a) a smaller proportion of municipal wastes among total wastes generated; (b) a significantly smaller proportion of reuse and recycling, except in hazardous wastes; and (c) a significantly smaller proportion of incineration than the EU average. These differences led to a higher rate of landfilling and a lower capacity for hazardous waste treatment through modern landfilling and incineration technologies. To the West, Hungary appeared underdeveloped based on its waste generation structure and "waste-efficiency'" indicators (primarily measured by its waste/GDP ratio). The common claim, here in the words of a study by regional experts, that "the situation in the Central and East-European countries resembles to a high degree the situation in OECD countries in the 1980s, when landfilling was the main disposal technique," is not completely off the mark (Eurowaste 2001).

This statement is misleading, however. First, it rests on the common misinterpretation of Hungary's socialist past as ignoring waste problems and lacking policy tools to deal with them. In the 1980s, Hungary actually pursued recycling and discouraged landfilling much more than it does now and, according to my estimates in chapter 5, more than the OECD did then as well. In sum, the difference between the European Union and Hungary was not simply that of quantity, indicating a lower stage on the same developmental trajectory, but of quality, owing to a difference in the respective developmental trajectories themselves.

Furthermore, Western European countries had not made much progress in developing alternatives to landfilling either, which at the turn of the millennium still was the treatment option of choice for close to two-thirds of municipal waste (European Environment Agency 1999). Finally, unlike Hungary, the European Union had not yet managed to uncouple its waste generation from economic growth: between 1993 and 2003, economic growth averaged 6 percent in the European Union, while waste generation grew by 10 percent annually. In Hungary, according to data provided in the NWMP, overall waste generation declined from 106 million tons in 1990 to 68.7 million tons in 2000, during which period economic growth, while initially negative, rebounded to around 5 percent through the second half of the 1990s. While an increase in waste generation was registered in the last few years of the nineties, no increase was expected in the first decade of the new millennium, according to the NWMP.

The data discussed above were not used as context at the time the European Commission established the accession requirements for former state socialist countries. The European Union departed from three assumptions: (1) Hungary, like other former socialist countries, had no environmental waste legislation to speak of; (2) it lacked the technical and institutional infrastructure necessary for implementing modern waste management methods; and (3) without Western assistance, Hungary was incapable of implementing progressive change. As a market analysis from 2001 stated, "Most of the current environmental difficulties arise from the fact that environmental policy was virtually non-existent under the communist regime" (Trade Partners UK 2001, 2).

Why were Hungary's achievements in regulating waste production ignored? One of the main reasons was that statistical data prevailed in the representation of centrally planned economies; but more importantly, that such statistics concentrated on ratios of waste to GDP, rather than on waste per capita or ratios of recycling of industrial waste—data that would have demonstrated faults with Western waste practices and highlighted the advantages of state socialism, or at least that could have presented a more balanced picture (see chapter 1). This way, perhaps, the functioning elements of socialist waste policies could have been preserved. Second, "indigenous" economists, mostly informed by neoliberal paradigms, themselves despised the state's intervention in the economy, including policies promoting waste reduction and reuse. Third, state socialist waste policies and practices, while not entirely unknown to Western academics and journalists, were not considered to be of an environmental nature, but rather were viewed as merely a curious element of central planning, and thus their significance was left unexplored. Finally, the increasingly visible and the truly horrendous environmental record of state socialism in Hungary, in the eyes of Western observers and Hungarian reference economists, simply dwarfed any positive achievements of the former regime's relationship to the environment. As a result, policymakers, both Hungarian and EU experts, came to the conclusion in the early 1990s that Hungary must start from a blank slate, which first required that the old be erased.

Based on the discrepancies between Hungarian and EU waste practices (if not principles), the European Union had two major concerns. First, it wanted to make sure that by admitting Hungary (and other former socialist countries) it would not unduly add to environmental problems caused by wastes. That the European Union had such fears is apparent from studies lamenting that, given present-day data, its waste output would double when the first wave of candidate countries joined. Not only would enlargement worsen the European Union's waste statistics, it was also feared that candidate countries' loose environmental standards would offer an undesirable competitive advantage over existing members. Paradoxically, it had been exactly this laxity of enforcement (though not of standards) that lured EU-constituent businesses to the region. Apparently, EU officials could not decide between the European Union's environmental principles and its economic interests. In 2002, it granted exemptions to Hungary, along with most other candidate countries, from fulfilling EU requirements concerning waste policies. Hungary received a four-year exemption from implementing legislation conforming with EU regulations on hazardous wastes and on the recovery and recycling of packaging wastes, as well as a fifteen-year grace period in the area of urban waste-water treatment.

Indeed, we cannot appreciate the full relevance of the enlargement unless we treat the European Union not merely as a bundle of legal and institutional arrangements, as is usually done in studies of the eastern enlargement, but also as a powerful global actor that represents and is supported by specific (rather than universal) economic interests. Western European critiques of the European Union often bring attention not merely to the commonplace of democratic deficit, that is, a lack of influence by citizens over decision making, but also to the corporate voices that do have control over many decisions and resources. Similarly, catching up with the European Union with regard to waste treatment capacities is not merely a humanitarian or an environmentalist goal. While the European Union sees itself as the environmental conscience of the world and has played important leadership roles in numerous environmental issues in the international arena, its actual legislation, policy, and aid vis-à-vis Eastern

Europe reflect Western European interests in exporting end-of-pipe technology. In this regard, I will now address two different modes of EU presence in former socialist countries, and examine the extent to which these different modes are complementary or contradictory to the European Union's presence as a set of laws. I will examine the likely effects in the future on Hungary's waste practices from, on the one hand, certain EU-constituent businesses and, on the other, European Union aid.

The economic prognosis for the postsocialist environmental cleanup sector already looked good right after the fall of state socialism: the market for environmental services in Eastern Europe and the former Soviet Union was expected to double in the first half of the 1990s (Trumbull 1994, 8) (see table 8.1). As no market analysis of Eastern Europe has since failed to mention, the big opportunity for environmental business in the region comes from former socialist countries' desire to join the European Union. "The goal of EU accession is the main driver for improvement of the environment in Hungary and the recent attention given to the latter (after a sluggish start) by the Hungarian authorities looks set to continue," says a UK analysis (Trade Partners UK 2001, 2). This is good news for investors. "The size of the Hungarian environmental services market was valued at US$700 million in 1997 and was expected to rise about 40 per cent to the end of 2000. Further growth between 2000 and 2010 is expected" (Trade Partners UK 2001, 3). A study published by Frost and Sullivan also emphasizes that "by far the most important driver of the [municipal waste management] market over the forecast period is expected to be EU expansion and harmonization, leading to the increasingly urgent need to raise standards and improve infrastructures" (quoted in Davies 2000, 3). A study commissioned by the U.S. Department of Commerce also implies that, were Western doors to close to Hungary, the country's environmental record would be unlikely to improve (Svastics 1999). As noted by the study's author, Kinga Svastics, "The fact that Hungary became a member of the OECD in 1996 and subsequently made a commitment to joining the European Union (EU) has increased government attention to environmental issues" (1999, 1). The same study explicitly laments that "municipal waste incineration is very scarce in Hungary" (Svastics 1999, 8). In the words of an American banker investing in the export of waste treatment facilities, answering doubts expressed as to whether East Europeans can pay for such technologies, "If they want to become part of the greater European community, I don't see they have much of a choice" (Schwartz, Koehl, and Breslau 1990).

As I analyzed above, Western waste incinerator firms placed the entire

Table 8.1. Market for Contaminated Site Cleanup in Europe*

Country	Number of sites	Costs of cleanup
Austria	400	404
Belgium	300	303
Bulgaria	2,000	1.8bn
Czechoslovakia	3,000	2.7bn
Denmark	240	243
Finland	200	202
France	1,000	899
Germany, West	10,200	5bn
Germany, East	50,000	7bn**
Greece	100	101
Hungary	2,750	2.4bn
Ireland	34	30
Italy	900	904
Netherlands	480	485
Norway	150	152
Poland	7,000	6.3bn
Portugal	80	81
Sweden	400	506
Switzerland	400	404
USSR	52,500	47bn

Source: *Environmental Markets in Europe*, September 1991, from Department of Trade and Industry, Environmental Unit, UK, quoted in Newman and Foster 1993, 334–335.

*The data show the number of contaminated sites (involving hazardous wastes) and estimated costs of cleanup in million pounds sterling.

**The three highest values are highlighted.

postsocialist region of Europe under a veritable siege. Unfortunately, EU accession was unlikely to deter such imports. The previously cited National Waste Management Plan (NWMP) for 2003–2008, the main goal of which was to harmonize Hungary's waste policies with those of the European Union, called for six new incinerators, even though in the parliamentary debate on the NWMP one Environmental Committee member considered the four or five mentioned in an earlier draft excessive (Parliamentary Committee Minutes 2001). Furthermore, the NWMP stated that "Hungary must have a nation-wide incineration capacity of 170 thousand [metric] tons/year"—a doubling of its pre-accession capacity (NWMP 2000, 28). The plan appears hardly more negotiable than five-year plans under state socialism:

> In certain sensitive regions of the country (e.g. where industrial activities are concentrated, where the geological conditions are special, where tourism represents a seasonal change, or where several of these factors are present simultaneously) construction of an incinerator can be postponed for a certain period of time, but *in the long term there is no alternative to the disposal of the remaining waste.* (NWMP 2000, 28; emphasis mine)

What compelled the NWMP authors to elevate the pumping-up of incinerator capacity to a national law? Was it the pressure of industrial lobbies in the end-of-pipe technology sector, or was it the Western opinion that Hungary was backward in terms of its incinerator capacity? Or was it the synergy between the backwardness discourse and the economic interests that put its stamp so powerfully on the future waste practices of the country? Either way, how such interests prevail, how this synergy comes about, and how the synergy is reproduced all need to be examined.

Processes of Change

First, the European Union tells Hungary what waste treatment capacities it needs in order to be accepted as truly European. Then, it provides the "aid" to fulfill the requirements. Finally, most of this aid makes its way back to EU-constituent producers of environmental technologies. Three main funds were established for assisting former socialist countries in their transitions and in adopting the *Acquis*. The earliest was PHARE (Poland/Hungary Aid for the Reconstruction of the Economy), followed by ISPA (Instrument for Structural Policies for Pre-Accession) for transportation and environmental objectives, and SAPARD (Special Accession Programme for Agriculture and Rural Development) for agricultural and regional development. Among Hungary's ISPA funds, waste management projects received priority. Out of the total ISPA contribution between 2000 and

2002 (547 million Euros), 30 percent was awarded to various waste management projects (not including waste-water treatment, another preference area).

Westerners were thus not merely entering the cleanup market: by replacing Hungarian legislation and standards with those of the European Union, they were creating it. I do not have access to data regarding whether technologies or firms from "old" (pre-enlargement) EU countries are the most common beneficiaries of these projects (and most of the bidding is still open). Clearly, however, firms from Western Europe have an advantage in this market. After all, they know best what will truly conform to EU standards. Market analyses also demonstrate that Eastern Europeans prefer Western environmental technology to domestic alternatives (Regional Environmental Center 1997). Furthermore, non-EU firms are excluded from bidding on projects to be completed with EU funds (unless through their European subsidiaries), much to the annoyance of the United States and Canada. North American market studies explicitly lament the small and decreasing share of U.S. companies in the Eastern European waste technologies market. With the departure of the U.S. giant Waste Management from the region at the end of the 1990s, this situation seems to be irreversible. Such an exclusion makes it clear that the primary aim of "environmental" aid is not for Eastern Europe to adopt the environmentally most beneficial solutions through completely open bidding, according to the principle of "best available technology." The goal is rather to turn the region into a market for Western European goods.[22]

The compromise of environmental principles becomes even clearer when we consider that the bidding announcements for these waste projects call for building new landfills. With the pretext that old, dangerous landfills had to be eliminated, the NWMP aimed at establishing a network of regional dumps, so all settlements would have a landfill for municipal solid waste within a 30-kilometer radius. The defenders of the NWMP argued that, at this density, landfills would become profitable (Parliamentary Committee Minutes, 2001). But if the goal to reduce waste amounts was to be achieved, would that not change the profitability calculations? Was the NWMP conforming to EU waste practices or to EU waste principles, and, if the latter, to which one?

May policymakers have been motivated more to follow the Proximity Principle than to decrease waste and dumping? The Proximity Principle, according to which waste should be disposed of as close as possible to where it is generated, works well in countries where there is already a network of legal and up-to-date dumps. However, in the candidate countries, where the existing network is insufficient either in safety standards or in capacity, it may act as an unintended inducement to build dumps, further marginalizing waste prevention goals. More importantly, as long as waste dumping receives generous EU funding, and waste reduction receives only symbolic gestures in programmatic documents, the policy emphasis on the expansion of landfill capacity will reinforce the existing motivation for end-of-pipe technologies. In the long run, it may lock in future waste practices, making a (hypothetical) move in a more preventative direction less and less feasible.

In this analysis, the NWMP was itself the realization of the practical consequences of both EU aid and EU business, cementing end-of-pipe technologies as the favored method of dealing with unwanted materials. In fact, the plan aimed to radically overhaul the existing economic incentives for recycling and reuse in order to relax restrictions and penalties waste producers would otherwise face. While constituting a new policy tool, an alternative to the existing system of product charges, passed at the end of December 2002, was weak. The Hungarian Parliament then voted against the further relaxation of the producers' responsibility in the product charges system. It is clear, nevertheless, that the pressure remains from industry to loosen waste legislation, and especially to forgo economic incentives for waste minimization and recycling.

In this often fierce struggle between industrial lobbies and environmentalists, the meaning of Europeanness was also contested. Since Europe is a powerful symbol, most participants in the debate tried to define their positions as closer to that of the European Union. There are several difficulties in evaluating such claims. First, it was never clear whether the reference was to EU law or to EU practice. In that regard, it may be said that the NWMP conformed not to EU ambitions—which, as mentioned, place reuse and recycling above incineration and dumping in the waste management hierarchy—but rather to EU practice, which still favors dumping.[23]

Second, in the case of waste policy tools, what policies conform to EU guidelines remained quite ambiguous. While the European Union laid down the desired principles and goals of waste management in directives that the member countries adopted in the course of a few years, how a member country's state apparatus attempted to achieve those goals remained within the scope of national authority, and thus varied. As a result, even though not all old EU members had put these principles into law, on the eve of the accession there were already diverse models in place in Western Europe in the different areas of waste management. Not all were equally effective and presumably not all were equally practical for Hungary. There was quite a variety of methods, especially for achieving EU objectives concerning packaging wastes and recycling. While Hungarian environmental activists continued to demand the maintenance and strengthening of the system of product charges and the reinstitution of deposit systems, their opponents (the association representing manufacturing interests, and, occasionally, ministry officials) pointed to various EU principles protecting the uninhibited workings of the market. During the screening process, for example, the European Union objected to Hungarian product charges, arguing that they ultimately acted as production subsidies. (Since product charges are supposed to be pumped back to the companies for extending their reusing and recycling capacities, they can be seen as a form of subsidy.) The European Union also prohibits obliging producers/distributors to levy deposit charges on packaging materials, since those may function as hidden import duties. This was the explicit reasoning behind the European Commission's ruling in 2004 that Germany must change its packaging deposit law because it is a barrier to intra-EU trade.

There was also the question of which set of laws and policy tools could actually guarantee that Hungary would fulfill its promise to achieve a 50 percent recycling rate for packaging waste by 2006 (in accordance with the temporary exemptions granted by the European Union). Considering all these constraints—in quotas, policy tools, and principles—and the existing diversity in practices, EU-conformity turned out to be a slippery concept. Thus, it was adaptable to political agendas of all kinds.

The Politics of Waste Distribution

With the hegemony of the chemical model complete by the second half of the eighties, waste started to be seen as increasingly negative, as something useless and as something to discard. Even a quick glance at the media representation of waste problems reveals this conceptual shift. During state socialism, even in its late period in which waste was already seen as a source of environmental degradation, articles about discovered and implemented waste-reuse possibilities, and even muckraking reports about "wasted materials," had abounded. Now, however, all one could find were articles suggesting that waste was something inherently negative and harmful, and thus to be gotten rid of. "Waste Trade: Rusty Markets," "Asbestos Waste Scandal," and "The Best Solution Is to Shoot the Garbage Up to the Moon" were some of the characteristic headlines.

Public discourse, furthermore, entirely shifted to issues of waste distribution, that is, to questions of what to do with already produced wastes. Issues of waste production, such as questions of how to prevent wastes or what controls should be in place for products or technologies that generated especially large volumes of wastes or hard-to-deal-with toxic by-products, became taboo. The free citizens of postsocialist democracy might have a say in where to dump or incinerate, and how the economic benefits of such facilities should be distributed, but they could never question "purely economic decisions" about waste-generating investments, and about what should be done with by-products. And those few who tried to expand the terms of the debate to issues of waste generation found themselves instantaneously charged with "infringing on the principle of free market" (Bödecs 1996, ix) and being backwards (Bánhidy 1996; Bödecs 1996, viii), and they were labeled as "religious fanatics" who based their arguments on emotions rather than on "expert objectivity" (Bánhidy 1996).

Indeed, the neoliberal economic rationalism paradigm has much to do with the taboo on regulating waste production. With the sanctity of private property, production, including the production of waste, became a private matter. This economic rationalism, however, was not the only possible path to take, as I indicated previously. Simply by reading the many EU declarations and the EU environmental programs promoted in glossy brochures, one could have been justified in expecting that the ecological modernization path would have been a foregone conclusion for the postsocialist transition. The type of capitalism under which the European Union was expanding to Eastern Europe, however, embraced neoliberal globalization and, equally importantly, had the waste incineration industry as one of its most profitable sectors.

Furthermore, nowhere was it acknowledged that late socialist environmental policies were already heading in the ecological modernization direction by virtue of their more "progressive," more prevention-centered environmental discourse. In fact, even the more moderate recommendation of a group of U.S. and Hungarian experts that the "assessment of the effectiveness and deficiencies of institutions established by the previous regime for the purpose of environmental protection is an inevitable precondition of designing new institutions" (Bochniarz and Kerekes 1994, 13) fell on deaf ears. As a result of this blind, tabula rasa approach, the Hungarian path toward preventative policies was abandoned, and the economic rationalism discourse prevailed. Since this paradigm expects environmental improvement solely from market incentives, the state was kicked out of regulating waste production, which in turn led to the abandonment of preventative policies.

The disappearance of the state in the first half of the 1990s had particularly grave effects on the long-term resolution of Garé's case. Should the state have done what a well-behaved state in capitalism is supposed to do: let the market run the show? Or, rather, should it have stepped in, thereby committing the biggest crime of postcommunist states: a "capricious intervention" thus "weaken[ing] or undermin[ing] the operation of market actors and market forces" (Schöpflin 1995, 67)? These were the alternatives the economic rationalism discourse presented at the beginning of the 1990s. If, for example, the state had pushed through cleanup, either by more drastic administrative action or by allocating state funds for it, it would have delegitimized the presence of a Western, profit-oriented business in Garé's vicinity, implying a familiar (from state socialism) politics of closing Western capital out and manually operating the economy.

However, in Garé's case the Hungarian state indeed opted for being a grade-busting student of liberalism, inasmuch as it let a Western incinerator firm keep forcing the idea of cleanup via profit-oriented incineration, thus delaying actual cleanup until a final decision based on the "rule of law" was made. In this local case of the politics of waste distribution, public discourse did not even include a discussion of alternative cleanup methods; it was simply limited to the question of who should benefit from an already decided waste liquidation method. With the emphasis having shifted away from restoring a healthy environment in the village, BCW successfully eschewed obeying orders to start cleanup or to at least stabilize the environmental situation by blaming the delay on the legal proceedings, more precisely on the opponents of the incinerator, who kept appealing decisions favorable to the company.

The state's role up until 2000 was exhausted in facilitating the public hearings and deliberating at various geographical levels of authority. The first decision, made by the Southern Transdanubian regional environmental authority, denied the permit for the incinerator; the second, made at the national level, granted the permit; and the third, which was the result of a civil lawsuit against the national authority that charged it with endangering public health and the environment, obliged the regional authorities to start the process of impact studies and public hearings all over again. Appealing this decision, Hungaropec eventually lost the case and the state forced BCW to clean up, while also setting aside funds for loans with favorable terms to assist the company. Subsequently, debates have occasionally erupted around whether and which "government-near" (*kormányhoz közeli*) companies would win the bid to transport the drums, or clean the soil, or burn the wastes. Such debates and the brakes on state capacity discussed in chapter 7—privatization, cutting back funding and staff of regulatory and enforcement bodies, the sanctity of private property—led to a substantial delay in the cleanup. The barrels were finally taken away but, as of August 2004, Garé was still waiting for 100,000 tons of soil to be decontaminated.

What we can learn from the waffling, the suggested illegal efforts to win the state's favor, and the heavy-handed accusations about bidding irregularities[24] is that various actors, even as they turn to private, entrepreneurial solutions or, alternatively, to grassroots ones, have a strong need for the state's larger involvement, which it cannot provide. In interviews I conducted, villagers from Garé and Szalánta seemed equally weary of the various meetings, voting, and the legal battles—sometimes resolved in their favor, sometimes in favor of their opponents—leaving them nostalgic for the seemingly simpler and faster, even if not democratic, decision-making system of state socialism. Many of those I interviewed even said that if state socialism had not collapsed, the dump would be long gone and the problem solved; but they rarely went as far as calling for the present state's more direct involvement. This might indicate a deep lack of trust in the state's capacity, but it might also indicate the effect of prominent anti-etatist, postcommunist ideologies.

The retreat of the state from the terrains of production and regional development freed even previously disempowered and silenced rural communities such as Garé to organize politically around environmental issues. It also made it possible for environmentalists to come to the aid of those villages such as Szalánta which previously had not enjoyed the expertise of urbanites, and to help them exercise their democratic rights in environmental decision-making processes. On the one hand, such an alliance, just like the alliance between Garé and international capital, indicates the acknowledgment that local communities require coalitions with broader visions, expertise, and political capital in order to realize their environmental interests. The villages' tug-of-war, on the other hand, indicates that the state should have taken on a more active mediating role.

Until the state became more active in 2000, by providing information and resources and delegating administrative capacity to finally start the cleanup, the new freedom had been paralyzing. The result had been a nonresult: the deferment of the cleanup under the pretext of striving for entrepreneurial and democratic decisions. If state socialism had mostly been characterized by power through the incalculable, professionally ungrounded, and politically unchecked decisions of the state, the first decade of postsocialism was characterized by what John Gaventa (1980) would call power through the "non-decisions" of a fragmented state held in check by the private sector.

Activists and environmental experts hoped the European Union would change all this and prevent Garé-type cases by strengthening the state in demanding and enforcing high environmental standards, and by explicitly demanding civil input and assisting NGOs. So far these expectations have not been fulfilled. First of all, as I indicated, Hungary, as did other post-socialist countries, received deferment from complying with various environmental standards, especially waste-related ones. Second, the European Union still provides funds only for end-of-pipe technologies, and its constituent corporations have benefited greatly from EU demands for a vigorous environmental cleanup sector.

The involvement by NGOs has mostly been a window-dressing measure. The European Commission has loudly solicited NGO participation in the accession negotiations. But, as these NGOs now lament, this has been merely a symbolic gesture. First, NGOs were excluded from committees deciding ISPA and SAPARD grants, where numerous decisions with long-term consequences were made. Second, the meetings between the Environmental Directorate General and green NGOs of the region have been futile. The NGOs, armed with data and expert studies in the best spirit of professionalism, demanded the introduction of accession requirements to safeguard their countries' biodiversity from the adverse ecological effects of meeting other EU requirements, in the areas of infrastructure (road construction) and agriculture. Yet the Commission repeatedly prevented the NGOs' comments and opinions made at these meetings from being printed in the resulting summaries of the minutes. It "did not want to be held accountable later for not fulfilling promises made there" (personal interview, Anonymous environmental activist, Szentendre, 2000). Ultimately, there were no practical steps taken to enforce NGO-suggested accession conditions. Furthermore, as I indicated above, when civil organizations have mobilized against waste dumps to be financed by EU funds, they have been looked at with suspicion and have been accused of representing various ideological extremes from left to right.

There is indeed a certain danger here of one particular political camp expropriating environmental claims to their advantage. How this process happens is worth describing. In the chemical model, the state, the corporations, and civil society are all locked in the vicious circle of producing waste that needs to be dumped or incinerated, regulating these technologies but not finding willing communities to live with waste elimination facilities. However, since such decisions are made based on science, democratic legislation, and public hearings, the entire regime of waste production and dealing with wastes appears perfectly rational and democratic. Consequently, this hegemonic discourse makes alternative solutions appear irrational and undemocratic. No wonder that after 1989 the Green movement in postsocialist countries, especially the segment of it critical of end-of-pipe technologies, lost its credibility despite its prominent role in bringing down state socialism.

The other consequence of the powerful stigmatization of environmentalism with irrationalism is that citizens and some environmentally concerned activists have become attracted to self-consciously irrational and undemocratic politics. One of the first Green parties, the Party of Hungarian Greens (PHG), went as far as making the historic connection between environmental pollution and the health of the nation. By 1992, this culminated in an agenda in which declining health and growing sterility were primarily interpreted as a problem of national survival, and in which concerns with the cleanliness of the body and nature quickly led to calls for racial purity.[25] Fortunately, Hungarians have not found this party attractive, although in 1994 preelection polls gave it 10 percent of voter support. By comparison, no Green party in Hungary has yet reached the 5 percent threshold necessary to get into Parliament. It must be realized that this chauvinist wing of the Greens is further discrediting the environmental movement.

It is clear that the conservative parties in Parliament have established hegemony by appealing to citizens' patriotism and their feelings of vulnerability as a nation. The fact that no left or liberal politician would represent the interests of villagers who oppose such waste treatment facilities already indicates the alliance of nationalism and environmentalism. In the last few years, it is the right-wing conservative party, FIDESZ (Fiatal Demokratàk Szövetsége—Federation of Young Democrats), that has consistently elevated various environmental controversies into parliamentary discussions and into the media. The FIDESZ Party has also been the one most consistently resisting incinerators and the newly planned dumps funded by EU monies. Surely there is an elective affinity between nationalism and the body discourse of the chemical model. Both thrive on a victimized subjectivity, and both are suspicious of Western corporations and intentions. Nationalism, furthermore, not only equates nature with the nation, but also equates threats to humans with threats to the nation those humans belong to. The European Union, or, better said, EU-philic politicians have not yet managed to earn the trust of green activists and citizens concerned about their immediate environment.

Lock-In

Is any of this a reversible trend? In my view, there are serious limits to what the European Union, even if it wanted to, could achieve in the interests of an environmentally saner society. The very privatization and liberalization the European Union demanded of candidate countries, and the simultaneous dominance of the chemical model helped to hegemony by Hungary's waste history, are together locked in the path I called economic rationalism, as well as the preference for end-of-pipe solutions in particular. One could argue that a truly preventative European Union may still do away with the negative tendencies of the 1990s. But while laws and policies are indeed reversible, their effects are rarely so.

The postsocialist transition and Hungary's subsequent Europeanization have not only been about markets and law. First, they have had much to do with the technological choices corporations have invested in, and this has meant that prospective later changes, such as waste-preventing innovation, would be technically difficult and costly. These corporations therefore would do whatever they can to prevent such a turn. Second, the radical economic and political transformations of the transition have required and called for a new kind of culture and a new kind of subjectivity. The particular way in which a postsocialist society has so far gone about joining the West produces a certain kind of consumer, employee, or manager. The thrifty and waste-conscious material culture that developed under state socialism may today seem backward and contrary to "European" consumerism, rendering preventative waste policies less attractive and achievable only later and at a much greater social cost. Given that the European Union encourages increasing consumption, it is hardly a surprise that, despite the Fifth Environmental Action Programme, waste generation is on the increase in the Western European countries. Similarly in Hungary, short of explicit policy tools to rein in consumption, it seems that even the more modest plans for increasing waste efficiency will fail.

Third, the environmental effects are themselves irreversible and call for a further strengthening of end-of-pipe solutions. The first ten years of postsocialism in Garé led to the spread of toxic waste and its seeping into groundwater, thus creating more wastes to be cleaned up (more soil, more water) than were there originally in 1990. Since the European Union provides no funds for waste prevention, and since no technology transfer is happening in this area, dumping and incineration will be more and more necessary. In sum, neither the developmental path nor the environmental effects of the past fifteen years are reversible.

The recent history of the state's effort to site one of the regional waste dumps projected in the NWMP suggests Garé has not been an exception or simply a leftover case from state socialism, but rather the prototype of what is now happening. Yes, eventually, there will be villages who will say yes. After all, thanks to globalization and EU policies, many villages will find, just as Garé did, that they cannot make a living from agriculture, and will feel attracted to the EU funds allotted for waste treatment facilities.

The European Union sends mixed messages to Hungary on waste policy issues. On the face of it, the European Union is for preventative waste policies and is concerned about the environmental effects of economic growth. This is the position espoused in the Environmental Action Plans, the directives, and the programmatic studies. However, in terms of actual practices, particularly investments and economic and infrastructure requirements, the European Union stands for unsustainable development and for putting economic interests before environmental interests. Given the contradictory sets of expectations placed on candidate countries, it is not surprising that environmental harmonization has lagged and that business interests have dominated the legislative process in the individual accession countries.

Ultimately, Hungary's waste transition is likely to be limited to its powerless localities being upgraded from technologically backward, communist wastelands to high-tech, European ones.

nine
Conclusion

After walking the reader through the waste history of Hungary, it is finally time to step back and put the research in context by interpreting the empirical data and by revisiting the concept of waste.

Evaluating Hungary's Waste History

In the foregoing chapters I have presented a history of Hungary's waste regimes from 1948 to the present. I have sliced this history along three dimensions—the production of waste, the representation of waste, and the politics of waste—and I have analyzed the limitations and contradictions of each waste regime—the metallic, the efficiency, and the chemical—through the BCW/Garé case study. Helping the reader in this review is a summary table (table 9.1).

In the fifties, the Hungarian Workers' Party's economic concern with growth and political concern with the control over resources required a new ethos and the creation of a New (Wo)Man who made the problems of production his/her personal concern, renouncing his/her individual needs. This puritan ethos, coupled with the Party's primitive materialism that bordered on material worship, endowed waste with a whole series of positive values. The problem of waste was not framed as a problem of its production; that was more or less accepted as one of the many necessary by-products of building communism. The problem was letting it "go to waste"—that is, leaving it unitilized. From this perspective waste was a found treasure, an extra resource to be mobilized for fulfilling the plans; in sum, a benevolent deus ex machina. The existence of waste, which could have been seen as a failure of central planning, was therefore interpreted as providing a resource that could only be fully appreciated and used in socialism, with the help of ingenious class-conscious workers. Because of the prevailing identification of waste with metal scrap, and the propaganda hailing hardness and the resistance of workers' bodies that could mold materials and nature to their will, I have termed this regime "metallic." In this regime waste was treated as use value, and the state saw it as its goal to keep wastes under central control by issuing waste delivery quotas and organizing the central redistribution of wastes in order to recirculate them in production. Public discourse concentrated on waste production, and waste liquidation was a taboo. As an unintended consequence, however, the policy tools, such as waste quotas, and the concept of waste led to an increased production of waste and to the accumulation of unnecessary, unreusable, and nonrecyclable wastes.

In the reform period, it became clear that the gap between capitalist and socialist countries and the latter's economic dependence on the former was only growing, a point the oil crisis drove home rather painfully. The Party's key concern was chipping away at the rate of this trend and demonstrating at all costs that the leaders were still competent and the country was able to compete. Now, the existence of waste was seen as yet another sign of backwardness, which could only be reduced by more growth. By treating waste as inefficiency, even if still basically a useful material, it could be reintegrated into the Party's plans of modernization and rationalization and into the liberalization project of reformers and enterprise management. By tackling the waste problem through technological innovation and eco-nomic tools, the country's technocracy could prove its competence. The efficiency regime was characterized by a monetized concept of waste: waste was seen as a cost of production, and waste reduction and reuse were seen as steps to increase efficiency. Policy tools emphasized the financial motivation of waste producers and included credits, subsidies, and price manipulation. As the fifties' strict use-value mentality was relaxed, waste liquidation became legitimate. Professionals with economic and technical expertise were encouraged to participate both in achieving goals of waste reduction and reuse and in facilitating safe dumping. In this regime, both

Table 9.1. Hungary's Waste Regimes

Waste Regimes	Production of Waste	Representation of Waste	Politics of Waste	Contradictions, Paradoxes, Crisis Tendencies
Metallic Regime 1948–1974	*Forms of waste:* Allocative; material *Social agency:* State is owner and "manager"; reuse is a political task and is movementized *Material agency:* Wastes that cannot be treated as always reusable and recyclable metal scrap escape reuse efforts, they accumulate and rot, causing environmental problems	*Identification of waste:* metal scrap; useful, pliable, multipurpose material, always seen as use value *Definition of waste problem:* Leaving wastes without reuse *Applied knowledge:* Schematic knowledge of metallurgy, accounting, administrative systems of work competitions; science is shunned in the name of extreme social constructivism	*Subject of public discourse:* Waste production *Taboo:* Liquidation, waste distribution *Tools:* Mobilization of workers, residents, quotas and competitions *Hidden goals:* Discipline, control over resources *Morality:* To waste wastes is immoral, rejects the capitalist worshipping of new materials	Quota fulfillment encourages the production of even more wastes Accumulation of unneeded and nonrecyclable wastes, which creates bottlenecks in production

Table 9.1. Continued

Waste Regimes	Production of Waste	Representation of Waste	Politics of Waste	Contradictions, Paradoxes, Crisis Tendencies
Efficiency Regime 1975–1984	*Forms of waste:* Allocative; material; waste resulting from wasteful technologies handed down by the West *Social agency:* State is owner, funder, and coordinator of waste programs; collection/reuse and reduction are economic tasks and are supported with extra state funds and are carried out by experts *Material agency:* Chemical production resists waste reduction; temporary disposal doesn't sufficiently contain toxic wastes; contaminated soil turns into waste	*Identification of waste:* Inefficiency, cost of production, monetized, commodity when reused (metallic model is residual, chemical is emergent) *Definition of waste problem:* Too much waste compared to output, inefficiency *Applied knowledge:* Professional microeconomics, engineering and hard sciences	*Subject of public discourse:* Waste production and distribution *Tools:* Economic tools, subsidies, credits, cost-benefit analyses, price manipulation, large-scale modernizations *Hidden goals:* Avoid economic crisis, create favorable economic relations with the West *Morality:* Wastes are the result of our backwardness; they need to be eliminated through economic rationalization	Increase efficiency while promoting growth → overall waste volume doesn't shrink and ratio of waste among raw materials does not increase Limited dumping → ecological time bombs

Table 9.1. Continued

Waste Regimes	Production of Waste	Representation of Waste	Politics of Waste	Contradictions, Paradoxes, Crisis Tendencies
Chemical Regime 1985–present	*Forms of waste:* Residual material; market allocative *Social agency:* Wastes are increasingly privatized; reduction and reuse are privatized; no coordinated state effort to regulate waste production *Material agency:* Waste incineration produces toxic by-products	*Identification of waste:* Useless, harmful commodity when dumped, incinerated *Definition of waste problem:* Pollution caused by wastes *Applied knowledge:* Professional macroeconomics (neoliberalism), engineering and hard sciences, public administration knowledge	*Subject of public discourse:* Waste distribution *Taboo:* Waste production *Tools:* Legislation to ensure democracy in environmental public hearings, to set technical standards *Hidden goals:* Remove intervention of the state in the economy, protect private property *Morality:* Wastes are the sign of Hungary's (physical and moral) dirtiness, thus they need to be eliminated through modern European technologies (incineration and dumping); cleanliness is a measurement of the country's degree of civilization and Europeanness	The state is removed, so central programs aiming at minimizing and reusing waste are erased; Western waste incinerator imports, regression to end-of-pipe technologies Accumulation of wastes on factory yards Prolonged environmental conflict

waste production and waste distribution were legitimate subjects of public discourse, even if democratic control over waste distribution was still absent and even if disposal and incineration continued to be the less preferred way to deal with wastes. Instead of waste disposal sites, legislation priori- tized temporary waste storage with the hope of finding reuse for the stored wastes. With the worsening economic situation, funds for technological innovation remained unavailable; thus these hopes evaporated, and the temporary and technologically inadequate dumps turned into long-term wastelands. Furthermore, as growth never ceased to be a macroeconomic objective, whatever beneficial effects that increases in efficiency had for absolute waste volumes were offset by increasing production. Preventative attitudes, such as waste reuse and reduction, remained problematic in certain industries, most notably in the chemical industry. Its representa- tives, along with other professionals, called for legitimate waste-liquidation facilities with increasing success. They justified their demands with a cer- tain concern for the environment, arguing that the forced preventative attitude to waste problems and the continued resistance to end-of-pipe technologies led to illegal and unprofessional waste disposal.

From the second half of the eighties, chemical industry representatives became prominent, as did scientists in general, in shaping waste policies, and the state eventually abandoned its earlier waste reduction and waste reuse projects. Waste liquidation became the primary point on the official agenda of waste politics. The chemical waste model, in which waste was primarily seen as a useless and even harmful material, became dominant. At the same time, as environmental consciousness strengthened and as the political purchasing power of environmental claims increased, an environ- mental movement coalesced around a different politics of waste distribu- tion from that of the chemical industry, in which residents and activists effectively resisted the siting of many new waste disposal and incineration facilities. This focus proved convenient for new, increasingly private, eco- nomic actors who wanted the state and the public out of the sphere of production. Privatization and the reign of the chemical waste model had rendered waste production—the generation of toxic substances, source reduction, reuse, and recycling—a taboo of waste politics. As a result, policies now concentrated on end-of-pipe technologies, rather than on production-centered preventative solutions, a trend that was also strength- ened by the increasing exports of waste treatment facilities from the West to Eastern Europe. Many feared that Hungary would become the West's dump site. After the breakup of the socialist camp, European integration moved to the center of the project of cultural and political reorientation.

The dimensions along which Hungary had to demonstrate its worthiness of becoming "European" were numerous. Salient among these, however, were the indexes of "being civilized." Besides the commonly imagined lofty goals, such as respect for the individual, the sanctity of private property, and democracy, there were more mundane, albeit rather visible measures of "being civilized." Cleanliness was probably the most important of them. The existence of waste was reintegrated into the new moral order by identifying waste with dirtiness; more precisely, with the dirtiness of state socialism. Admitting the country's dirtiness was a self-purifying confession; cleaning up the country's wastes was breaking with the dirty past. As I have shown through Garé's case, the pro-incinerator rhetoric mobilized a symbolic dichotomy in which the positive side was represented by the adjectives "European," "clean," and "entrepreneurial," with the adjectives "socialist," "dirty," and "state-dictated" on the negative side. I have demonstrated that, although in principle the European Union favors waste prevention and recycling, its aid and its technological presence in the region prioritizes end-of-pipe technologies—that is, an increase of waste disposal and waste incineration facilities. In sum, EU accession has so far meant no divergence from the chemical model.

What are the limits of the foregoing analysis? Let me concentrate on three questions. (1) First of all, does it apply more or less in the same way to other formerly socialist countries? (2) Does the foregoing evaluation mean that state socialism was not really wasteful and environmentally disastrous? (3) Does my evaluation mean that a production-centered, preventative approach is inherently alien from capitalism? Furthermore, what would the answer to this latter question imply for comparisons between capitalism and state socialism?

First of all, as I have demonstrated, state socialism was not of a piece even within one country. The differences among the three models of waste indicate significant shifts in the relationship between economy and politics and between economy and culture; or, more concretely, a change in the relationship between the party-state and experts, and between the party-state and citizens as workers, consumers, and residents. To the extent that these shifts were partially driven by political/ideological changes—such as a certain détente after Stalinism—and by external economic impacts—such as the oil crisis—they necessarily affected all socialist countries. Whether these factors had the same impact on the waste discourses and waste politics of other members of the socialist bloc, however, remains to be answered by direct empirical investigation.

I only collected data from Hungary; therefore, I can respond to the question of generalizability only to the extent that my research unearthed documents and articles referring to other former socialist countries. There are not many of these, but they do suggest that in the fifties a metallic and use-value-oriented waste approach dominated in the Soviet Union and Czechoslovakia as well. Similarly, in the eighties, waste reduction and reuse became a shared concern for European socialist countries, at least to the extent of a COMECON (Council for Mutual Economic Assistance (1949–1991) waste management program being declared. The only difference I found in approaches to material conservation in the eighties was that, while in Hungary waste problems were tackled through economic tools, in the GDR, the Soviet Union, and Bulgaria such administrative tools as waste delivery quotas were renewed or sustained, even as Hungarian experts often posited the developed waste-recycling system of the GDR as a model to follow.[1]

Second, I do want to emphasize that state socialism produced wastefully in many respects and created an ecological crisis in many parts of Eastern Europe. However, I am suspicious of comparisons with Western capitalism whose aim is to establish which social order is more wasteful and environmentally more destructive or which social order is more open to environmental claims making. Not only are measures of wastefulness and environmental damage difficult to operationalize, but whether such hypothetical measurements would be meaningful without an adequate analysis of the roots of wastefulness and its victims is also dubious. Both from a theoretical and a practical point of view, it is best to analyze the wastefulness and related pathologies of capitalism and socialism on their own terms. Such a sui generis analysis has been my goal in this book. The theoretically and practically relevant question is not the "how much" question but the "how," "what," and "why" questions.

As for a political comparison, again, it is undoubtedly true that in Western capitalism there are more and stronger democratic institutions that can be used for environmental claims making, such as for protesting the siting of a waste facility. But how much are such institutions worth if their scope of authority is limited to policies that can, at the most, remedy but not prevent waste problems? If waste production—that is, how much and what kind of wastes can be produced—is excluded from public discourse, the most that democracy can achieve is to regulate what to do with the wastes already produced. In state socialism there was no democratic control over wastes, but the state's main effort was to deal with wastes preventatively within the sphere of production, and such efforts were partially successful. (Though it was unfortunate that the state shied away from regulating waste distribution, that is, treatment, disposal, and incineration.) The real political difference therefore resides not in the size and kind of claims-making institutions but in the scope of public discourse.

Finally, as I emphasized in my introductory chapter, I have carefully avoided certain ways of posing questions and claims that could, even if involuntarily, essentialize either state socialism or capitalism. One way to do this was to put the time dimension into the analysis. I have described the changes in Hungary's waste regimes under state socialism, I have referred to changes in waste models in the West—what many have called "ecological modernization"—and, finally, I have contrasted the capitalism of today's Hungary with that of today's West. Recent data indeed suggest that a production-centered environmental discourse is taking hold in Western capitalism and Japan, but whether these developments will take place with the exclusion of the state and the public from the regulation of production or whether this trend will be, so to speak, democratized, remains to be seen.

But it's only fair to go back further in time in the case of the West as well. Older readers with personal experience, or readers familiar with U.S. or European economic history, may suggest that there have also been periods in the West in which a metallic model was dominant, at least in some industries. The war economies of the United States and European countries, in which recycling was not only prioritized but promoted by the state, are probably the most obvious examples. Among the earliest records I found dealing with industrial waste problems in the United States were several analyses and programmatic studies evidencing a production-centered approach to waste dating to the twenties and thirties. The largest study was done by the Committee on Elimination of Waste in Industry of the Federated American Engineering Societies in 1921 (American Engineering Council 1921). The study, which, interestingly, used the term "waste" in a rather broad sense, including both loss of material and of labor in production, was indeed greatly concerned with reducing and "eliminating" waste in industry.

In light of such pieces of evidence, it might be argued that the production-centered, reuse- and recycling-encouraging discourse of the fifties in Hungary was either an extended effect of the war and/or the result of a certain stage of industrialization. Such factors, however, do not explain why waste disposal remained a taboo in the first half of Hungarian state socialist history. After all, the above-mentioned U.S. study, while clearly prioritizing "elimination," also dedicated attention to the safety of waste disposal, evidencing that a focus on waste production does not necessarily delegitimize waste distribution.

Observers may claim that the taboo on waste disposal was due to an absence of information. To the contrary, information on the dangers of chemical wastes and on disposal practices was available to Hungarian engineers and policymakers. The abstracts of chemical industry and chemistry journals that the Technical Library[2] in Budapest subscribed to reveal that such topics were researchable in Hungary at least from the early sixties. It is not information per se that was missing—after all, even engineers had the data—but what was lacking was the kind of discursive environment in which these data were meaningful, that is, translatable into practice.

It would be foolish to deny that these factors—the war economy, "backwardness," or lack of information—had something to do with the emergence and long-lasting impact of the metallic waste model and the taboo on waste disposal. Understanding these events only in these terms, however, would mean that Hungary's waste history was reducible to the absence of certain crucial elements of Western capitalism. Such a view cannot explain the agency behind the metallic model: that is, why this model not only emerged but also was guarded and protected, and what political struggles formed around the issue of waste. In light of the archival data and my case study, the previously analyzed cultural-cognitive characteristics of Soviet-type socialism and the day-to-day political tasks of the Communist Party in Hungary stand out as the most important factors. We must not, however, ignore the agency of waste as material. This is what I turn to in my closing statement.

Waste as a Hybrid Entity

What does this history tell us about waste that we didn't know before? I trust this history has aptly demonstrated that waste is a social category—which was my initial intention. What economic mechanisms affect how much and what kinds of wastes are produced, how one form of waste turns into another, how waste is defined, how the problem of waste is constructed, and what actors should be authorized to define and deal with the definition of waste problems all depend on factors that cannot simply be reduced to technology. Culture, morality, ideologies, economic interests, social inequalities, and power struggles permeate the very concept of waste and thus its very materiality. As a result, solving waste problems can never become the exclusive domain of engineers.

But in the process of the research, I found that waste is more than just a social construction. It also has a relatively independent material aspect, which puts limits on how it can be defined and physically tampered with. It is not just that wastes bite back—that is, that they resist purely human or social intention—but their materiality impacts what those intentions may be. In the fifties, what the Party intended to do with wastes, for example, had much to do with the fact that metal scraps were its most visible form, both because of the war ruins and because of the ever-muscular heavy industry's generation of metal wastes. Furthermore, what I have called the metallic regime, therefore, was not merely a social arrangement, but a "mangle," in Andrew Pickering's (1985) formulation: its laws and institutions did not simply *misrepresent* all wastes as metallic, they did not simply act upon some preexisting form of waste, but they actually produced wastes in a particular way. They had the unintended consequence of producing more wastes and of letting them accumulate and turn into other waste materials (for example, rot, contaminated groundwater, and so forth), just to mention the most obvious connection. The material reality brought into being this way then had much to do with how later economic actors saw the waste problem. While they wanted to reduce wastes, and to bring some order into how wastes were stored or dumped, the cultural legacy of the metallic waste regime—namely, the ethos that prohibits wasting wastes by dumping them—only allowed the temporary storage of wastes, rather than providing final dump sites with higher technological protection against environmental damage. This environmental damage then provided sufficient fodder for those calling for ending waste reuse and waste reduction efforts, instead advocating the "ultimate solution": incineration. Social and material agency are thoroughly interwoven in Hungary's waste history. It is in this sense that we are justified in calling waste a hybrid, rather than an exclusively social or exclusively technical entity.

What is the implication for politics? Primarily, we ought to end the presently existing invidious division of labor: producers determine the material composition of wastes, while the state and the public take care of the social infrastructure dealing with waste problems. Corporations claim the right to choose materials and technologies, and thus to produce wastes according to their needs and interests. The state or the public, in their turn, can prescribe quotas about recycling rates, they can define what constitutes recycling, and they can regulate the parameters of "safe dumping" or "safe incineration." However, they have no or a very limited impact on the materiality of wastes, that is, how toxic by-products are and how much are produced. You cannot leave the material control of waste in one hand, and its social control in the other. This will only create more unintended consequences and thus will make policies, price regulation, and siting decisions inefficient. To insist that we only have to get the policy environment right or that we need to put production into state ownership ignores the material implications of whatever social arrangements we come up with, and that these material implications constantly change. We cannot, for example, simply demand recycling. As I showed, that too can have unintended negative material and environmental consequences. Since waste is both social and material, its regulation and management must be integrated. Production itself must be politicized. Citizens must be able at the least to access information about the material characteristics of wastes, and ideally, to participate in deliberating about how much we need to consume of certain materials, what compounds should not even be produced, and, ultimately, how to create a safer material world. We need to socialize, that is, democratize decisions about materials, and vice versa. We need to materialize political decisions and infuse them with what we may call a material impact assessment. And we have to do so over and over again.

Notes

1. Was State Socialism Wasteful?

1. The energy intensity index is the amount of material or energy used per unit of GDP.

2. In environmental policy circles, the term "end-of-pipe technologies" refers to the management and treatment of already produced emissions and waste, rather than to their prevention, which would require an intervention into product design and the production process. More about this distinction later.

3. Greens active in the Garé case included Green Circle, based in the nearby city Pécs, and the Green Alternative Party.

4. I am using the word "exotic" in Gudeman's (1986) sense, as something markedly different and alien to Western cognitive models.

5. These are the *Christian Science Monitor*, the *New York Times*, the *Los Angeles Times*, the *Wall Street Journal*, and the *Washington Post*.

2. Toward a Social Theory of Waste

1. An exception is Berki 1992.

2. I have elaborated on these links in an article (Gille 1997).

3. An exception is Tickle and Welsh 1998.

4. "Tap" and "sink" refer to the two functions of nature, as a source of resources and as a dumping ground for emissions and wastes.

5. In the absence of earlier data, I had to accept post-collapse data for socialist countries, that is, data from 1990. Then the economic decline was not yet as deep, and the "logic" of the economy was still unchanged enough for 1990 waste output data to serve as a proxy for the pre-1989 data. In the next chapter I will analyze such absences of data.

6. An obvious candidate for such a factor was the economic, and more directly the industrial, structure of a country. Industries vary a great deal in terms of the amount of waste per unit of output, which makes countries with a larger share of waste-intensive industries appear more wasteful than those with a smaller share. Having put together a number of tables with too many empty cells or too many footnotes indicating differences in measurement, I had to admit that there was just no easy way to quantify industrial structure according to waste intensity; in fact, even the classification of the origin of wastes is subject to significant enough variation from country to country to make cross-national comparisons unreliable. Again, more about the problems of measurement and comparison in chapter 2.

7. The 1966 edition of *Kingzett's Chemical Encyclopaedia* provides the following explanation for the term "Wastes (Industrial)": "Many industries related to chemistry produce wastes that are troublesome, not only to the industries themselves but also to the surrounding communities. As industrial areas become more and more congested this matter becomes a serious problem." Here waste is not a problem in itself, but

congestion is, although what industrial areas become congested with—people, buildings, or perhaps wastes—is left unclear. The problem of waste is that it is in the wrong, i.e., congested, place, it lacks value, and therefore the solution is its disposal.

8. Of course, one characteristic feature of consumer societies is that the intended time of usage is getting shorter. See my analysis of Toffler (1970) and Packard (1960) below.

9. For a useful theorization of the life of objects, primarily commodities, see Appadurai (1986).

10. Other economic models treat by-products as *overproduced* commodities which then "can be disposed of, that is, the prices of these will be zero" (Schefold 1987, 1031, explaining von Neumann), or stipulate that "joint products can be disposed at zero cost" (Schefold 1987, 1031, explaining Koopmans). That is, they "allow for" recycling and dumping, but it is assumed that either could be done at no expense to the producer or that, at least, those costs need not be integrated into the accounting of usual production costs.

11. Gourlay castigates dictionaries and working definitions of hazardous wastes and special wastes by various supranational agencies, such as the Organisation for Economic Cooperation and Development (OECD) and the World Health Organization (WHO), for including disposal in the definition of waste, thus "fudg[ing] the issue by including the potential and the existing within the same category" (Gourlay 1992, 23). This is a fallacy in thinking I referred to above as "operationalism."

12. He makes the claim that waste "can be taken into account by analyzing the social relations that 1) govern the degree to which real engines deviate from ideal engines by failing to minimize the waste produced, 2) govern what happens to waste (dumping, recycling, reusing, purifying, etc.), and 3) govern responsibility for waste" (Murphy 1994, 110). An "ideal" engine is one that works exactly as it is supposed to according to abstract equations—that does not mean that it creates no waste, nor that there could be no environmentally sounder technological alternatives.

13. This is the exact opposite of another sociologist's, Allan Schnaiberg (1980), conceptualization of waste as additions (rather than withdrawals) from the ecosystem.

14. Hence Filtzer's definition of waste: "by waste we refer to the tendency within the Soviet economy to consume means of production and labor power without commensurate production of finished product" (1986, 134).

15. Such "decorative" or nonproductive uses of materials and time have probably always been an element in production. Without denying that consumerism predated capitalism (an argument forcefully made by Chandra Mukerji [1983]), there is a key difference between the roles of such "extras" in capitalism and in earlier economies. As Baran and Sweezy (1966) would argue, it is only in monopoly capitalism that such a form of consumption becomes the condition of the viability of the economy as a whole.

16. In his terminology, resource regimes are social institutions that determine what natural resources are considered valuable by society, lay down the principles of valuation, and resolve the resulting value conflicts. Their core is a structure of rights and rules, which implies a certain distribution of advantages and disadvantages. These are, consequently, always subject to pressures for reinterpretation and change. Therefore, according to Young, they possess qualities that social institutions in general do, such as

deviance, formal and informal channels and decisions, and unintended consequences of operation.

17. I have elaborated on these links in an article (Gille 2000).

3. METALLIC SOCIALISM

1. They identify seventeen movements, but in addition, I found twelve more specific ones in the archives of the Industry and Transportation Department of the Party (Pető and Szakács 1985, 177–78). The list I collected from other archives includes: Maintenance workers for the 100,000 kilometers; Maintenance workers for quality; "A-B" movement (for the acceleration of forwarding parcels); Let's do the rush without repair work; Increase of the average production of trains; Increase of the net kilometer per gross ton-kilometer ratio; The 180 quintal movement (one freight car should move at least 180 quintals); Varashova movement (the increase of the lifetime of machines); Kovalyev movement (transferring work methods to colleagues); Tsuktin movement (self-supervision, quality contest); Fast-working movement (turning on lathes more quickly); and Protect and take care of the goods (the safe packaging and transportation of goods).

2. Hungary's political and ultimately military alliance with Nazi Germany was rewarded with the return of most of the territory lost in the 1920 Treaty of Trianon to Czechoslovakia, Romania, and Yugoslavia between 1939 and 1941; these territories were restored to those countries at the end of the war.

3. Relations *of* versus *in* production is Burawoy's distinction (1985). The former are the social relations between the producers and the appropriators of surplus, primarily manifest at the macro-level of society, while the latter include the more specific nature of the production process, the division of labor, remuneration, the ways in which workers increase their earnings and decrease effort, the internal labor market of a plant, and, in general, the ways of making employees work.

4. The term "local industry" was reserved for plants in private or cooperative ownership that mostly produced consumption goods for local needs. More about this can be found in the discussion below, "The Politicization of Waste: Disciplining Cooperatives and Private Shops."

5. The Mátyás Rákosi Steel Works consisted of several plants, only one of which was the steel mill. Other plants within the complex produced pipes and bicycles. The plant's namesake ruled the Party and the country from 1948 to 1953.

6. Let Gudeman's description of an agricultural practice in Panama stand as an example of such models of waste's location in production. The Panamanian peasants' model of livelihood applies the scheme of hair growing on humans' heads to cycles of their agricultural production.

The metaphor fitted the cycle by which land moved from equal access to temporary usufruct and back to nature. Agriculture is an activity in which nature is temporarily tamed or humanized by removing the forest cover. Although both human hair and crops are cultivated under the guidance of persons, their force for growing comes not from themselves (the hair, the seed) nor from their cultivator (the barber, the laborer) but from that in which they grow (the head, the earth). . . .

> Humans contribute their barber-like skills, but the crops are not labor-generated;
> this is a natural process which depends on a force that is outside local control.
> (Gudeman 1986, 6)

There are two forms of wastes in this production process. One is weeds, the other is stubble. The difference between harvest, on the one hand, and weeding and clearing stubble, on the other, is expressed in the description of the depth of the haircut. The harvest is termed cutting (*cortar*), removing the stubble is compared to shearing off hair (*pelar*), and weeding, if done the best way, is described as "cutting the roots by breaking the casing of the head" (*casquear*). After shearing, the remaining stubble is burned. After the second year of use, the plot remains stubble for several years until the forest grows back.

Because production is not seen as an activity of humans, but rather as an activity of nature, waste appears as a natural phenomenon, and tasks emanating from wastes—weeds and stubble—seem to be all part of the cycle of production and the cycle of land use and rest. Gudeman does not provide details about what is done to the stubble, but this example suffices to demonstrate that the metaphor of production is transferred to that of waste. Waste is orderly, natural, and fertile, even if not directly needed by humans.

7. The novelty lay not in assigning use value to waste, an attitude familiar to Hungarians due to long periods of deprivation, but in the state assuming this role and politicizing waste reuse.

8. Both are Marxist categories. Use value refers to the concrete ability of a product to satisfy human needs, while exchange value refers to the value of a product, usually monetary, for which it could be exchanged on the market.

9. Endre Vészi's novel *Géza Gazda's Forints* (1952) is about the Stalinist hero of material conservation and waste recycling, of whom more later.

10. The representation and deconstruction of this worker-hero that is perhaps best known to Western audiences is Polish director Andrzej Wajda's film *Man of Marble* (1977).

11. Several authors have noticed this social constructivist attitude toward nature in Marx's writings, and explained it with Marx's need to distinguish his materialism from biological reductionism (O'Connor 1988).

12. Note that point (d) is practically identical to the last quoted paragraph of the No. 2.500-21/1954 decree discussed above. This just means that this draft did not become legislation in its original form, and even in a changed form only two years later.

13. In fact there were two kinds of paralysis, as indicated by the example of the leather-reusing cooperative: (a) the secondary production of goods made out of these materials had to be stopped when access to these materials became limited; and (b) the original production process in which these waste materials were generated was hampered by their accumulation on factory yards.

14. Carruthers and Espeland (1991) compare two dimensions of double-entry book-keeping, the rhetorical and the technical. They argue that in the history of double-entry bookkeeping, the significance of its rhetorical value exceeded that of its technical value. Similarly to Anthony G. Hopwood and Peter Miller (1994), they also emphasize that accounting not only reflects changes in social institutions, but has also "helped engender and legitimate them" (60).

15. This practice also prevailed in the Soviet Union, as described by Berliner (1957), and it has continued in Russia after the collapse of central planning, although for different reasons (Burawoy and Krotov 1992).

16. The capacities the center was most concerned about were the grinding, foundry, and rolling facilities in metallurgy.

4. The Primitive Accumulation of Waste in Metallic Socialism

1. These included campaigns as diverse as Communist Saturdays, during which workers worked for free for some centrally decided political goal, or the collection of signatures and donations for the people of Vietnam during the Vietnam War or for starving children in Africa.

2. Under state socialism, citizens normally received, and thus expected, such social benefits as day care, changing rooms, meals during the workday, compensation for health impacts peculiar to the industry, vacation resources such as designated resorts, etc. from their employers. Thus, in a situation of chronic labor shortage, such resources were crucial in attracting and retaining employees.

3. At the time, Hungarian enterprises were obliged to exchange their hard currency earnings with the state bank.

4. I contacted several U.S. companies that produced 1,2,4,5-TCB to ascertain whether BCW's waste-intensive technology was the same process they used, or whether they were able to produce it with a smaller waste/final output ratio. My requests for such information were denied (see my arguments about secrecy and lack of data about production waste in chapter 2).

5. The Efficiency Model

1. Fradi is a sports team traditionally favored by the working class.

2. Ivan Klíma in *Love and Garbage* actually sees both the West and the East as full of indestructible rubbish. After a visit to Detroit's Ford factory and incinerator, his hero says, "They probably melt down the crushed metal to make iron and new steel for new cars, and thus rubbish is transformed into new rubbish, only slightly increased in quantity" (1991, 18). Here the car, as the symbol of Western consumerism, is viewed as rubbish, while in another part of the novel, he identifies state socialism as a heap of rubbish:

> One of the rubbish searchers had just caught a red flag with his hook. With a great effort he extricated it from underneath the mass of ashes and other filth, rolled it round his pole, and when he'd got it out eventually waved his wife over and together they unrolled the rag. When they opened it out in the wind we could see that it was really a red flag which was now flying above the mountain of garbage. (Klíma 1991, 143)

3. *Man of Marble* is the title of the previously mentioned 1977 film about the fate of a Stakhanovite work hero, directed by Polish filmmaker Andrzej Wajda.

4. This refers to the communist organization for young children.

5. The first official and largely ineffective move toward this distinction between collection and reuse was made in 1971. On its twentieth anniversary, MÉH decided to change its name to MÉH Secondary Raw Material Utilizing Company. "The change in

the name expresses among other things that today the industrial preparation and the processing of reusable, so-called secondary raw materials is as important as the buying of these materials" (*Népszabadság* 1972, n.p.).

6. For a concise review of the history of Hungarian economic reforms see Comisso and Marer (1986).

7. These data don't include red mud (the main by-product of bauxite mining). By comparison, OECD countries on the average recovered 10 percent of their industrial hazardous wastes in 1990. It is true, however, that Hungary's definition of hazardous wastes was at that time more inclusive than the OECD's.

8. "Technical ones" is the literal translation of the Hungarian *műszakiak*, and it is the official label for employees with degrees in engineering. In the early period of state socialism, people in administrative positions at state authorities usually did not hold science degrees.

9. György Konrád and Iván Szelényi (1979) put this change in terms of a shift from *telos* to *techne*, comparable—in Weberian terms—to a shift from substantive to formal rationality.

6. The Limits of Efficiency

1. In Hungarian it (sort of) rhymes: "A hulladék nem szemét, átveszi és pénzt ad érte a MÉH."

2. Industrializing the countryside was not a new idea in the sixties. However, while in the fifties the establishment of new factories in rural areas was encouraged for political reasons—namely, to break up peasant majorities—in the sixties the goal was to achieve greater equality in living standards between villages and cities and to rationalize the geographical distribution of economic activities, as well as to improve air quality.

3. This move was doubly supported by the state's polices. First of all, Hidas was on the list of preferred relocation targets; second, coal processing plants, due to the imminent exhaustion of Hungary's coal mines, were prioritized as facilities for which new industrial uses had to be found. The Budapest Chemical Works applied for subsidies or preferential credits that promised to support relocation projects consistent with these policies, but once again in vain.

4. The land had been held partly in state and partly in cooperative ownership.

5. I am making Hungarian socialist regional development policies appear more seamless and their history more unilinear than they really were. The goals, rationale, and methods of regional development policies went through several changes, and the actual outcome of these policies often did not reflect the original intentions of the planners. Gábor Vági, who was likely the best informed and most theoretically and critically attuned sociologist on this topic, analyzed the changes as well as the relationship between central intentions and local outcomes in several essays (1982; 1991).

6. This is a bulletin where major decisions and laws were announced to the public. I am somewhat doubtful whether this decision was indeed published in such a widely circulated publication; it is possible that my interviewee referred to an internal bulletin of the county. In *Közlöny* I found no mention of the dump, or of any other such sites.

7. The Budapest Chemical Works actually got its permit in 1979, but the first negotiation was held in Szalánta in June 1978.

8. Thane Gustafson (1981) finds that, interestingly, geographers and other scientists

in the Soviet Union brought up agricultural interests in the defense of nature, particularly in their protest against hydroelectric power plants. Yet the mechanism, of environmental claims succeeding only when they dovetailed with primary state policy, is the same: the reason why they could be successful was that from the 1960s "hydropower expansion . . . interfered with the leaders' new plans for expanded agricultural development in the European zone of the country—a fact that underscores the close link between the rise of environmental issues and the Brezhnev agricultural program" (48).

9. Bosta is another village, located approximately as near to the dump site as Garé is, which suffered a similar administrative disempowerment to Garé's. The "Chronicle" was a standard form, an administratively mandated yearly summary produced by the leadership.

7. The Chemical Model

1. The dam was to be built jointly by Hungary and Czechoslovakia on the Danube at Gabcikovo (on the Slovakian side) and Nagymaros (on the Hungarian side), and this demonstration was one of numerous actions organized by the Danube Movement, and the key civil organization in the movement, the Duna-Kör (Danube Circle). The dam was originally planned in the fifties to produce electricity and improve navigability, but the plans remained dormant until the 1980s. The Danube Movement, which resisted the dam for environmental, economic, and political reasons, became the largest environmental movement in Hungary's history, and galvanized the many actions and demonstrations that are credited by many with bringing the socialist regime down.

2. I am borrowing Ann Anagnost's distinction between producing and consuming bodies (1995).

3. Teréz Reich, the leader of the protest, described Ófalu in this way:

Ófalu is a small village of 500 inhabitants. It was only ten years ago that a road was even built to the village. There are no water pipes, and the only water is polluted. Most inhabitants commute because they can't find a job in the village. Ninety percent of the people belong to the German minority. In the village, there is only one intellectual, but she doesn't work there. No teacher, no doctor, no other representative of the intelligentsia can be found there. There are three villages within 10 kilometers of each other (Ófalu, Mecseknádasd and Óbánya), that have only one governing body; they belong to one council. (Reich 1990, 59)

4. The media had been dealing with environmental concerns in quite a matter-of-fact fashion since the mid-seventies, and scholarly journals had been regularly publishing articles on one or another scientific aspect of environmental protection. The conclusion of these articles and reports was invariably the need for integrating environmentalism into economic management and technological innovation.

5. The 1975 Helsinki Accords, commonly credited with starting the process of détente, acknowledged the status quo of European borders, and thus reduced the military threat to socialist regimes in return for those regimes' improvement of their human rights records.

6. The Right Livelihood Award, also known as the "Alternative Nobel Prize," was established in 1980 to honor and support people whose actions embody the principles of living rightly, that is, respecting other people and the natural world.

7. Here I am borrowing Hungarian sociologist Sándor Berki's incisive metaphors (Berki 1992).

8. A summary of waste-related laws of the European Union is available at: http://ec.europa.eu/environment/waste/legislation/c.htm.

9. This is why, for example, the eighties saw a massive increase in hazardous waste imports to the United Kingdom.

10. The reported amount exported by the developed countries to developing countries in the early nineties was 120,000 tons annually, but according to the Dobris Assessment, there is "increasing evidence that the magnitude of these transfrontier movements is far larger than recorded" (Stanners and Bourdeau 1995, 352). No data exists for the total amount exported to Eastern Europe, but the fact that Western Europe exported one million tons of hazardous wastes just to the GDR in 1988 gives us an idea of the magnitude of this trade.

11. In 1993 in the United States, the EPA actually put an eighteen-month moratorium on incinerator construction, partly because of resistance and partly because an overcapacity had been created.

12. Since the monetary union, that is the adoption of the Euro, requires low budget deficits—not higher than the average of the three lowest among the EU countries—efforts to meet its conditions have led to the cutting of welfare benefits, even in Germany, which proposed the requirements.

13. The Privatization Act was not actually passed until 1995. For a brief summary of the periods of Hungarian privatization, see www.unc.edu/courses/2002spring/rues/230/001/PRIVATIZATION/Hungary/hungaryecon.html.

14. According to a high-ranking official in the Environmental Ministry, the same obstruction could be observed in the process of drafting Hungary's comprehensive waste management law.

15. The stakes involved in the order of privatization and the restructuring of environmental protection are analyzed through the example of the Czech Republic and Slovakia by Richard Andrews (1993).

16. The Budapest Chemical Works' share in Hungaropec's capital stock is 26 percent; this is the minimum, according to Hungarian laws, at which BCW can still have a say in the increase of the capital stock.

17. My calculation is from Greenpeace data (Gluszynski and Kruszewska 1996).

18. In addition, the only modern waste incinerator that was built before 1989 in Hungary—in Dorog—was first privatized and then sold to a French company. The country's first modern hazardous waste dump in Aszód met a similar fate.

8. "Building a Castle out of Shit"

1. More about this rival facility below.

2. In fact, as one of the authors of the technical part of the environmental impact assessment told me, all he or others can work with are technical parameters received from the investor, and they do not have a way of checking whether these data are indeed correct.

3. The reference is to the Hungarian saying, "One cannot build a castle out of shit."

4. Data and currency rate are from 1996.

5. Garé could afford not collecting local taxes for the previous few years thanks to the compensation (more precisely the interest on it) it received from Hungaropec. The amount gathered from such taxes would have been a meager amount anyway (120,000 Forints).

6. Data are from the economic-social impact study (Fact Bt. 1995).

7. The importance of the (free) paper was that this district never had its own newspaper, and that in the post-1989 economic situation very few people could afford buying the large-circulation regional daily that covers issues in their villages.

8. My use of the term is closest to Jameson's (1991). He argues that political action requires cognitive mapping—"nam[ing] the system" (418); that is, a spatial imagination of the self in relation to an increasingly globalized social reality.

9. The term "entrepreneur" (*vállalkozó*) had a very positive connotation in the years immediately preceding and following the collapse of state socialism. Its primary meaning was not so much business for profit as working on one's own initiative, independently of the state. This positive connotation is here exploited to hide the fact that the proposal is actually about a profit-making venture.

10. Most concretely, the new road mentioned in chapter 5, and possibly other kickbacks that cannot be confirmed.

11. The Swiss-Hungarian joint venture planned to build an incinerator just a few kilometers away, in Kökény, but the project was abandoned by the late 1990s after allegations of corruption, while the Dorog incinerator was an already functioning facility about 200 kilometers to the north, much closer to Budapest.

12. The estimated number of nongovernmental organizations (NGOs) worldwide, as well as their financial resources, has been steadily increasing since the 1970s, with a real takeoff in the 1980s. It is practically impossible to know the exact number of environmental NGOs, partly because environmental and developmental or other issues are often tackled together in the same organizations, and partly because of their independence. Also, NGOs are not accounted for in registries, such as those maintained by the UN or other international associations, partly because of their often temporary existence—that is, because they transform themselves with relative ease as projects dictate. However, we know that there were 5,000 NGOs registered at the Rio Summit, but we also know that just in India, there are 12,000 such organizations, which should help us imagine their magnitude and salience.

13. The abbreviation "NIMBY" stands for "Not in my backyard," the rather malicious name for people's resistance to the establishment of toxic facilities near their residence. This label attributes a certain shortsightedness to such residents, inasmuch as they are portrayed as not resisting such facilities elsewhere.

14. This conflict (1703–1711) was fought by serfs and lower and middle nobility to liberate Hungary from Habsburg Austrian rule. France's Louis XIV had a tacit alliance with Hungarian rebel leader Ferenc Rákóczi, but stayed away from establishing formal diplomatic relations with the new, short-lived, independent Hungarian government, which the latter badly needed to combat its international isolation.

15. A reference to the post–World War I Trianon peace treaty of 1920.

16. One key aim was to undermine peasant majorities in rural areas.

17. According to a Hungarian official of the Hungarian Mission in Brussels, it was

not until high-ranking politicians in candidate countries started openly advocating the "possibility of life outside the EU," that is, in 1999, that the Commission sped up the negotiations (personal interview, Gábor Baranyai, Brussels, 2003).

18. As pointed out by the members of the Hulladék Munkaszövetség (Work Association on Waste), the most important Hungarian NGO dealing with waste issues, the data are incomplete and do not add up ("Mennyi hulladék képződik Magyarországon?" 2002). Indeed, I found it hard to navigate the data provided. In light of these valid criticisms, I report only the basic figures.

19. According to Hungarian lawmakers, this is made up of agricultural and forestry residues entirely recycled through biological cycles.

20. Roughly one-quarter of it was comprised of red mud resulting from aluminum production.

21. Reliable and comparable data on incineration are very hard to come by even according to the EU's own offices (Brodersen, Crowe, and Jacobsen 2001).

22. This is not to imply that North American technologies are necessarily environmentally friendlier.

23. This was pointed out by several of the participants of the meeting of the Parliamentary committee evaluating the draft of the NWMP in June 2001 (Parliamentary Committee Minutes 2001). However, the final plan does not establish a clear and concrete preference for recycling.

24. Besides rumors, the only detectable signs of corruptibility were two sudden resignations. A high-ranking employee of the regional environmental authority, and the key contact for BCW, resigned the day the permit was denied to Hungaropec; and the last official signature of the head of the national-level authority before his unexpected resignation was on the document that granted Hungaropec the permit.

25. Among the concerns and demands of the PHG were racial purity and increasing male potency and fertility through improving environmental quality, banning the use of harmful salt produced by "neo-Zionists" around the world to poison others, and forcing AIDS patients entering the country to wear yellow tags (recalling for many the yellow stars that Jews had to wear in Nazi-ruled countries prior to and during World War II).

9. Conclusion

1. As an article made the contrast in 1985, "Bulgaria and GDR have waste quotas for enterprises, in Hungary the waste collection plans are to be fulfilled by the economy as a whole" (*Hajdú-Bihari Napló* 1985, n.p.).

2. This library, called OMIKK (Országos Műszaki Információs Központ és Könyvtár [National Technical Informational Center and Library]), collects, catalogues, abstracts, and translates technical, scientific, and industrial data from all over the world; it is open to the public and provides services for engineers working in various fields of employment.

Sources and References

INTERVIEWS BY AUTHOR

Anonymous. 1995. Personal interview. Budapest.
——. 1996. Personal interview. Garé.
——. 2004. Personal interview. Maglód.
Anonymous environmental activist. 1996. Personal interview. Pécs.
——. 2000. Personal interview. Szentendre.
Anonymous official of Environmental Ministry. 1997. Personal interview. Budapest.
Anonymous official of Ministry of Industry. 1996. Personal interview.
Bakonyi, Árpád. 1996. Personal interview. Budapest.
Balla, Zoltán. 1995. Personal interview. Budapest.
Baranyai, Gábor. 2003. Official of the Hungarian Mission. Personal interview. Brussels.
Durkó, Mrs. Miklós. 1996. Personal interview. Budapest.
Eifert, Gyula. 1995. Personal interview. Budapest.
Farkas, Hilda. 2003. Environmental Ministry official. Personal interview. Budapest.
Kassai, Miklós. 1996. Personal interview. Pécs.
Kelemen, Ferenc. 1997. Personal interview. Budapest.
Kovács, László. 1996. Personal interview. Budapest.
Romhányi, Gábor. 1995. Personal interview. Budapest.
Szabó, Mrs. [pseudo.]. 2004. Personal interview. Budapest.
Szterjopulosz, Krisztoforosz. 1996. Personal interview. Budapest.
Takáts, Attila. 1996. Personal interview. Budapest.
Valovits, Emil. 1997. Interview (by telephone). Budapest.

LAWS

1951. No. 113.900/1951 decree of the Director of the Central Planning Office.
1951. No. 102.700/1951 decree of the Director of the Central Planning Office.
1952. No. 107/1952 decree of the Central Arbitration Committee.
1954. No. 2.500-21/1954 decree of the Director of the Central Planning Office.
1981. Decree on Hazardous Wastes.
1992. §35 of the LIV. Law.
2000. National Waste Management Plan (NWMP) of Article 56 in the 2000 Waste Act.

Sources and References

ARCHIVES

(With abbreviations used in the text)

BFL: Budapest Főváros Levéltára (Budapest Capital City Archives), Budapest. (Formerly Budapest Főváros Tanácsa Levéltár [Archives of the Council of Budapest Capital City].)

BML: Baranya Megyei Levéltár (Baranya County Archives), Pécs. (Formerly Baranya Megyei Tanácsa Levéltár [Archives of the Council of Baranya County].)

BVM: Budapesti Vegyiművek Levéltára (Archives of the Budapest Chemical Works), Budapest.

MDP-MSZMP: MDP-MSZMP Levéltár (Communist Party Archives), Budapest. (Now part of Politikatörténeti és Szakszervezeti Levéltár [Political History and Trade Union Archives].)

PVL: Pécs Városi Levéltár, Pécs.

SZOT: Szakszervezetek Országos Tanácsa Levéltára (Archives of the National Council of Trade Unions). (Now part of Politikatörténeti és Szakszervezeti Levéltár [Political History and Trade Union Archives].)

UML: Újkori Magyar Levéltár (Modern [Postwar] Hungarian Archives), Budapest. (Now part of Magyar Országos Levéltár [Hungarian National Archives].)

REFERENCES

Aftalion, Fred. 1991. *A history of the international chemical industry*. Philadelphia: University of Pennsylvania Press.

Ákos, Károly, ed. 1962. *Kislexikon A–Z* (Small lexicon, A–Z). Budapest: Akadémiai Kiado.

Állami Vagyonügynökség (State Privatization Agency). 1993. A környezetvédelmi követelmények érvényesüléséről az állami vállalatok privatizációja során (On the fulfillment of environmental requirements during the privatization of state enterprises). *Környezet és Fejlődés* 5, no. 4:31–34.

Alley, Kelly D. 1994. Ganga and Gandagi: Interpretations of pollution and waste in Benaras. *Ethnology* 33, no. 2:127–45.

Amato, Ivan. 1997. *Stuff: The materials the world is made of*. New York: Basic Books.

American Engineering Council. 1921. *Waste in industry, by the Committee on Elimination of Waste in Industry of the Federated American Engineering Societies*. Washington, D.C.: Federated American Engineering Societies.

Anagnost, Ann. 1995. A surfeit of bodies: Population and the rationality of the state in post-Mao China. In *Conceiving the new world order: The global politics of reproduction*, ed. F. D. Ginsburg and R. Rapp. Berkeley: University of California Press.

Andrews, Richard N. L. 1993. Environmental policy in the Czech and Slovak Republic. In *Environment and democratic transition: Policy and politics in Cen-*

tral and Eastern Europe, ed. Anna Vári and Pál Tamás. Boston: Kluwer Academic Publishers.

Appadurai, Arjun. 1986. *The social life of things: Commodities in cultural perspective.* Cambridge: Cambridge University Press.

Argyrou, Vassos. 1997. "Keep Cyprus clean": Littering, pollution, and otherness. *Cultural Anthropology* 12, no. 2:159–78.

Aronson, Hal R. 1997. Constructing racism into resources: A portrait and analysis of the environmental justice movement. Ph.D. dissertation, University of California, Santa Cruz.

Árvai, József. 1990. *Hulladékgazdálkodás* (Waste management). Budapest: Budapesti Műszaki Egyetem, Mérnöktovábbképző Intézet.

A szövetkezeti anyaggazdálkodás és értékesítés főbb kérdései (The key questions of material management and sale in the cooperative sector). 1953. Budapest: Könnyűipari Kiadó.

Az önköltséget vizsgálták két üzemcsoport gyakorlatában (Production costs examined in the practice of two plants). 1983. *Vegyiművek*. June 20, 2.

B. Sz. [pseud.] 1985. Szemétimport (Garbage import). *Népszava*. July 20, n.p.

Bakonyi, Árpád. 1991. Hulladékok és másodnyersanyagok hasznosítása a gazdaságban (The utilization of wastes and secondary raw materials in the economy). *Anyaggazdálkodás és Raktárgazdálkodás* 19, no. 1:9–11.

Bánhidy, János. 1996. Letter to Kukabúvár. *Kukabúvár* 2, no. 2:15.

Baran, Paul, and Paul Sweezy. 1966. *Monopoly capital.* New York: Monthly Review Press.

Barany, Zoltan D. 1994. Living on the edge: The East European Roma in postcommunist politics and societies. *Slavic Review* 53, no. 1:321–44.

Bataille, Georges. 1988. *The accursed share: An essay on general economy.* New York: Zone Books.

Beck, Ulrich. 1992. *Risk society.* London: Sage Publications.

Berend, Iván T. 1979. *A szocialista gazdaság fejlődése Magyarországon 1945–1975* (The development of the socialist economy in Hungary, 1945–1975). Budapest: Kossuth Könyvkiadó.

Berki, Sándor. 1992. Trójai falovak, szent tehenek és más állatfajok (Trojan horses, sacred cows and other animal species). In *Leltár* (Confession), ed. Vera Gáthy. Budapest: MTA Társadalmi Konfliktusok Kutató Központja.

Berliner, Joseph S. 1957. *Factory and manager in the USSR.* Cambridge, Mass.: Harvard University Press.

Black, John. 2002. Efficiency. *A Dictionary of Economics.* Oxford University Press, 2002. *Oxford Reference Online.* Oxford University Press. University of Illinois–Urbana Champaign, January 27, 2006. www.oxfordreference.com/views/ENTRY.html?subview=Main&entry=t19.e957.

Blauner, Robert. 1967. *Alienation and freedom: The factory worker and his industry.* Chicago: University of Chicago Press.

Blumberg, Louis, and Robert Gottlieb. 1989. *War on waste: Can America win its battle with garbage?* Washington, D.C.: Island Press.

Bochniarz, Zbigniew, and Sándor Kerekes. 1994. Deficiencies in the existing system of environmental protection in Hungary. In *Designing institutions for sustainable development in Hungary: Agenda for the future*, ed. Zbigniew Bochniarz, R. Bolan, Sándor Kerekes, and József Kindler. Budapest: Környezettudományi Központ.

Bödecs, Barnabás. 1996. Szeméthegyen innen, termékdíjon túl (Before waste piles, beyond product charges). *Kukabúvár Melléklet önkormányzatok számára* (Supplement for local governments) 2, no. 2: vii–ix.

——. 1997. A HuMuSz javaslatai a hulladéktörvény szakmai koncepciójához (The proposals of HuMuSz for the conceptualization of the waste management law). *Kukabúvár* 3, no. 3: n.p. http://www.kukabuvar.hu/cikk/8066; accessed March 2005.

Bodnár, Judit. 2000. *Fin de millénaire Budapest: Metamorphoses of urban life.* Minneapolis: University of Minnesota Press.

Boer, J. Tom, Manuel Pastor, Jr., James L. Sadd, and Lori D. Snyder. 1997. Is there environmental racism? The demographics of hazardous waste in Los Angeles County. *Social Science Quarterly* 78, no. 4:793–810.

Bognár, Nándor. 1978. Minden grammból termék: Kár a szemétbe dobni—Korszerű anyagtechnológiák (From every gram a product: It's a pity to throw it in the trash—modern material technologies). *Magyar Hírlap.* February 9, n.p.

Bor, Ambrus. 1979. Visszaköröztetés (Recycling). *Magyar Nemzet.* October 15, n.p.

Bőripari Dolgozók Szakszervezete (Leather Workers' Union). 1951. *A Gazdamozgalom elmélyítésével segítsük elő ötéves tervünk sikerét* (Let's foment the success of our five-year plan by deepening the Gazda movement). Budapest: Egyetemi Nyomda.

Böröcz, József. 1992. Dual dependency and property vacuum: Social change on the state socialist semiperiphery. *Theory and Society* 21, no. 1:77–104.

——. 1993. Simulating the great transformation: Property change under prolonged informality in Hungary. *Archives européennes de sociologie/Europäisches Archiv für Soziologie/European Archives for Sociology* 34, no. 1 (May):81–107.

Böröcz, József, and Melinda Kovács, eds. 2001. *Empire's new clothes: Unveiling EU enlargement. Central Europe Review.* www.cereview.org/ebookstore/ebooks_main.html; accessed April 2003.

Bowker, Geoffrey C., and Susan Leigh Star. 1999. *Sorting things out: Classification and its consequences.* Cambridge, Mass.: MIT Press.

Brodersen, Jens, Matthew Crowe, and Henrik Jacobsen. 2001. *Hazardous waste generation in EEA member countries.* Copenhagen: European Environment Agency.

Bryant, Bunyan, and Paul Mohai, eds. 1992. Race and the incidence of environmental hazards: A time for discourse. Boulder, Colo.: Westview Press.

Bullard, Robert D. 1990. *Dumping in Dixie: Race, class, and environmental quality.* Boulder, Colo.: Westview Press.

Burawoy, Michael. 1985. *The politics of production.* London: Verso.

Burawoy, Michael, Alice Burton, Ann Arnett Ferguson, Kathryn J. Fox, Joshua Gamson, Nadine Gartrell, Leslie Hurst, Josepha Schiffman, Leslie Salzinger, and Shiori Ui. 1991. *Ethnography unbound: Power and resistance in the modern metropolis.* Berkeley: University of California Press.

Burawoy, Michael, Joseph Blum, Sheba George, Zsuzsa Gille, Teresa Gowan, Lynne Haney, Maren Klawiter, Steve Lopez, Sean O'Riain, and Millie Thayer. 2000. *Global ethnography: Forces, connections and imaginations in a postmodern world.* Berkeley: University of California Press.

Burawoy, Michael, and Kathryn Hendley. 1992. Between perestroika and privatisation: Divided strategies and political crisis in a Soviet enterprise. *Soviet Studies* 44, no. 3:371–402.

Burawoy, Michael, and Pavel Krotov. 1992. The Soviet transition from socialism to capitalism: Worker control and economic bargaining in the wood industry. *American Sociological Review* 57, no. 1:16–38.

Callon, Michel, John Law, and Arie Rip, eds. 1986. *Mapping the dynamics of science and technology: Sociology of science in the real world.* Basingstoke, UK: Macmillan.

Carruthers, Bruce G., and Wendy Nelson Espeland. 1991. Accounting for rationality: Double-entry bookkeeping and the rhetoric of economic rationality. *American Journal of Sociology* 97, no. 1:31–69.

Casper, Monica, ed. 2003. *Synthetic planet: Chemical politics and the hazards of modern life.* London: Routledge.

Catton, William R., Jr., and Riley Dunlap. 1978. Environmental sociology: A new paradigm. *The American Sociologist* 13, no. 1:41–49.

"The Chronicle of the Village of Garé." 1981. Baranya Megyei Levéltár (BML), Pécs.

Colborn, Theo, Dianne Dumanoski, and John Peterson Myers. 1997. *Our stolen future: Are we threatening our fertility, intelligence, and survival? A scientific detective story.* New York: Penguin.

Comaroff, John, and Jean Comaroff. 1992. *Ethnography and the historical imagination.* Boulder, Colo.: Westview Press.

Comisso, Ellen, and Paul Marer. 1986. The economics and politics of reform in Hungary. In *Power, purpose and collective choice: Economic strategy in socialist countries,* ed. Ellen Comisso and Laura D'Andrea Tyson. Ithaca, N.Y.: Cornell University Press.

Committee on Elimination of Waste in Industry of the Federated American Engineering Societies. 1974 (1921). *Waste in industry.* Easton, Pa.: Hive Publishing Co.

Costner, Pat, and Joe Thornton. 1993. *Playing with fire: Hazardous waste incineration.* Washington, D.C.: Greenpeace USA.

Cronon, William. 1983. *Changes in the land: Indians, colonists, and the ecology of New England.* New York: Hill and Wang.

———. 1991. *Nature's metropolis: Chicago and the Great West.* New York: W. W. Norton.

Sources and References

Darwin, Charles. 1996 (1859). *Natural selection*. Phoenix: Orion Books.

Davies, Steve. 2000. *The private sector and waste management in Central and Eastern Europe 2000*. London: PSIRU. http//www.psiru.org.

Davis, John W. 1999. *Fast track to waste-free manufacturing: Straight talk from a plant manager*. Portland, Ore.: Productivity Press.

DeBardeleben, Joan. 1985. *The environment and Marxism-Leninism: The Soviet and East German experience*. Boulder, Colo.: Westview Press.

———. 1991. *To breathe free: Eastern Europe's environmental crisis*. Baltimore: Johns Hopkins University Press.

Demeritt, David. 2002. What is the "social construction of nature"? A typology and sympathetic critique. *Progress in Human Geography* 26, no. 6:766–89.

Department of Wage, Production, and Economics of the Central Council of Hungarian Trade Unions. 1953. Report on the situation of socialist work competitions. Szakszervezetek Országos Tanácsa (SZOT). Levéltára, Budapest.

Des Chene, Mary. 1997. Locating the Past. In *Anthropological locations*, ed. A. Gupta and J. Ferguson. Berkeley: University of California Press.

Di Chiro, Giovanna. 1996. Nature as community: The convergence of environmental and social justice. In *Uncommon ground: Rethinking the human place in nature*, ed. William Cronon. New York: Norton.

DiMaggio, Paul. 1994. Culture and economy. In *Handbook of economic sociology*, ed. Neil Smelser and Richard Swedberg. Princeton, N.J.: Princeton University Press.

Dlusztus, Imre. 1989. *Vizlépcsőd. Bősi ülésszak* (Your dam: Bős session). Szeged, Hungary: Novum Kft.

Dömötör, Ákos. 1980. *A MÉH nyersanyaghasznositó tröszt története (1950–1980)* (The history of the MÉH Raw Material Utilization Trust, 1950–1980). Unpublished report.

Douglas, Mary. 1966. *Purity and danger: An analysis of concepts of pollution and taboo*. New York: Praeger.

Dowd, Douglas. 1989. *The waste of nations: Dysfunction in the world economy*. Boulder, Colo., and London: Westview Press.

Drábek, Zdenek. 1988. The natural resource intensity of production technology in market and planned economies: Austria vs. Czechoslovakia. *Journal of Comparative Economics* 12, no. 2:217–27.

Dryzek, John S. 1997. *The politics of the earth: Environmental discourses*. Oxford: Oxford University Press.

Dunn, Elizabeth. 1999. Slick salesmen and simple people: Negotiated capitalism in a privatized Polish firm. In *Uncertain transitions*, ed. Michael Burawoy and Katherine Verdery. Lanham, Md.: Rowman and Littlefield.

Dürrschmidt, Jörg. 1999. The "local" versus the "global"? "Individualised milieux" in a complex "risk society": The case of organic food box schemes in the South West. In *Consuming cultures: Power and resistance*, ed. Jeff Hearn and Sasha Roseneil. Basingstoke, UK: MacMillan.

Dworák, József. 1991. Magyarország hulladékgazdálkodása (Hungary's waste management). *Anyaggazdálkodás és Raktárgazdálkodás* 19, no. 2:20–26.

Egy év alatt 130 milliárd dollár értékü másodnyersanyag a népgazdaságnak (Raw materials worth $130 million per year for the people's economy). 1974. N.p.

Elefánti, Ervin. 1952. A mérlegmódszer szerepe és jelentősége az anyagellátás tervezésében. Az anyaggazdálkodás új rendszere (The role and significance of the balance system in planning material redistribution: The new system of material management). Budapest: Jogász Szövetség.

———. 1953. Az anyagtervezés néhány problémája (Some problems of material planning). Budapest: N.p.

Elek, Lenke. 1976. Pillantkép egy kis üzem nagy gondjairól (Snapshot of the big problems of a small plant). Magyar Hírlap. February 10, n.p.

Ember, György. 1952. Gazda-mozgalom a vasiparban (The Gazda movement in the iron industry). Budapest: Népszava and Szakszervezetek Országos Tanácsa Lap-és Könyvkiadó Vállalata.

Environmental Committee of the Hungarian Parliament. 2001. Minutes of the June 13th meeting on the National Waste Management Plan of the Article 56 in the 2000 Waste Act. Unpublished paper, Budapest. http//emil.alarmix.org/sajto/jegyzokonyv2001jun13.html.

European Environment Agency. 1999. Environment in the European Union at the Turn of the Century. Report No. 2. Unpublished paper, Copenhagen, Denmark.

Eurowaste. 2001. The final report on the project: Waste management policies in Central and Eastern European countries: Current policies and trends. Prague: DVC CR. www.eurowaste.org.; accessed April 2003.

Executive Committee of the Council of Baranya County. 1978. Minutes from January 3, 1978. Baranya Megyei Levéltár (BML), Pécs.

Fact Bt. 1995. A Garé térségében építendő hulladékégető társadalmi hatástanulmánya (The social impact study of the incinerator to be built in the vicinity of Garé). Pécs: Fact Bt.

Fagan, G. Honor. 2004. Waste management and its contestation in the Republic of Ireland. Capitalism, Nature, Socialism 15, no. 1 (March):83–102.

Fahidy, József. 1976. A jövő útja: hulladékból nyersanyag (The path of the future: Raw material from waste). Népszabadság. March 30, n.p.

Fehér, Ferenc, Ágnes Heller, and György Márkus. 1983. Dictatorship over needs. New York: St. Martin's Press.

Fejes, Endre. 1964. Rozsdatemető (Generation of rust). Budapest: Magvető.

Ferenczi, József. 1985. Szemét a szomszédból: Kényszerböl—kísérletként (Garbage from the neighborhood: Of necessity—as an experiment). Kisalföld. September 10, n.p.

Feshbach, Murray, and Alfred Friendly, Jr. 1992. Ecocide in the USSR: Health and nature under siege. New York: Basic Books.

Filtzer, Donald. 1986. Soviet workers and Stalinist industrialization: The formation of modern Soviet production relations. London: Pluto Press.

———. 1992. Soviet workers and de-Stalinization: The consolidation of the modern system of Soviet production relations, 1953–1964. Cambridge: Cambridge University Press.

Sources and References

Fogaskerék. 1951. No title. October 13, 2.

Fővárosi Tanács Végrehajtó Bizottsága (Executive Committee of the Council of Budapest). 1967. Report on municipal waste depositories, presented at the meeting on November 22, 1967. Budapest Főváros Levéltára (BFL), Budapest.

Fraser, Nancy. 1989. *Unruly practices: Power, discourse and gender in contemporary social theory.* Minneapolis: University of Minnesota Press.

French, Hilary F. 1990. *Green revolutions: Environmental reconstruction in Eastern Europe and the Soviet Union.* World Watch Paper No. 99. Washington, D.C.: World Watch Institute.

Frey, R Scott. 1998. The export of hazardous industries to the peripheral zones of the world-system. *Journal of Developing Societies* 14, no. 1:66–81.

Frow, John. 2003. Invidious distinction: Waste, difference and classy stuff. In *Culture and waste: The creation and destruction of value,* ed. Gay Hawkins and Stephen Muecke. Oxford: Rowman and Littlefield.

Gábor, István R. 1990. A magánvállalkozás és a polgárosodás kilátásairól (On the prospects of private entrepreneurship and bourgeoisification). *Valóság* 33, no. 6:49–55.

Gandy, Matthew. 1994. *Recycling and the politics of urban waste.* London: Earthscan Publications.

Gaventa, John. 1980. *Power and powerlessness: Quiescence and rebellion in an Appalachian valley.* Chicago: University of Illinois Press.

Gazda, Géza. 1951. Használjunk fel minden gramm hulladékot! (Let's use every gram of waste!). *Szabad Nép.* August 14, 1.

Geertz, Clifford. 1983. *Local knowledge: Further essays in interpretive anthropology.* New York: Basic Books.

Gervais, Caroline. n.d. *An overview of European waste and resource management policy (executive summary).* Royal Society for Nature Conservation. www.forum forthefuture.org.uk/uploadstore/Ex%20Sum%20–%20An%20Overview%20of %20European%20Waste%20and%20Resource%20Management%20Policy.pdf.

Gille, Zsuzsa. 1997. Two pairs of women's boots for a hectare of land: Nature and the construction of the environmental problem in state socialism. *Capitalism, Nature, Socialism* 8, no. 4:1–21.

———. 2000. Cognitive cartography in a European wasteland: Multinationals and Greens vie for village allegiance. In M. Burawoy et al., *Global ethnography: Forces, connections and imaginations in a postmodern world.* Berkeley, Calif.: University of California Press, 240–67.

———. 2005. Detached flows or grounded place-making projects? In *Towards a sociology of environmental flows: A new agenda for 21st century environmental sociology,* ed. Arthur P. J. Mol and Gert Spaargaren. Cambridge, Mass.: MIT Press.

Gille, Zsuzsa, and Sean O'Riain. 2000. Global ethnography. *Annual Review of Sociology* 28:271–95.

Gluszynski, Pawel, and Iza Kruszewska. 1996. *Western pyromania moves East: A case study in hazardous technology transfer.* Greenpeace. www.rec.hu/poland/wpa/pyro-toc.htm.

Goldman, Marshall I. 1972. *The spoils of progress: Environmental pollution in the Soviet Union.* Cambridge, Mass.: MIT Press.

Goldman, Michael, and Rachel Schurman. 2000. Closing the "great divide": New social theory on society and nature. *Annual Review of Sociology* 26:563–84.

Gömöri, András. 1974. Nincs kincs. Legenda és valóság a budapesti szeméttelepekröl (No treasures: The legend and reality of the garbage dumps of Budapest). *Magyar Hírlap.* January 24, n.p.

Gomulka, Stanislaw, and Jacek Rostowski. 1988. An international comparison of material intensity. *Journal of Comparative Economics* 12, no. 4:475–501.

Gottlieb, Robert. 1993. *Forcing the spring: The transformation of the American environmental movement.* Washington, D.C.: Island Press.

———. 2001. *Environmentalism unbound: Exploring new pathways for change.* Cambridge, Mass.: MIT Press.

Gourlay, K. A. 1992. *World of waste: Dilemmas of industrial development.* London: Zed Books.

Gudeman, Stephen. 1986. *Economics as culture: Models and metaphors of livelihood.* London: Boston and Henley, UK: Routledge and Kegan Paul.

Gustafson, Thane. 1981. *Reform in Soviet politics: Lessons of recent policies on land and water.* Cambridge: Cambridge University Press.

Hajdú-Bihari Napló. 1985. No title. April 20, n.p.

Hajer, Maarten. 1995. *The politics of environmental discourse: Ecological modernization and the policy process.* Oxford: Clarendon Press.

Hann, Chris, ed. 2002. *Postsocialism: Ideal, ideologies and practices in Eurasia.* London: Routledge.

Haraszti, Miklós. 1977. *Workers in a workers' state.* London: Penguin.

Haraway, Donna J. 1991. Situated knowledges: The science question in feminism and the privilege of partial perspective. In *Simians, cyborgs, and women: The reinvention of nature.* New York: Routledge.

Harper, Krista. 1999. From green dissidents to green skeptics: Environmental activists and post-socialist political ecology in Hungary. Ph.D. dissertation, University of California, Santa Cruz.

Hartsock, Nancy C. M. 1987. The feminist standpoint: Developing the ground for a specifically feminist historical materialism. In *Feminism and methodology,* ed. Sandra Harding. Bloomington: Indiana University Press.

Harvey, David. 1989. *The condition of postmodernity.* Oxford: Basil Blackwell.

Havas, Henrik. 1988. *A Bős-Nagymaros dosszié, avagy egy beruházás hordalékai.* (The Bős-Nagymaros file, or the sediments of an investment). Budapest: Codex Rt.

Hawken, Paul, Amory Lovins, and L. Hunter Lovins. 1999. *Natural capitalism: Creating the next industrial revolution.* Boston: Little, Brown and Co.

Hawkins, Gay, and Stephen Muecke, eds. 2003. *Culture and waste: The creation and destruction of value.* Oxford: Rowman and Littlefield.

Hawley, Gessner Goodrich. 1993. *Hawley's condensed chemical dictionary,* ed. R. J. Lewis, Sr. New York: Van Nostrand Reinhold.

Sources and References

Hellebust, Rolf. 1997. Aleksei Gastev and the metallization of the revolutionary body. *Slavic Review* 56, no. 3:501–18.

Hill, Sarah. 2003a. Metaphoric enrichment and material poverty: The making of colonias. In *Ethnography at the Border*, ed. Pablo Vila. Minneapolis: University of Minnesota Press.

———. 2003b. The wasted resources of *Mexicanidad*: Consumption and disposal on Mexico's northern frontier. In *The social relations of Mexican commodities: Power, production, and place*, ed. Casey Walsh, Elizabeth Emma Ferry, Gabriela Sota Laveaga, Paola Sesia, and Sarah Hill. La Jolla, Calif.: Center for U.S.-Mexican Studies, University of California, San Diego.

Hopwood, Anthony G., and Peter Miller. 1994. *Accounting as social and institutional practice*. Cambridge and New York: Cambridge University Press.

Horton, Stephen. 1997. Value, waste and the built environment: Marxian analysis. *Capitalism, Nature, Socialism* 8, no. 2 (30): 127–39.

Horváth, Annamária. 1985. Amíg egyeztetik a fogalmakat (While the concepts are being harmonized). *Népszava*. April 25, 4.

Horváth, János. 1981. "Összefoglaló" (Summary). In *Tűz- és robbanásveszélyes, valamint mérgező gyógyszeripari hulladékok megsemmisítésével kapcsolatos gondok, problémák* (Troubles and problems associated with the elimination of inflammable, explosive, and toxic pharmaceutical wastes), ed. J. Nuridsány. Budapest: Magyar Gyógyszeripari Egyesülés.

Hrabal, Bohumil. 1990. *Too loud a solitude*. San Diego: Harcourt Brace Jovanovich.

Hughes, Gordon. 1990. *Are the costs of cleaning up Eastern Europe exaggerated? Economic reform and the environment*. London: Centre for Economic Policy Research.

Humphrey, Caroline. 1991. "Icebergs," barter, and the mafia in provincial Russia. *Anthropology Today* 7, no. 2:8–13.

———. 1999. Traders, "disorder," and citizenship regimes in provincial Russia. In *Uncertain transitions*, ed. Michael Burawoy and Katherine Verdery. Lanham Md.: Rowman and Littlefield.

———. 2002. The unmaking of Soviet life: Everyday economies after socialism. Ithaca, N.Y.: Cornell University Press.

Hungaropec. 1993. *Tájékoztató a Garéban tervezett ipari hulladékégetőről* (Information on the incinerator planned in Garé). Budapest: Burson-Marsteller.

Jameson, Fredric. 1991. *Postmodernism, or, the cultural logic of late capitalism*. Durham, N.C.: Duke University Press.

Jancar, Barbara. 1987. *Environmental management in the Soviet Union and Yugoslavia: Structure and regulation in federal Communist states*. Durham, N.C.: Duke University Press.

Jávor, András. 1954. *Az anyagtakarékosság és önköltségcsökkentés műszaki feladatai a vegyiparban* (The technical tasks of material conservation and cost reduction in the chemical industry). Budapest: Felsőoktatási Jegyzetellátó Vállalat.

Jócsik, Lajos. 1977. *Egy ország a csillagon* (A country on the star). Budapest: Szépirodalmi Könyvkiadó.

Jonesburg, Harry. 1992. *The waste streams of ignorance*. Dayton, Ohio: Les Livres.

Juhász, Ádám, Dr. 1981. Az anyagtakarékosság lehetőségei és feladatai az iparban— Tézisek (Conference on the potentials and tasks of material savings—Theses). In *Az információ 1981. évi helyzete—Az anyaggazdálkodás helyzete és fejlesztésének irányai* (The situation of information in 1981: The situation and directions of development of material savings). Budapest: MTESZ.

Juhász, Judit, Anna Vári, and János Tölgyesi. 1993. Environmental conflict and political change: Public perception on low-level radioactive waste management in Hungary. In *Environment and democratic transition: Policy and politics in Central and Eastern Europe*, ed. Anna Vári and Pál Tamás. Boston: Kluwer Academic Publishers.

Kaderják, Péter. 1997. Economics for environmental policy in the Central Eastern European transformation: How are the context and textbook prescriptions related? In *Economics for environmental policy in transition economies: An analysis of the Hungarian experience*, ed. P. Kaderják and J. Powell. Cheltenham, UK: Edward Elgar.

Kiguberált milliárdok (Scavenged billions). 1981. *Heti Világgazdaság*. March 21, 28–29.

Kindler, József. 1994. Evaluation of economic, social, and political preconditions for a successful implementation of the institutional reform. In *Designing institutions for sustainable development in Hungary: Agenda for the future*, ed. Zbigniew Bochniarz, R. Bolan, Sándor Kerekes, and József Kindler. Budapest: Környezettudományi Központ.

Kingzett, Charles Thomas. 1966. *Kingzett's chemical encyclopaedia: A digest of chemistry and its industrial applications*, ed. D. H. Hey. London: Bailliere, Tindall and Cassell.

Klarer, Jürg, and Patrick Francis. 1997. Regional overview. In *The environmental challenge for Central European economies in transition*, ed. Jürg Klarer and Bedrich Moldan. Chichester, UK: John Wiley and Sons.

Klarer, Jürg, and Bedrich Moldan. 1997. *The environmental challenge for Central European economies in transition*. Chichester, UK: John Wiley and Sons.

Klíma, Ivan. 1991. *Love and garbage*. New York: Alfred A. Knopf.

Kolstad, Charles F. 2000. *Environmental economics*. Oxford: Oxford University Press.

Komárom D. L. 1971. No title. March 11, n.p.

Komarov, Boris [Zeev Wolfson]. 1980. *The destruction of nature in the Soviet Union*. White Plains, N.Y.: M. E. Sharpe.

Konrád, György, and Iván Szelényi. 1979. *The intellectuals on the road to class power*. New York: Harcourt Brace Jovanovich.

Koopmans, T. C. 1951. Analysis of production as an efficient combination of activities. In *Activity analysis of production and allocation*, ed. Tjalling Charles Koopmans. New York: John Wiley and Sons.

Korányi, Tamás G. 1987. Égetőgondok (Burning issues). *Ötlet*. February 26, 34–35.

Kornai, János. 1959. *A gazdasági vezetés túlzott központosítása: Kritikai elemzés*

Sources and References

könnyűipari tapasztalatok alapján (The overcentralization of economic management: Critical analysis based on experiences from light industry). Budapest:
Közgazdasági és Jogi Könyvkiadó.

———. 1980. *Economics of shortage*. Amsterdam: North-Holland.

———. 1986. A gazdaságos anyagfelhasználás és a technológiák korszerüsítésének
eredményei és feladatai az iparban (The results and tasks of economical material use and technological modernization in industry). In *VI. Anyaggazdál-
kodási Akadémia előadásai* (Lectures of the Sixth Material Management Academy), ed. Attila Sallay. Debrecen, Hungary: Szervezési és Vezetési Tudományos Társaság, Magyar Tudományos Akadémia.

———. 1990. The affinity between ownership forms and coordination mechanisms:
The common experience of reform in socialist countries. *Journal of Economic
Perspectives* 4, no. 3:131–47.

környei [pseud.]. 1976. A környezetvédelem nagy gondja: Mi legyen a veszélyes
hulladékokkal? (The big problem of environmental protection: What should be
done with hazardous wastes?). *Magyar Nemzet*. December 9, 5.

Kozma, Judit. 1982. Gazdag lelőhely (Rich source). *Népszabadság*. July 9, n.p.

Kristóf, Imre. 1982. Az anyaggazdálkodás eredményei az iparban a hetvenes évek-
ben (The achievements of material management in the industry in the seventies). *Ipargazdaság* 34, nos. 8–9:60–64.

KSH (Központi Statisztikai Hivatal) (Central Bureau of Statistics). 1952. Jelentés a
szövetkezetek tevékenységéről (Report on the activities of cooperatives). Budapest: Központi Statisztikai Hivatal.

———. 1953. Jelentés a szövetkezetek tevékenységéről (Report on the activities of
cooperatives). Budapest: Központi Statisztikai Hivatal.

———. 1983. Statisztikai fogalmak meghatározásának jegyzéke (List of definitions for
statistical categories). Budapest: Központi Statisztikai Hivatal.

———. 1988. Központi fejlesztési programok. A melléktermék-és hulladékhasznosí-
tási program 1987. évi eredményei (Central development programs: The results
for the year 1987 of the by-product and waste reuse program). Budapest: Központi Statisztikai Hivatal.

Kuletz, Valerie L. 1998. *The tainted desert: Environmental and social ruin in the
American West*. London: Routledge.

L. Gy. 1951. No title. *Szabad Nép*. May 6, 5.

Ladó, László, Gábor Romhányi, and Katalin Büchner. 1983. *Az anyagforgalmi
diagramok a környezetvédelemben* (Material flow charts in environmental protection). Budapest: Környezetvédelmi Minisztérium.

Lampland, Martha. 1995. *The object of labor: Commodification in socialist Hungary*. Chicago: University of Chicago Press.

Larrimore, Mark. 1999. Sublime waste: Kant on the destiny of the "races." In
Civilization and oppression, ed. Catherine Wilson. Alberta: University of Cal-
gary Press.

Latour, Bruno. 2004. *Politics of nature: How to bring the sciences into democracy*.
Cambridge, Mass.: Harvard University Press.

Latour, Bruno, and Steve Woolgar. 1979. *Laboratory life: The social construction of scientific facts.* Beverly Hills: Sage Publications.

Ledeneva, Alena V. 1998. *Russia's economy of favours: Blat, networking and informal exchange.* Cambridge: Cambridge University Press.

Lehoczki, Zsuzsa, and Zsuzsanna Balogh. 1997. Hungary. In *The environmental challenge for Central European economies in transition,* ed. J. Klarer and B. Moldan. Chichester, UK: John Wiley and Sons.

Lemon, Alaina. 2000. Talking transit and spectating transition: The Moscow metro. In *Altering states: Ethnographies of transition in Eastern Europe and the former Soviet Union,* ed. Daphne Berdahl, Matti Bunzl, and Martha Lampland. Ann Arbor: University of Michigan Press.

Lewis, Flora. 1990. The red grime line. *New York Times.* April 10, A(21)L.

Lipschutz, Ronnie D., and Judith Mayer. 1996. *Global civil society and global environmental governance: The politics of nature from place to planet.* Albany, N.Y.: SUNY Press.

Lukács, Georg. 1971 (1922). *History and class consciousness.* Cambridge, Mass.: MIT Press.

Luton, Larry S. 1996. *The politics of garbage: A community perspective on solid waste policy making.* Pittsburgh: University of Pittsburgh Press.

Mándi, Péter. 1951. A pártszervezetek feladatai az anyagtakarékosság terén (The tasks of the party organs in the area of material savings). *Pártépítés* 7:15.

Marcus, George E. 1998. *Ethnography through thick and thin.* Princeton, N.J.: Princeton University Press.

Marcuse, Herbert. 1964. *One-dimensional man.* Boston: Beacon Press.

Markham, Adam. 1994. *A brief history of pollution.* New York: St. Martin's Press.

Massey, Doreen. 1994. *Space, place and gender.* Minneapolis: University of Minnesota Press.

Matthes, F., and L. Mez, eds. 1996. *Ten years after the Chernobyl disaster: Electricity in Eastern Europe.* Berlin: Heinrich-Böll-Stiftung, with Öko-Institut and Forschungsstelle für Umweltpolitik.

McMichael, Philip. 1996. Globalization: Myths and realities. *Rural Sociology* 61, no. 1:25–55.

Megéri takarékoskodni, csakhogy veszítsünk rajta? (Is it worth being thrifty just to lose money at it?). 1979. *Vegyiművek.* N.d., n.p.

Melosi, Martin V. 1981. *Garbage in the cities: Refuse, reform, and the environment, 1880–1980.* College Station: Texas A&M University Press.

Mélykúti, Attila. 1986. A mérgezett föld dokumentumai 2. Veszélyes vagy nem veszélyes hulladék? (The documents of poisoned soil, part 2: Hazardous or nonhazardous waste?). *Népszabadság.* August 23, 6.

Mengham, Rod. n.d. *Ilya Kabakov: A short critical biography.* www.ilya-emilia-kabakov.com/biography.pdf.

Mennyi hulladék képződik Magyarországon? (How much waste is generated in Hungary?). 2002. *Kukabúvár* 8, no. 3 (Fall). www.kukabuvar.hu/2002/osz?page=3.

Sources and References

Merchant, Carolyn. 1989. *Ecological revolutions: Nature, gender and science in New England*. Chapel Hill and London: University of North Carolina Press.

——. 1996. Reinventing Eden: Western culture as a recovery narrative. In *Uncommon ground: Rethinking the human place in nature*, ed. William Cronon. New York: Norton.

Miklós, Dezső. 1975. Ennyire gazdagok vagyunk? Kihasználatlan tartalékunk: a gumihulladék (Are we this rich? Our unutilized reserve: rubber waste). *Népszava*. November 20, n.p.

Miller, Benjamin. 2000. *Fat of the land: Garbage in New York: The last two hundred years*. New York and London: Four Walls Eight Windows.

Miller, Richard K. 1995. Incineration: Industry execs see bright future for incineration. *Waste Age*. January 1, n.p. www.wasteage.com/mag/waste incineration industry execs/; accessed April 2003.

Mills, C. Wright. 1967. *The sociological imagination*. Oxford: Oxford University Press.

Mol, Arthur P. J. 1995. *The refinement of production: Ecological modernization theory and the chemical industry*. Utrecht: Van Arkel.

Molnár, Patricia. 1979. Fáradhatatlanul—a fáradt olajért (Untiringly—for used oil). *Népszava*. October 3, n.p.

Molotch, Harvey. 2003. *Where stuff comes from: How toasters, toilets, cars, computers, and many other things come to be as they are*. New York: Routledge.

Mónus, Miklós. 1983. Elsődlegesen fontos másodnyersanyag (Secondary raw material of primary importance). *Népszava*. June 30, 12.

Moroney, John. R. 1990. Energy consumption, capital and real output: A comparison of market and planned economies. *Journal of Comparative Economics* 14, no. 2:199–220.

Morris, Meaghan. 2003. Back cover endorsement. In *Culture and waste: The creation and destruction of value*, ed. Gay Hawkins and Stephen Muecke. Oxford: Rowman and Littlefield.

Moser, Walter. 2000. The acculturation of waste. In *Waste-site stories: The recycling of memory*, ed. Brian Neville and Johanne Villeneuve. Albany, N.Y.: SUNY Press.

MTI (Magyar Távirati Iroda) (Hungarian News Agency). 1981a. Intézkedések a veszélyes hulladékok ellenőrzéséről, újrahasznosításáról (Measures concerning the control and reuse of hazardous wastes). *Népszava*. November 13, n.p.

——. 1981b. Hasznosítják az ipari hulladékot (Industrial wastes reused). *Népszava*. July 25, n.p.

Mukerji, Chandra. 1983. *From graven images: Patterns of modern materialism*. New York: Columbia University Press.

Murphy, Raymond. 1994. *Rationality and nature: A sociological inquiry into a changing relationship*. Boulder, Colo.: Westview Press.

Murray, Robin. 1999. *Creating wealth from waste*. London: Demos.

Mutch, David. 1990. Cleaning up the environment seen as major task in a united Germany. *Christian Science Monitor*. May 17, 4.

N. Gy. [pseud.]. 1981. Teljesítik terveiket. Ötmillió forintos anyagtakarékosság—Egyedi termékek a Szerves A üzemben (They are fulfilling their plans: Material savings of five million Forints—Unique products in the plant "Organic A"). *Vegyiművek.* October 12, 1.

Nadiri, M. Ishaq. 1987. Joint production. In *The new Palgrave: A dictionary of economics,* ed. John Eatwell, Murray Milgate, and Peter K. Newman. London: Macmillan.

Nagle, Robin. Forthcoming. To love a landfill. In *Healing Natures,* ed. Robert France. Cambridge, Mass.: MIT Press.

Nazarea-Sandoval, Virginia D. 1991. Some lessons to be learned (still) in integrating women's concerns into farming systems research. *Journal of Asian Farming Systems Association* 1:153–77.

Népszabadság. 1972. No title. January 14, n.p.

Népszabadság. N.d. No title. March 10, n.p.

NÉTI [pseud.]. 1987. Az anyag nem vész el, csak drágább lesz: Feltáratlan kincses-bányáink (The material does not get lost, it only gets more expensive: Our unexplored treasure mines). *Mai Magazin.* March 6, n.p.

Neville, Brian, and Johanne Villeneuve, eds. 2000. *Waste-site stories: The recycling of memory.* Albany, N.Y.: SUNY Press.

Newman, Oksana, and Allan Foster. 1993. *European environmental statistics handbook.* London, Detroit, and Washington, D.C.: Research International.

Nove, Alec. 1980. *The Soviet economic system.* London: George Allen and Unwin.

The Number 12/1966 decree of the President of Nitrokémia. 1966. *Nitro Közlöny.* N.d., n.p.

Nuridsány, János. 1981. Bevezetés (Introduction). In *Tűz-és robbanásveszélyes, valamint mérgező gyógyszeripari hulladékok megsemmisítésével kapcsolatos gondok, problémák* (Troubles and problems associated with the elimination of inflammable, explosive and toxic pharmaceutical wastes), ed. J. Nuridsány. Budapest: Magyar Gyógyszeripari Egyesülés.

O'Brien, Martin. 1999. Rubbish-power: Towards a sociology of the rubbish society. In *Consuming cultures: Power and resistance,* ed. J. Hearn and S. Roseneil. Basingstoke, UK: MacMillan.

O'Connor, James. 1988. Capitalism, nature, socialism: A theoretical introduction. *Capitalism, Nature, Socialism* 1, no. 1 (Fall): 11–38.

——. 1989a. Political economy of ecology. *Capitalism, Nature, Socialism* 3:93–107.

——. 1989b. Uneven and combined development and ecological crisis: A theoretical introduction. *Race & Class* 30, no. 3:1–11.

Olessák, Dénes. 1982. A veszélyes hulladékok kezelésének helyzete és fejlődési irányai Magyarországon (The situation and directions of development of the treatment of hazardous wastes in Hungary). *Építés és Minőség.* no. 3:41–43.

Omole, T. A. 1983. *Waste recycling in the food chain.* Ife, Nigeria: University of Ife Press.

Országos Közegészségügyi Intézet és Budapest Fővárosi Tanács VB (National Institute of Public Health and the Executive Committee of the Council of Budapest). 1961. Szemét- és Hulladékkezelési Ankét (Conference on the Management of Garbage and Waste). Budapest Főváros Levéltára (BFL), Budapest.

Packard, Vance. 1960. *The waste makers*. New York: David McKay.

Pálffy, Judit. 1981. Sok öntvényen pazarló a ráhagyás (Wasteful allowance on many castings). *Esti Hírlap*. March 7, n.p.

Pearce, Frank. 1990. Responsible corporations and regulatory agencies. *Political Quarterly* 61, no. 4:415–30.

Pécsi Zöld Kör. n.d. A király meztelen (The emperor has no clothes). Pécs, Hungary: Pécsi Zöld Kör.

Pellow, David Naguib. 2002a. *Garbage wars: The struggle for environmental justice in Chicago*. Cambridge, Mass.: MIT Press.

——. 2002b. *The Silicon Valley of dreams: Environmental injustice, immigrant workers, and the high-tech global economy*. New York: New York University Press.

Pető, Iván, and Sándor Szakács. 1985. A *hazai gazdaság négy évtizedének története* (The four-decade history of the national economy). Budapest: Közgazdasági és Jogi Könyvkiadó.

Pickering, Andrew. 1995. *The mangle of practice: Time, agency, and science*. Chicago: University of Chicago Press.

Pickvance, Chris. 1996. Environmental and housing movements in cities after socialism: The cases of Budapest and Moscow. In *Cities after Socialism*, ed. G. Andrusz, M. Harloe, and I. Szelényi. Cambridge, Mass.: Blackwell.

Pieper, Weiner. 1987. *Das Scheiss Buch: Entstehung, Nützung, Entsorgung menschlicher Fäkalien* (The shit book: The origin, use and disposal of human fecal matter). Löhrbach, Federal Republic of Germany: Medienexperimente.

Pintér, Lajos. 1951. Példaképünk a Szovjetunió ellenőrzésének első népbiztosa: Sztálin (Our model is the First Commissar of Public Inspection of the Soviet Union: Stalin). *Motor* 6, no. 53:3.

Ponting, Clive. 1991. *The green history of the world: The environment and the collapse of great civilizations*. New York: Penguin.

Porter, Richard C. 2002. *The economics of waste*. Washington, D.C.: Resources for the Future Press.

Pusztai, Éva. 1972. Vevőre vár a vashulladék (Iron waste awaits buyers). *Déli Hírlap*. April 7, n.p.

Radio Free Europe. 1979. Hungarian Monitoring (transcripts). July 7, 1979.

——. 1981. Hungarian Monitoring (transcripts). October 3, 1981.

——. 1983. Hungarian Monitoring (transcripts). April 28, 1983.

Radocsai, László. 1952. Selejtelszámolás a kohó-és gépipari vállalatoknál (The accounting of rejects at enterprises in the smelter and machine industries). *Számvitel* 3, no. 11:831–43.

Redclift, Michael. 1996. *Counting the costs of global consumption*. London: Earthscan.

Regional Environmental Center. 1997. *Demand for environmental technologies in the Czech Republic, Hungary, Poland and Slovakia: A Showcase Europe market research project.* Budapest: Regional Environmental Center.

Reich, Teréz. 1990. Community action for environment and health: A case study from Hungary. In *Environment and health in Eastern Europe: Proceedings of the symposium on occupational health during societal transition in Eastern Europe,* ed. B. Levy and C. Levenstein. Pécs, Hungary: United States–Eastern Europe Exchange for Occupational and Environmental Health; and Boston: Management Sciences for Health.

Remetei, Ferencné. 1986. A hulladék és másodnyersanyagok programjának eredményei és tapasztalatai 1981–1985 (The results and experiences of the waste and secondary raw materials program, 1981–1985). *Ipari és Építőipari Statisztikai Értesítő.* December, 465–81.

Remmert, Hermann. 1980. *Ecology, a textbook.* Trans. M. A. Biederman-Thorson. Berlin and New York: Springer-Verlag.

Repa, Edward W. 2001. *The U.S. solid waste industry: How big is it?* An Environmental Research and Education Foundation study that more accurately determines the size of the U.S. solid waste industry—Special report. *Waste Age,* December 1. wasteage.com/mag/waste_us_solid_waste/index.html.

Rév, István. 1989. The anti-ecological nature of centralization. In *The new détente: Rethinking East-West relations,* ed. Mary Kaldor, Gerard Holden, and Richard A. Falk. London: Verso; and Tokyo: United Nations University.

Ricklefs, Robert E. 1993. *The economy of nature: A textbook in basic ecology.* New York: W. H. Freeman.

Ries, Nancy. 1997. *Surviving economic hardship in Russia.* Washington, D.C.: National Council for Eurasian and East European Research.

Román, Marian. 1985. Egy kisváros nagy gondja. Vihar a dorogi szemétégető körül (The big problem of a small town: Storm around the garbage incinerator of Dorog). *Népszabadság.* April 23, 6.

Sajó, András. 1994. Legal aspects of environmental protection in Hungary: Some experiences of a draftsman. In *Designing institutions for sustainable development in Hungary: Agenda for the future,* ed. Zbigniew Bochniarz, R. Bolan, Sándor Kerekes, and József Kindler. Budapest: Környezettudományi Központ.

Sampson, Steven. 1999. The social life of projects: Importing civil society to Albania. In *Civil society: Challenging Western models,* ed. Chris Hann and Elizabeth Dunn. London: Routledge.

Schefold, Bertram. 1987. Joint production in linear models. In *The new Palgrave: A dictionary of economics,* ed. John Eatwell, Murray Milgate, and Peter Newman. London: Macmillan.

Schnaiberg, Allan. 1980. *The environment: From surplus to scarcity.* New York: Oxford University Press.

Schnaiberg, Allan, and Kenneth Alan Gould. 1994. *Environment and society: The enduring conflict.* New York: St. Martin's Press.

Schöpflin, George. 1995. Post-communism: A profile. *The Public* 2, no. 1:63–72.

Schor, Juliet. 2000. *Do Americans shop too much?* Boston: Beacon Press.

Schultz, Irmgard. 1993. Women and waste. *Capitalism, Nature, Socialism* 4, no. 2(14):51–63.

Schwartz, John, Carla Koehl, and Karen Breslau. 1990. Cleaning up by cleaning up. *Newsweek.* June 11, 40–41.

Schwartz, Katrina Z. 2006. *Nature and national identity after communism: Globalizing the ethnoscape.* Pittsburgh: University of Pittsburgh Press.

Scott, James C. 1998. *Seeing like a state: How certain schemes to improve the human condition have failed.* New Haven, Conn.: Yale University Press.

Sebestyén, Tibor. 1973. Anyagmentés—nagyban (Salvaging materials—On a large scale). *Figyelő.* February 14, n.p.

Seuss, Dr. 1979. *Oh Say Can You Say.* New York: Beginner Books.

Simons, Marlise. 1993. West offers plan to help clean up East Europe. *New York Times.* May 4, n.p.

Sláma, Jirí. 1986. An international comparison of sulphur dioxide emissions. *Journal of Comparative Economics* 10, no. 3:277–92.

Socolow, Robert. 1994. Six perspectives from industrial ecology. In *Industrial ecology and global change,* ed. R. Socolow, C. Andrews, F. Berkhout, and V. Thomas. Cambridge: Cambridge University Press.

Solomon, Laurence. 1990. The best Earth Day present: Freedom. *Wall Street Journal.* April 20, A14.

Sólyom, József. 1975. Szemlélet és százmilliók (Perception and hundreds of millions). *Népszabadság.* November 5, n.p.

Spaargaren, Gert, and Arthur P. J. Mol. 1992. Sociology, environment, and modernity: Ecological modernization as a theory of social change. *Society and Natural Resources* 5, no. 4:323–44.

spider [pseud.]. 2003. A mocsok szemét (The dirty garbage). www.axelero.hu.

Spies, Sherrill, Steve H. Murdock, Steve White, Richard Krannich, Jeffry Dean Wulfhorst, Krissa Wrigley, F. Larry Leistritz, Randy Sell, and JoAnn Thompson. 1998. Support for waste facility siting: Differences between community leaders and residents. *Rural Sociology* 63, no. 1:65–93.

Staniszkis, Jadwiga. 1991a. *Dynamics of the breakthrough in Eastern Europe: The Polish experience.* Berkeley: University of California Press.

——. 1991b. "Political capitalism" in Poland. *East European Politics and Societies* 5, no. 1:127–41.

——. 1992. *The ontology of socialism.* Oxford: Clarendon Press.

Stanners, David, and Philippe Bourdeau. 1995. *Europe's environment: The Dobris Assessment.* Copenhagen: European Environment Agency.

Stark, David, and László Bruszt. 1998. *Postsocialist pathways: Transforming politics and property in East Central Europe.* Cambridge: Cambridge University Press.

Strasser, Susan. 1999. *Waste and want: A social history of trash.* New York: Metropolitan Books.

Svastics, Kinga. 1999. *Waste management, Hungary, industry sector analysis.* www.tradeport.org/ts/countries/hungary/isa/isar0005.html.

Szabad Nép. 1951a. No title. May 19, n.p.

Szabad Nép. 1951b. No title. May 8, n.p.

Szabad Nép. 1951c. No title. May 12, n.p.

Szabad Nép. 1951d. No title. October 10, 5.

Szabad Nép. 1951e. No title. June 7, 5.

Szasz, Andrew. 1994. *Ecopopulism.* Minneapolis and London: University of Minnesota Press.

——. 1995. The iconography of hazardous waste. In *Cultural politics and social movements,* ed. Marcy Darnovsky, Barbara Epstein, and Richard Flacks. Philadelphia: Temple University Press.

Szasz, Andrew, and Michael Meuser. 2000. Unintended, inexorable: The production of environmental inequalities in Santa Clara County, California. *American Behavioral Scientist* 43, no. 4:602–32.

Szász, Károly. 1981. Tűz -és robbanásveszélyes, valamint mérgező gyógyszeripari hulladékok megsemmisítésével kapcsolatos gondok, problémák (Troubles and problems associated with the elimination of inflammable, explosive, and toxic pharmaceutical wastes). In *Tűz -és robbanásveszélyes, valamint mérgező gyógyszeripari hulladékok megsemmisítésével kapcsolatos gondok, problémák* (Troubles and problems associated with the elimination of inflammable, explosive, and toxic pharmaceutical wastes), ed. János Nuridsány. Budapest: Magyar Gyógyszeripari Egyesülés.

Százezres érték a hulladék között (Values worth hundreds of thousands among the wastes). 1951. *Szabad Nép.* October 24, 5.

Székely, Attila. 1991. Az ipari hulladékgazdálkodás helyzete és problémái (The state and problems of industrial waste management). *Anyaggazdálkodás és raktárgazdálkodás* 19, no. 12:22–27.

Székely, Gábor. 1951. Harc az egyéni megtakarítási számlák széleskörü bevezetéséért (Struggle for the wide implementation of individual savings accounts). *Számvitel* 2, no. 8:647–52.

Szirmai, Viktória. 1999. A *környezeti érdekek Magyarországon. "Fontosabb, hogy megéljünk"* (Environmental interests in Hungary: "It's more important that we get by"). Budapest: Pallas Stúdió.

Szlávik, János. 1991. Piacosítható-e a környezetvédelem? (Is environmental protection marketizable?). *Valóság* 34, no. 4:20–27.

Taga, Leonore Shever. 1976. Externalities in a command society. In *Environmental misuse in the Soviet Union,* ed. Fred Singleton. New York: Praeger.

Takáts, Attila. 1990. A hulladékok káros hatása elleni védelem jogi, müszaki és gazdasági szabályozása (The legal, technical and economic regulation of protection against the harmful effects of wastes). In *Hulladékgazdálkodás* (Waste management), ed. J. Árvai. Budapest: Budapesti Műszaki Egyetem, Mérnöktovábbképző Intézet.

Tarr, Joel. 1996. *The search for the ultimate sink: Urban pollution in historical perspective.* Akron, Ohio: University of Akron Press.

——. 1997. Searching for a sink for an industrial waste. In *Out of the woods: Essays in environmental history,* ed. Char Miller and Hal Rotham. Pittsburgh: University of Pittsburgh Press.

Sources and References

Tenner, Edward. 1996. *Why things bite back: Technology and the revenge of unintended consequences.* New York: Alfred A. Knopf.

Thomas, Jim. 1993. *Doing critical ethnography.* Newbury Park, Calif.: Sage.

Thompson, Michael. 1979. *Rubbish theory: The creation and destruction of value.* Oxford: Oxford University Press.

Tickle, Andrew, and Ian Welsh. 1998. *Environment and society in Eastern Europe.* New York: Longman.

Ticktin, Hillel. 1976. The contradictions of Soviet society and Professor Bettelheim. *Critique* 6 (Spring): 17–44.

——. 1992. *Origins of the crisis in the USSR: Essays on the political economy of a disintegrating system.* Armonk, N.Y.: M. E. Sharpe.

Toffler, Alvin. 1970. *Future shock.* New York: Random House.

Trade Partners UK. 2001. *Environment market in Hungary.* www.tradepartners. gov.uk/text/environment/hungary/profile/overview.shtml.

Trumbull, Mark. 1994. Global cleanup spots find revenue-hungry U.S. firms at the door. *Christian Science Monitor.* March 24, 8.

Tudományos Ismeretterjesztő Társulat. 1980. *Környezetvédelmi előadói segédanyag* (Subsidiary material for lectures on environmental protection). Budapest: Tudományos Ismeretterjesztő Társulat.

Turner, Victor. 1990 (1969). The ritual process: Structure and anti-structure. In *Culture and society: Contemporary debates,* ed. Jeffrey C. Alexander. Cambridge: Cambridge University Press.

Újlaki, László. 1976. Az ószerestől a MÉH-ig. A jövő: az anyag szervezett körforgása (From ragmen to MÉH: The future: The organized circulation of material). *Népszabadság.* March 10, 8.

v. a. [pseud.]. 1988. Folytassa MÉH! Vége a hulladékstopnak (Carry on, MÉH! End of the waste moratorium). *Magyar Hírlap.* January 6, n.p.

Vági, Gábor. 1982. *Versengés a fejlesztési forrásokért: Területi elosztás—társadalmi egyenlötlenségek* (Competition for development funds: Spatial allocation, social inequalities). Budapest: Közgazdasági és Jogi Könyvkiadó.

——. 1991. *Magunk, Uraim: Válogatott írások településekről, tanácsokról, önkormányzatokról* (Ourselves, my Sirs: Selected writings on settlements, councils, and self-governments). Budapest: Gondolat.

Vályi. 1951. No title. *Szabad Nép.* N.d., 2.

Van Gennep, Arnold. 1960. *The rites of passage.* Chicago: University of Chicago Press.

Vasmunkások Szakszervezete (Iron Workers' Union). 1951. *A Gazda-mozgalom a vasiparban* (The Gazda movement in the iron industry). Budapest: Népszava.

Vegyiművek. 1971. No title. March 1, 1.

Vegyiművek. 1972. No title. April 22, n.p.

Verdery, Katherine. 1996. *What was socialism, and what comes next?* Princeton, N.J.: Princeton University Press.

Veress, József. 1982. A környezetvédelmi szabályozásról—vállalatgazdasági nézöpontból (On environmental regulation—from a microeconomic angle). *Iparpolitikai Tájékoztató* 19, no. 11:46.

Vészi, Endre. 1952. *Gazda Géza forintjai* (Géza Gazda's Forints). Budapest: Nép-művelésügyi Minisztérium.

Völgyes, Iván. 1974. *Environmental deterioration in the Soviet Union and Eastern Europe.* New York: Praeger.

Wallach, Amei. 1996. *Ilya Kabakov: The man who never threw anything away.* New York: Harry N. Abrams.

Walsh, Edward J., Rex Warland, and D. Clayton Smith. 1997. *Don't burn it here: Grassroots challenges to trash incinerators.* University Park: Pennsylvania University Press.

Wedel, Janine R. 1998. *Collision and collusion: The strange case of Western aid to Eastern Europe, 1989–1998.* New York: St. Martin's Press.

Weinberg, Adam S., David N. Pellow, and Allen Schnaiberg. 2000. *Urban recycling and the search for sustainable community development.* Princeton, N.J.: Princeton University Press.

Weissenbach, Thomas. 2001. *Waste management facilities: Electronic catalogue.* Copenhagen: European Environment Agency.

White, Richard. 1980. *Land use, environment and social change: The shaping of Island County, Washington.* Seattle: University of Washington Press.

White, Robert M. 1994. Preface. In *The greening of industrial eco-systems,* ed. B. R. Allenby and D. J. Richards. Washington, D.C.: National Academy Press.

Williams, Raymond. 1973. Base and superstructure in Marxist cultural theory. *New Left Review* no. 82:3–16.

Wilson, C. Anne, ed. 1991. *Waste not, want not: Food preservation from early times to present day.* Edinburgh: Edinburgh University Press.

Wolcott, Harry F. 1999. *Ethnography: A way of seeing.* Walnut Creek, Calif.: Alta-Mira Press.

Woodruff, David. 1999. Barter of the bankrupt: The politics of demonetization in Russia's federal state. In *Uncertain transitions,* ed. Michael Burawoy and Katherine Verdery. Lanham, Md.: Rowman and Littlefield.

Worster, Donald. 1984. History as natural history: An essay on theory and method. *Pacific Historical Review* 53 (February):1–19.

———. 1985. *Rivers of empire: Water, aridity and the growth of the American West.* New York: Pantheon.

Wynne, Brian. 1989. Frameworks of rationality in risk management: Towards the testing of naive sociology. In *Environmental threats,* ed. Jennifer Brown. London: Belhaven Press.

Yaeger, Patricia. 2003. Trash as archive, trash as enlightenment. In *Culture and waste: The creation and destruction of value,* ed. Gay Hawkins and Stephen Muecke. Oxford: Rowman and Littlefield.

Young, Oran R. 1982. *Resource regimes: Natural resources and social institutions.* Berkeley: University of California Press.

Ziegler, Charles E. 1992. Ideology, postcommunist values and the environment. In *Ideology and system change in the USSR and Eastern Europe,* ed. Michael E. Urban. London: St. Martin's Press.

Index

Page numbers in italics refer to illustrations.

Index

European Community. *See* European Union
European Environment Agency, 15, 188
European Union, 154; Copenhagen Criteria,
   155; enlargement of, 9, 185–195, 196, 199,
   202, 209, 222n12, 223n17; European Community, 155, 180; waste legislation in, 155–
   158

Federated American Engineering Societies,
   211
Fejes, Endre, 105–106
Fiatal Demokratàk Szövetsége (FIDESZ)
   (Federation of Young Democrats), 200
Filtzer, Donald, 29–31

Garé: history of, 133–135, 163–165; planned
   incinerator in, 165–174, 178–185; toxic
   waste dump in, 3, 121, 133–136, 138–139,
   150–163
Gastev, Aleksei, 62
Gazda, Géza, 42, 43, 55, 65, 90
Gazda movement, 43, 56–59, 63, 71, 76, 85–
   91, 111, 125
Gazda movement prices, 82
German Democratic Republic (GDR), 2,
   210, 222n10, 224n1
global ethnography. *See* ethnography
globalization, 157, 163, 166, 196, 202
Gourlay, K. A., 18, 25
Green Alternative Party (GAP), 179–180
Green Circle, 179, 215n3
Greenpeace, 180

Hazafias Népfront (People's Patriotic Front)
   (HNF), 109, 138, 152
Hidas, 99, 132–134, 137–138, 165, 220n3.
   See also Budapest Chemical Works
Homo Sovieticus, 79. *See also* Socialist Man
Hrabal, Bohumil, 107
Hungarian Revolution of 1956, 8, 91, 105
Hungaropec, 166, 168–170, 173–185. *See
   also* Budapest Chemical Works
hybridity of waste, 25–28, 212–214

industrial ecology, 122–123, 162. *See also* ecological modernization
industrialization, 2, 91, 183, 211
intelligentsia, 88, 118–121, 124, 137, 146,
   204, 208
ISPA (Instrument for Structural Policies for
   Pre-Accession), 192, 199

joint production. *See* concept of waste, in
   economics

Kabakov, Ilya, 106–107
Kádár, János, 8, 91, 105, 108
Klíma, Ívan, 107–108
Kökény, 170, 174, 183, 223n11
Kommunista Ifjúsági Szövetség (KISZ), Com-
   munist Youth Organization, 109
Kornai, János, 29–30

labor discipline, 51, 65–66, 71–78, 87, 100–
   101
labor unions, 55, 57, 72, 81, 85, 86, 88, 89
liminality of waste, 20–24, 34

Magyar Tudományos Egyesületek Szövetsége
   (MTESZ) (Hungarian Alliance of Technical and Scientific Associations), 119, 121,
   162
Marxism: socialist ecology, 25, 32; and socialist environmental destruction, 4, 8, 12,
   218n11
Mátyás Rákosi Steel Works, 54, 55, 56, 63
Melléktermék -és Hulladékhasznosító Vállalat
   (MÉH) (By-Product and Waste Utilization
   Company), 41, 45, 53
Menzel, Jiri, 39, 106–107
metal scrap, 3, 9, 39, 46, 47, 48, 58, 63, 70, 74,
   78, 204
metallic concept of waste, 9, 28, 57–62, 80;
   in metallic waste regime, 100–101, 124,
   130, 141, 142, 145 (*see also* waste regimes);
   unintended consequences of, 84–88, 90,
   92
metallurgy, 61–62, 84, 101, 219n16; Siemens-
   Martin furnaces, 56, 61, 111, 130
morality, 64, 118, 178–179, 209, 212 (*see also*
   Homo Sovieticus); of waste, 14, 21–24, 32,
   34. *See also* liminality of waste
Murphy, Raymond, 25

National Waste Management Plan (NWMP),
   191–193
New Economic Mechanism of 1968. *See* economic reforms
NIMBY (Not in my backyard), 181

O'Connor, James, 32
oil crisis, 204, 209
operationalism, 18

Index

Zsuzsa Gille is Associate Professor of Sociology at the University of Illinois–Urbana Champaign. She is co-author of *Global Ethnography: Forces, Connections, and Imaginations in a Postmodern World.*